The Discombobulated Development of a CPA

A Memoir

KEN COOPER

DENVER, COLORADO

The Discombobulated Development of a CPA
A Memoir

CONTENTS

Prologue   1

Chapter 1: Bruises, Bites, Broken Bones and Bedpans   7

Chapter 2: H2Oh My Gosh! (My Love/Hate Relationship with Water)   23

Chapter 3: My Not Always Positive Experiences with Athletics   37
   Sub Chapter 3.1: "Hunting Is for the Birds!"   37
   Sub Chapter 3.2: "Hoosiers" (Or, Some Adventures with Hoops)   42
   Sub Chapter 3.3: "Three Strikes Are a Good Thing"   53
   Sub Chapter 3.4: "Three Strikes Are a Bad Thing"   56
   Sub Chapter 3.5: "Footballs Sure Bounce Funny"   66
   Sub Chapter 3.6: "It Takes Balls to Play this Game"   70

Chapter 4: Breasts and other Pleasant Surprises   77

Chapter 5: A Two Step Plan to Become Brilliant   95
   Sub Chapter 5.1: "Beware 20th Century Fox"   96
   Sub Chapter 5.2: "Now Just Where All Does this Route Cover?"   101
   Sub Chapter 5.3: "When Is a Golf Club Not a Golf Club?"   106
   Sub Chapter 5.4: Drug Trafficking, Bogus Markdowns and Late Lunches   110

Chapter 6: "Psst! The Greek Sent Me"   121
   Sub Chapter 6.1: Hell Week   128
   Sub Chapter 6.2: Living in the House   130
   Sub Chapter 6.3: "Do, Re, Mi, Fa"   131
   Sub Chapter 6.4: Activities with the Fairer Set   132
   Sub Chapter 6.5: Spring Break   140

Chapter 7: The Yellowstone Years   147
   Sub Chapter 7.1: A Hand of Bridge that Definitely Shaped My Life   148
   Sub Chapter 7.2: "Welcome to Pack Camp"   156
   Sub Chapter 7.3: Eight Hand Picked Studs and Yours Truly   160
   Sub Chapter 7.4: "Meanwhile, Back at the Ranch"   168
   Sub Chapter 7.5: A Whole Lotta Shakin Goin On   172
   Sub Chapter 7.6: When Fred Astaire Met Ginger Rogers   182
   Sub Chapter 7.7: Jellystone Adventures with Yogi Bear   188
   Sub Chapter 7.8: Choosing the Right Time and the Right Place   195

Chapter 8: Up Close and Personal with Celebrities   197

Chapter 9: Departing Downtown, Bound for the Boonies   209
   Sub Chapter 9.1: "Hey, It Beats Walking!"   209
   Sub Chapter 9.2: "OK, George, We'll Keep It Just Between Us."   210
   Sub Chapter 9.3: "What Was It You Said the Easter Bunny Left Me?"   212

Chapter 10: Things Better Left Unsaid or Undone (With 20-20 Hindsight)   221

Chapter 11: "I Doubt That I'll Ever Forget THIS Class!"   227

Chapter 12: Memorable Dining Experiences for Better or Worse   231

Chapter 13: "Colder than a Witch's Chest" (and other Weather Related Events)   247
   Sub Chapter 13.1: "Anyone for Christmas in Iowa?"   247
   Sub Chapter 13.2: "So Just How Cold WAS It?"   250
   Sub Chapter 13.3: "Let It Snow, Let It Snow, Let It Snow"   254
   Sub Chapter 13.4: "Snow: Tolerable; Wind: Terrible"   256

Chapter 14: Juvenile Attempts (No Age Requirement) at "Talking Dirty"   267

Chapter 15: This and That, In Order of Interest, (Or Lack Thereof)   281
   Sub Chapter 15.1: Not "Butt," as in Slut; But "Butte," as in Cute   281
   Sub Chapter 15.2: "Who Invited Her?" (And Other Female "Oops" Mishaps)   284
   Sub Chapter 15.3: "I've Gotta Stop Doing That!"   289
   Sub Chapter 15.4: Dragnet Protected the Innocent; I'm No Joe Friday   296
   Sub Chapter 15.5: "Luck of the Draw"   299
   Sub Chapter 15.6: "Must Be a Terrible Toothache!"   305
   Sub Chapter 15.7: My Doomed Youthful Love Affair with a Car   307
   Sub Chapter 15.8: "What Was That Again?"   311

Prologue

****

I grimaced as I watched Ted sauntering toward me across the steep terrain of Mount Washburn, part of one of the higher mountain ranges in Yellowstone National Park.

"About time you showed up." I commented sarcastically. "If I could entice these pathetically sunburned legs up this motherlovin mountain, with my blue jeans impersonating P120 grit sandpaper each step of the way, the least you could do was to get here on time. You'd think we were out in the boonies or something."

Without missing a beat, Ted responded, "Hey, I didn't force you to spend the whole afternoon yesterday down at the Firehole River with nothing but a swim suit on your miserable body, and a few too many cold beers in your cooler. So don't go bitchin to me about your damn sunburn."

"Remind me of this conversation the next time YOU have a lapse of good judgment, which, knowing you as I do, will not be too far off."

"It's a deal. Now let's dig into our lunchtime's enticing entrée, and see whether our stomachs will be appreciative or not."

Briefly thereafter, we had settled our scrawny butts on the ground in such a manner that we could individually lean back against our own huge White Pine Tree, of which there happened to be two in this immediate locale. We had been separated all morning, but had planned to meet for lunch at this prearranged spot in order to compare the results of our morning inspections.

As I was untying the rag knot of the cloth bag containing yet another soggy sandwich (an all-too-typical result of having unintentionally crushed the little cardboard half pint container of milk packed with said sandwich), I glanced over my right shoulder, and rather imagined that I was observing a slowly approaching animal of substantial size.

I then looked back at Ted, noting that his eyes had suddenly grown to the diameter of middle sized Frisbees ®. I quickly realized what it was that I had just seen, but not fully comprehended. Yes indeed, it was a massive GRIZZLY BEAR! (In a different setting, I would probably add the adjective "magnificent" as well, but from where we were sitting, it was not that setting.)

You can imagine the feelings experienced by Ted and me at that moment: an adrenalin jolt causes hair on the neck, arms and assorted body parts to stand at attention; while droplets of perspiration begin trickling down the body like a battalion of snails commencing a marathon. (If you haven't recently been in a situation where you were up close and personal with a live Grizzly, think of a scary movie in which the sweet young thing steps into a darkened room where the monster, the killer, or a startled cat suddenly makes his presence known.)

Almost simultaneously, we muttered "Holy shit!" or some other highly intelligent expression of concern, and immediately jumped to our feet.

****

"Wait a minute! Wait a minute! Stop the music!"

No, that wasn't either Ted or me, expressing such an action stopping statement, but rather the now long deceased entertainer with the self described "super schnozzola," Jimmy Durante, who often used that phrase or something similar to change the direction of what was transpiring during a musical number or skit in his show.

Like Durante, I am about to Stop the Music as it relates to this episode of "Two Guys and a Grizzly," because I am getting way ahead of myself. Oh, I promise to revisit this part of my life story in its proper place, complete with all the grisly Grizzly details, but I think it might be better to back up a little to allow you to have a better perspective of just what makes me tick.

****

The original title of my book was to have been *The Secret Life of a CPA*, until I noticed that nearly everyone and everything, from Walter Mitty, whose story first appeared about the same time I took my initial breath, to "Bees" just a few years ago, not to mention countless celebrities and even puppets, have all had their secrets told to the reading and/or movie populace.

I instead decided on *The Discombobulated Development of a CPA---A Memoir*, which better describes its contents anyway.

To be right up front, I AM a CPA, albeit a retired one. The point of this book is not to describe CPAs, but rather to share with you events that occurred during the quarter century after I had attained the age of three or four. When taken as a whole, you can then decide for yourself if I became a CPA because of them, in spite of them, or if they had no impact on my career choice whatsoever. Of course there is option four, which would be, "Who gives a rat's ass?"

First, however, some definitions and observations might prove to be beneficial:

I should clarify that "CPA" is an acronym for Certified Public Accountant (not "Constant Pain in the Ass" as we were often identified by clients), a profession somewhat like that of being an Attorney at Law, only in a different area of expertise.

A CPA tends to be involved in such fun-filled activities as awesome audits, tricky taxes and cool consulting contracts. If not actually a member of a CPA firm (i.e. Public Accounting), one may secure a financial position with a privately or publicly held business. I filled both roles during my career, moving from Peat Marwick Mitchell (a CPA firm) to Dillon Companies (a supermarket chain, subsequently merged with the Kroger Companies).

The accountant in a book or movie, while not necessarily the villain, is unlikely to be the hero; and if being cast by Hollywood, would almost certainly not be a Charlton Heston, Bruce Willis or Brad Pitt, but more probably a Don Knotts, or, if the studio is being kind to accountants that month, perhaps a Steve Carrell.

Although there may be no stereotypical accountant or CPA, it is probably safe to say that if an unbiased individual was given a rating sheet for a room full of people from all walks of life, the odds that a CPA would be ranked as the most charismatic person in that room would be next to zero. On the other hand, the same might well be said of a brain surgeon.

When I was discussing the contents of this book with some writers one afternoon, a young lady named Rachael remarked that a negative stereotype of CPAs was not exactly fair. She said she knew several accountants personally, and most of them seemed ALMOST normal. Now there's a ringing endorsement for the aspiring CPA.

Having always been interested in movies, let me warn you that there will be numerous references to many of them in this book.

Now that I've completed that bit of insight, it is time to proceed.

****

I grew up in the 1940s and 1950s, back when, as the bumper sticker says, "Air was clean and sex was dirty," so I may appear far more naïve than your average small town youth. Much of what amazed me during my prolonged coming of age would sound incredibly absurd ("Well, duh!") to the generation(s) who followed me, including any of our four grandchildren.

Having long since placed the bear bit on hiatus for now, let's back up a few years, (if this were an old movie, the screen would now get a bit blurry, as if looking through a suddenly disturbed pool of water), and proceed with my discombobulated development.

As is always the case prior to the commencement of a seminar or other activity, someone says "Before we start, there are a couple of housekeeping items we need to relate. The bathrooms are located....etc." Well I, too, have a couple of housekeeping items.

Those reading this memoir may envision me as an only child, as there is no mention of siblings anywhere. That is an erroneous assumption. Allow me to clarify:

I had a very loving older brother (by roughly three years) who contracted Encephalitis shortly after I was born. By the time I reached the age of four, when the events of this book begin to unfold, his "Sleeping Sickness" (how my parents described his illness to me) had advanced to the point that he had to be institutionalized at a hospital in Boulder, Montana. His tragic "life," if you could call it that, ended in that same institution before he attained the age of thirty. I cannot count the number of times I've thought how wonderful it would have been, had I been blessed throughout life with a big brother with whom to share things.

Absent the presence of that older brother in our home, I pestered my parents endlessly about my desire for them to add another sibling to the family. Due to some complications during my birthing process, my mother could have no more children, but my constant prodding brought the consideration of adoption into play. A few years later, after numerous interviews and reams of red tape, my wishes culminated in a little sister becoming part of our family. Sadly, when this sweet little two year old arrived on the scene, I was already twelve, and had developed both friendships and outside interests which prevented the two of us from being as close as we might have been, had our ages been closer. Her incredible life story could fill several books, but this is not one of them.

Finally, there is the amazing lady with whom I've shared married life for over half a century. Although as you would expect, she appears in many segments of this memoir, it is really not "our story" being related. That may be fodder for another book someday, but not this one. So please do not be critical of her for any of the following topics, organization or phraseology; it is MY memoir, so the blame lies entirely on me.

****

5

If there WERE ever to be a book strictly about the two of us (which I doubt will ever happen, as I'm getting too old for all this); what with me being from out west and frequently seen in childhood wearing a cowboy hat, whereas she hails from a small Indiana town, we could open it by showing us back in the age of innocence, and entitle it:

"COWBOYs and INDIANans"

******

Chapter 1

Bruises, Bites, Broken Bones and Bedpans

As no child throughout history had previously made it into adulthood without the requisite bloody nose, black eye, broken rib or worse, I considered it my civic duty to keep that record intact. In fact, I became so successful doing so, that shortly before I was to become a happily married man, the uncle of my bride-to-be asked her if she REALLY thought it wise to commit herself to such an accident prone individual as what I had demonstrated to be on far too many occasions. Fortunately for me, she overlooked this shortcoming of mine, among many others; and for over half a century has brought much happiness into my life, along with tender love and care, as was frequently needed.

****

My grandmother surprised me on my sixth birthday with an amazing present. If you want to get technical, it really wasn't my birthday for another two days. However, on our way to have dinner at the home of friends in a residential part of Missoula, Montana, we stopped at the post office to get our mail. Included in the letters and other items in P.O. Box 615 that day was a card, indicating that a package, too large for our box, was to be picked up at the Parcel Window. Much to my delight, the item awaiting us was addressed to me.

As we drove over to home of our hosts, I politely performed all the skillful pleading and logical reasoning talents available to someone literally just hours shy of achieving super-charged six year old-hood. My parents smilingly acquiesced, allowing me to open the large container immediately after we had made the proper greetings.

Contents: a bicycle, my first; the brand: Schwinn, the epitome of bike lovers; its color: flaming red, with a few white stripes thrown in for style; my mental state: ecstatic; and, had the much later appearing MasterCard commercial been in existence at the time, the look on my face with my new bike: priceless.

After completing the unit's required assembly in the yard of our hosts, my dad had me get astride the bike. He then ran beside me as I was introduced to the mechanics of balancing, pedaling and steering.

As it was one of those bikes I could grow into, so to speak, I obviously needed something on which to stand, in order to get my leg over the seat to the other pedal. Fortunately there was a tree stump close to the porch of the home where we were visiting, so I had the perfect launch pad to commence a ride.

Feeling adequately trained by my dad in the basics of operating my wonderful present, I mounted it and, after a wobbly first few yards going solo, began riding confidently. I rode all the way around the block, smiling, as my parents and their hosts applauded my success. I continued circling the block a couple more times before my audience felt confident enough in me, that they retired inside for wine, cocktails or just adult visiting, knowing that I would continue enhancing my newly acquired skill for the foreseeable future.

In the course of my training experience, there had been but one minor exclusion regarding the operation of the bike; or if it had been included, it had been lost in the excitement of all the other directions given me. This topic had to do with the termination of the riding experience, sometimes referred to as STOPPING. After I don't know how many circumnavigations of that particular city block had taken place, I finally began thinking about ending the vicious cycle/circle in which I was involved.

My first thought was to attract the attention of those former spectators, now inside the house. I would call out things like "Hey, look at this!" or "Here comes the champion!" as I approached the porch from in front of the house next door. When that failed to produce the desired result, I considered alternate options, and determined that my best bet was to slow down as much as possible without having the bike fall over and try to place my foot on the stump from which I had commenced my ride sometime earlier.

Let me just say that my plan ALMOST worked. I was still traveling just a little too fast as I reached my foot out to the target; while it briefly rested on the stump, my momentum was too great to allow a complete stop, and I toppled over into the grassless ground surrounding the stump. The bike, having already developed a close relationship with me during our short period of acquaintance, landed on top of me, with the handlebars whipping around, such that one handle whacked me in the shoulder.

It would come as no surprise to guess that my tears were first to arrive at the scene, followed shortly by moderately loud cries of pain. However, this noise was still of apparently insignificant magnitude to attract the attention of the adults, as no one came running to the door to question the source of the commotion out front.

Having realized that I was on my own, at least for the short term, I crawled out from beneath my bicycle, dried my eyes, checked for visible damage to my body or the bike, and, finding none, pushed it back to the porch.

As I was climbing the steps, my mother came to the door, saying "We were just about to come and check on you, as dinner is almost ready and they are having your favorite, corn on the cob. Come inside, wash your hands and you can still ride some more after dinner if you want. How did your ride go?"

"Oh, it was great! I could go pretty fast on that long part of the sidewalk around the corner." I didn't mention that I might want to talk to Dad about a couple of little details, before again riding solo.

****

There is an odd sounding, and infrequently occurring ailment, which seems more prevalent amongst boys than girls, and tends to appear during the ages of five through fifteen. *Osgood Schlatter Disease* is its name.

This disease appears in the form of a bump or swelling just below the knee, and is quite sensitive to pressure. It is more often found in active children, particularly those playing sports involving running and jumping. It can be treated with rest, ice, anti-inflammatory medications (e.g. ibuprofen) and, in more severe instances, a brace or cast, along with the use of crutches. The tenderness, if not the bump, typically disappears once a child has stopped growing.

Over the next couple of years, I had not only perfected the stopping and dismounting aspects of cycling; I had even become (at least to my mind) a biking daredevil of sorts.

Unbeknownst to me, just a little over a hundred miles southeast of Missoula, a contemporary named Bobby Knievel was also perfecting his biking skills in the mining town of Butte. I seem to have heard somewhere, that he later changed his moniker to Evel Knievel, and eventually gained a bit of notoriety, not to mention some decent revenue, performing various jumps with his bike.

Long before the time I became aware of any of this information, and perhaps lacking the dedication of young Knievel, I had moved on from such biking activities myself. However, it does pose the question that had we ever met during those formative years, we may well have become a daredevil team, and I'd never have become a CPA, nor have experienced the thrills associated with that profession.

In any event, despite having honed these newly developed riding skills, some element beyond my control would occasionally cause an accident to occur. Following one such incident, I had skinned up my left knee pretty badly, and even following the disappearance of the resulting scab, I still had significant pain just below the knee. I finally told my mother about the tenderness and the bump which had not gone away. A trip to the doctor's office introduced us to my new friend, Osgood Schlatter.

I avoided braces, casts and crutches, skipped the ibuprofen (or whatever they had that fit the bill back in the mid 1940s) and tended to be too busy playing to have time for ice and rest. My doctor basically said that I ought to avoid activities that caused me pain, but otherwise I should eventually grow out of it. The main thing I could not then, and even today cannot execute, was deep knee bends. I also tended to flinch whenever a doctor performed those reflex tests with the rubber hammer type gadget. No problem when he hit my ankles or my right knee, but "Be careful with my left knee, please."

****

Dogs are said to be man's best friend, but dogs and little boys seem to develop an even closer relationship than simple friendship. I always enjoyed a special togetherness with the dogs which have shared our home with me over the years. However an incident with a particular German shepherd skewed my focus towards dogs, such that I have a greater affection for some breeds than for others.

Our home at this time was in Pattee Canyon, a somewhat remote area just south and west of Missoula. About two miles down the canyon toward town from us, a local photographer had built a lovely residence a couple of years after we had completed ours. In the course of time they invited our family over for dinner and to see their completed project. They had a little boy about two years my junior and a German shepherd. We had an enjoyable visit, and I certainly was made to feel welcome by all members of their family, including the friendly canine.

Several weeks later I was with my mother, as we headed down the canyon to Missoula. She said we would be stopping at Susan's home to drop off a recipe she had promised our hostess during our earlier visit. We parked the car on the side of the road and began walking up the driveway to their house. The German shepherd came bounding down to greet us (or so I thought), but instead of being hospitable, as had been the case during our previous time together, he jumped up and took a chunk out of my shoulder.

As might be expected: I began crying loudly; Susan was running down to grab her dog; my mother was trying to comfort me; blood was oozing from the bite on my shoulder (I'd like to say GUSHING for dramatic purposes, but it really was simply oozing, so we'll leave it at that); and I have no idea what ever happened to the recipe we had come to deliver.

Needless to say, I recovered fully from this altercation, but long before I had ever heard of such breeds as Rottweiler or Pit Bull, I decided to always give a wide berth to German shepherds in the future. (I know that "Rin Tin Tin" was a wonderful animal, and that numerous good deeds were performed by that heroic dog on the silver screen and television, but impressionable children such as I had difficulty erasing such a memory.)

Whether due to the aforementioned declining level of hospitality by "Killer" (my own personal name for this four-legged antagonist), or just because our families didn't have a lot in common, I don't recall that we ever visited their home again. Nevertheless, when riding my bike down the canyon to Missoula to go swimming several times a week, I had no option but to pass their residence to reach my destination.

I would pedal a little extra hard (maybe a lot extra) beginning about 100 yards up canyon from their driveway, and as I was almost adjacent to their home, would put my feet up on the handlebars and coast past with an ever watchful eye out for Killer. Lest you wonder what happened on the return (uphill) trip, I nearly always found a way to hitch a ride back home with my mother, or any neighbor who worked in Missoula, and lived somewhere between our house and that of Killer.

Although I have avoided any further unpleasant encounters with German shepherds up to and including adulthood in the Denver area, my generally quiet and pacifistic wife was walking our cocker spaniel one pleasant Colorado afternoon, when a German shepherd suddenly raced out from the open gate of a backyard fence, with obvious menace directed towards our pet, "Lady." This attack took place before the Fanny Pack had been popularized, so my wife was instead carrying her purse.

As the teeth bearing, loudly barking shepherd approached them; Lady's protector (aka my bride) stepped in front of her and began swinging her purse at the aggressor, while yelling something along the lines of "Don't you even THINK of hurting her!" It sure is great to have such a brave stalwart member in our family! (Note to reader: If you were to replace "shepherd, German" with "snake, garter", then all bets are off.)

****

In the early 1950s our country had become almost paranoid about Infantile Paralysis, or Polio. The March of Dimes Campaign had pictures of little children in leg braces or iron lungs as its focal points. Visits to swimming pools were risky and thus severely curtailed. Even a simple activity such as going to the movies came with a stern warning to not let your head rest on the back of the theater seat.

In spite of adhering to all the various precautions, I apparently contracted this dreaded disease. I say "apparently," in that while I was effectively quarantined in our home for well over two months, during which my parents had strict orders from the doctors to keep me isolated, fill me with fluids and keep me from any form of activity (including walking the few steps from my bedroom to the bathroom), I somehow escaped the fate of becoming paralyzed, or the all too often end result of an early end to life.

Now perhaps the doctors were in error in their original diagnosis, despite numerous lab results to substantiate what they had determined was my condition. Doctors and lab technicians have been known to make mistakes. I, however, choose to believe that I happened to be just one of the very few extremely fortunate individuals who, for whatever reason, were spared the agony of an iron lung, paralysis, braces and premature death, in the days before Doctor Jonas Salk came out with his fantastic vaccine. To say that I am thankful beyond words would be a tremendous understatement.

Those two or three months of quarantine had plenty of downside (you can put bedpan utilization pretty close to the top of that list), but, conversely, I got a lot of attention in the process.

For example, when my isolation period continued into the beginning of the school year, I received a large box of letters of support, and some cookies, from my grade school class. Naturally, all of them had been written in the Palmer Method of Penmanship, required of all elementary students in those days. Even super attractive girls who might otherwise have had no problem totally ignoring one such as I, sent encouraging letters ending with "X's" and "O's" telling me they could hardly wait for me to return to school with them.

Once the crisis was over, I was eventually cleared to return to school and to otherwise ease back into an active life. To say that I took advantage of my notoriety, celebrity, good fortune or fifteen minutes of fame (though that phrase had not yet been uttered back then) would be yet another understatement.

In retrospect, I probably, no, let's make that definitely, displayed the worst possible attitude for one who should have been thankful, appreciative, gracious, attentive, obedient, or any of the logical attributes of one so blessed.

Instead, I caused disruption in my classes while telling others of my illness, looked for special treatment from teachers, expected ongoing recognition of my suffering from friends young and old, and generally went out of my way to destroy the goodwill built up for me from having had polio. (Although I was probably too youthful, and just cute enough, to avoid being labeled an asshole, I was obviously acting like a jerk.)

After allowing these antics to continue for nearly two weeks, my teacher asked me to give her a few minutes after school to discuss with me how I was progressing towards various assignments, tests to be made up and so forth.

While she did cover those topics, what she really did was chew me up and spit me out for my behavioral shortcomings. She explained that I was alienating friends, falling further and further behind in my class work (which would result in being held back rather than advancing with the rest of my classmates) and otherwise tearing down my previously favorable reputation. She, for one, would not put up with it any longer, and doubted that any friends I had not already pushed away would either.

It was my choice, she said, and she was leaving it up to me to get my act together, rather than bringing my parents in for a visit. She told me she still had full confidence in me, but that I had really disappointed her, and she hoped her high opinion of me had not been misguided.

Now this particular teacher, whose name was Pearl Felker, was considered to be one of the top instructors, if not *the* very best, in the entire county by former students, administrators and other faculty throughout Missoula. An elementary school student (at least those of the male persuasion) does not normally exhibit concern one way or another about teacher selection, but when I had learned during the summer (prior to the polio scare) that I had been assigned to her class, I must admit I had been elated.

The idea that I had been such a disappointment to this amazing lady, and that the high regard she seemed to have had for me had taken such a negative hit right off the bat, concerned me more, I think, than the likelihood of being held back a year in school or any repercussions with my parents as a result of this whole situation.

In any event, I did actively pursue some behavior modification beginning the very next day, and experienced an exceptional year of instruction in the classes conducted by this outstanding teacher.

As I attended both high school and college in Missoula, I had the opportunity to drop in on her several times over the ensuing years, to thank her for getting my attention during that negative hiccup in my life, and for pointing me toward every opportunity to succeed, if I was but willing to put forth the necessary effort.

Many years later, when my wife and I were visiting Missoula, we called on Mrs. Felker, then retired, at her home. In addition to the pleasure of seeing her again, I could finally introduce to my wife this talented and wise individual, who was most responsible for directing my path during what was a key period of my youth.

****

When I was in college, Physical Education classes consisted of such enjoyable activities as badminton, swimming, golf, tennis and more. In high school, however, unless one happened to be on the varsity (or at least the "B Squad") for football, basketball or track, it was definitely not much to anticipate five days per week.

I was certainly not one of the choice athletes in any of the aforementioned sports. In fact, I think the comment, "He may not be very tall, or particularly strong, but he sure is slow!" was created to describe me to a T.

Those high school phys ed classes meant a couple of undesirable things to me. First of all, I could never hope to attain

15

straight A's and inclusion on the High Honor Roll, while I was required to take a class in which I was unlikely to get better than a C. Although no one ever flunked P.E.; neither did anyone, other than the elite super jocks, have a high probability of receiving an A.

The second negative was the content of said classes. Calisthenics, defined as "gymnastic exercises for health" were the order of the day, every day. Yes, once all the jumping jacks, pushups, squats, set ups and related exercises had been completed, we might break up into teams for volleyball, basketball or something more fun and competitive, but more often than not, we spent a higher percentage of the hour on the former than the latter.

Our high school had always had a pretty decent tumbling squad. (This was long before gymnastics, an expanded version of tumbling, had become popular at not only this level of the educational journey, but at far younger ages. Our granddaughter, Danielle, happens to be an outstanding gymnast; whereas I was lucky if I could stand on my head for ten seconds. So much for genetics!)

Perhaps to show those not actively involved in the program just how difficult it was, our P.E. instructor deigned to include some basics of tumbling in the spring of each school year.

One such skill, so to speak, was to have a designated boy stand on the shoulders of another for a certain number of seconds, before dismounting by jumping forward to the mat. Of course that young man had to somehow attain his position atop those shoulders before the countdown began.

Had it been my decision, I might have suggested that the party of the first part climb up several steps on the bleachers, while the party of the second part positioned himself at the end of that row of bleachers, thus allowing party one to step directly onto party two's shoulders. As an alternative, a ladder could have been utilized in a similar manner.

Instead of either of these very common sense approaches, I, the party of the second part, was instructed to stand in a balanced position, feet apart, in a semi-squat. My partner could then simply (or so we were advised) place one foot on my outer thigh, while holding my opposite hand for balance; step up, such that his other foot could reach my waist; then climb up to my shoulders with the first foot, formerly positioned on my thigh, and follow with the second which had been digging into my waist. Also in the game plan was that I would help him in his ascent with my arms. A piece of cake, right?

For openers, it seemed that the whole procedure might have been slightly less abrasive on my thigh, waist and shoulders, had my partner been barefoot, rather than wearing shoes, albeit sneakers, but we simply followed the directions as we understood them.

After a few unsuccessful attempts, at last my partner triumphantly positioned both feet on my shoulders, much to my amazement. I might add that, at this juncture, he seemed more than moderately heavy.

As he released my hands and was attempting to straighten his legs to begin "the count," he began to lose his balance. Rather than jumping down directly in front of me, so we could try again, he instead pushed off, much like a swimmer might do at the beginning of a race, in order to propel himself as far out into the pool as possible.

I never took a Physics class in high school, but somewhere along the line I heard about Newton's Third Law of Motion, dealing with the fact that "for every action, there is an equal and opposite reaction" or words to that effect. I was to learn first hand about this law of physics right there in physical education class, of all places.

As my associate was moving forward from his push, I was being thrust backwards with great rapidity, possessing neither balance nor sense of direction. I impulsively threw my hands behind me, and while my action may have broken my fall, it also broke my left wrist.

Rather than spell out in endless and unnecessary detail my recovery period, I'll fast forward beyond the visit to the doctor to apply a cast; pass over my feeble attempts in the ensuing weeks to learn to eat an ear of corn with a single hand; skip the futile experiments of trying to poke a pencil or other extended length object down the inner portion of the cast to relieve the irritating itching; leave out adjectives describing the foul odor of stale perspiration inside the cast; and simply state the fact that I was not considered a good candidate for summer employment with this temporary, but limiting, handicap.

Despite this short-term disability, my dad was kind enough to "hire" me to paint our two-story house. He described how I could comfortably hang the paint bucket on my cast, hold the brush in my teeth and climb the ladder with my free hand. Once I had reached painting level, I could then lean against the ladder while affixing the linseed oil/stain liquid to the structure. Although I was certainly not the world's fastest housepainter, he paid me by the hour rather than by the job, which was quite thoughtful on his part. I was able to complete the project before my cast was scheduled for removal.

A winter view of the back of our house which I painted that summer with one arm in a cast, while using a tall and often swaying ladder.

One final aspect of this event was the actual cast removal procedure. My doctor welcomed me to his office, while picking up and turning on, what looked and sounded to me, like a portable, rotary buzz saw.

When my reflexes caused me to pull my arm away, he smiled and assured me that while the mechanism was noisy and might SOUND disconcerting (whatever that meant), that there was absolutely no cause for alarm. He stated that I might feel a slight "hot" sensation as he was cutting the cast, but that it was simply the result of the friction of the rotating blade against the plaster-like substance of the cast. He was definitely not going to be touching my skin.

(Just a brief aside: There was, at that time, a television commercial for the R.J. Reynolds Tobacco Company, which advised listeners that doctors preferred Camel cigarettes over any other brand, and that they smoked for pleasure, just like everyone else. The obvious message these "Wizards of Madison Avenue" were foisting off on the public had a logical premise and following conclusion: "Doctors represent good health. Doctors smoke Camels. Therefore Camels must be good for you." While I had not yet succumbed to the evils of tobacco, I generally trusted doctors. After all, they had brought me through polio without any lingering effects, and that was more than good enough for this child.)

While I may have had my doubts about the item of equipment described above, I put my arm, and my faith, in the hands of this learned man of science, and allowed him to cut away. In retrospect, I should have asked for a wooden stick or other more sanitary item to bite on, as it sure felt to me that he was cutting my skin; but what did I know? I hadn't gone to med school.

As he put down the tool and pried open the cast, there was a roughly three-inch-long bloody gash in my forearm. He looked stunned; he apologized profusely, saying the cast must not have been as thick as he thought it was. He then treated my shriveled up, and now even further wounded arm, and sent me on my way.

Please do not judge me too harshly for the following: I would prefer it not to be thought that I would ever hold a grudge (hey, accidents happen); however, when I heard a few short years later that this doctor had passed away via heart attack, long before what one would consider being in the old age category, I looked down at the scar on my arm and smiled. I wondered if he was one of those doctors who preferred Camels.

****

19

I've never been one to get terribly excited about "Pomp and Circumstance," referring not to the concert or musical definition, but rather big splashy events, up to and including Weddings of British Royalty. (Note to wife: My excitement over OUR wedding was another thing altogether, sweetheart. Admittedly, there were a total of only eight people involved in our wedding, including you, my lovely bride, and me; but that is a different story.)

Our wedding locale near Moose, Wyoming, contrasting the very small "Chapel of Transfiguration" in the foreground, with the massive Grand Tetons in the background

Back to the "Pomp" thing. When it comes to graduations, job changes, retirements and the like, my druthers would be to bypass them unless they are unavoidable. Not that I would normally go to any extreme to extricate myself from such an event, but when my own college graduation was at hand, I guess fate took a hand to help me avoid attending that particular ceremony.

I began feeling feverish and more than just being "under the weather" the night preceding my last final (is that redundant?) exam, and barely made it through the test the following morning. I returned to my apartment to crash, but kept feeling worse by the hour. One of my roommates showed up a couple of hours later, following his particular exam; after checking me out, he insisted he was taking me to the infirmary.

It turned out to be a fairly serious case of pneumonia. I wound up spending a week in the college infirmary, followed by another week in one of Missoula's fine hospitals, before being given a clean bill of health, along with the warnings: "Take it very slow to avoid a recurrence. Walk, don't run. Drink plenty of fluids of the non-alcoholic variety. Get plenty of rest." You know the drill.

Having mentioned earlier that my future wife's uncle had warned her concerning my apparent predilection towards medical treatment, it is only fair to relate that this may have been the first hint of what was in store for her.

You see, she was originally scheduled to travel from Indiana, following her own pomp and circumstance filled graduation, directly to Yellowstone National Park, where we were both employed for the upcoming summer. Instead, she had to modify her itinerary, such that she flew to Missoula in order to assist in driving us both down to Yellowstone.

She didn't get all that upset with me over the disruption I had brought into play, saying she was "just glad I hadn't gone and died before we could become better acquainted."

****

The office of the Canyon Village Nurse to which
I made frequent trips for various injuries during
my Yellowstone days. I probably should have put
her on a retainer.

Chapter 2

H2Oh My Gosh!

(My Love/Hate Relationship with Water)

*From an early age, I could never pass up the
opportunity to toss "Ox in the Otter" or snag
a container of this refreshing elixir from a fast
moving stream (discounting any concern about
Giardia, of course).*

    I am probably fortunate that I didn't get dishpan body
before surviving my first decade or two. For those of you
unfamiliar with the term "dishpan hands," it was the result of

spending too much time immersing one's hands in dishwater, a washing machine or some other container of liquid.

I always had an appreciation of, and respect for, water and its both positive and negative aspects:

* A key ingredient in some of the world's best mud pies

OK, let's see. I'm supposed to
mix one part liquid, three
parts dirt, and stir carefully.

* A refreshing after-exercise thirst quencher (decades before sports drinks came into being)

* A critical element in protection from a forest fire (assuming that evacuation of the area had not been required, thus preventing us from using our various hoses)

* A scarce habitat for the tiny trout residing in the small stream behind our house (the volume of which diminished dramatically during the hot days of late summer)

* A frightening force of nature during what could become a flash flood following heavy rains falling in the canyon in which we lived

* A necessary element for dirt removal (coupled with soap) during my Saturday night (or more frequently as needed, which was usually the case) baths. (By the way, when we initially moved to our canyon home, our bathtub was unavailable for immediate use, as my parents wanted rockwork on the wall above the tub itself, so for the first month, we had to substitute our kitchen sink for a bathtub.)

There's nothing like a little racy

nudity to promote a book, right?

Pattee Canyon is an area which today is overrun with family residences, but when we first arrived in the early 1940s, it was a remote, sparsely populated wilderness, served by a dirt/gravel

25

road. My parents built (or had built for them) two different homes in the canyon.

The first was constructed in 1940. A change to my dad's work resulted in our departure from Montana a couple years later; when we returned and attempted to repurchase our original home from its current owners, they rejected our request hands down.

We were, however, able to obtain acreage about a quarter of a mile further up the canyon, and that became the site of the home in which I basically spent my formative years.

Although electricity was soon to arrive, we survived with mini power plants (OK, they were small generators) which ran on gasoline. I didn't understand the mechanics of such machines then, and have never bothered to figure them out since. Within a year of moving in (the second time, that is), we had the "real stuff" so it doesn't matter anyway.

Also, at both houses, we had a well to provide water for drinking and cleaning things ranging from clothes to dishes to bodies. However for lawn watering, gardening, car washing and that sort of thing; we pumped water from Pattee Canyon Creek.

****

One of my earlier recollections connected with water was the providing of assistance to my mother in the washing of clothes.

We had a washing machine with an agitator in the tub and an attached wringer to remove excess water. I was warned numerous times of the dangers of the wringer, and how to "pop" it loose, should my fingers get caught therein.

(In my never ending quest to accumulate totally worthless bits of information, I have often wondered how the phrase "Don't get your tit caught in the wringer!" would translate to modern machinery and political correctness. About the best thing with which I could come up, was something along the lines of "Avoid the need to extricate your mammary gland from the drying mechanism in your laundry room." I guess you could say that it somehow loses a bit in translation.)

26

In any event, after extensive training in the operation of said machinery, I was allowed to perform the entire cycle (after my mother had started things by placing the sheets, towels, clothes or what have you, into the scalding hot water, and adding the proper amount of soap).

In addition to the wash tub, there was also a large double sink. In one of the sink basins was just plain old water, but in the second was some sort of bluing liquid, which made clothes white. Do not ask me how adding something blue to water resulted in whiter clothes, but it worked.

I would use a stick, perhaps the length of a plunger handle (which maybe it was) to reach into the very hot (and now rather dirty) wash water, extract an item, and quickly poke a corner of that material into the wringer, which would then pull the item on through, and allow it to fall into the basin of regular water for a rinse of sorts.

Once all the contents of the wash tub had been moved to the first rinsing basin, I could empty the wash tub into the floor drain and move to the next step.

This phase was far more pleasant than the earlier step, as pulling clothing items from the now warm rinse water was much easier on the hands than it had been removing them from the scalding hot washing tub. I often "spoke" to the articles of clothing, advising them that they were about to escape the ravages of cycles one and two, and were poised to enter the cool blue waters of paradise.

I mention this washing machine activity in which I participated for two reasons:

* Unlike a more curious little lad who might have tried experimenting with ink, to see if it had the same rinse result on "whiter than white" clothing as whatever my mother used in the bluing phase, I simply followed directions, with no thought of improvising (was that the accountant in me coming out at an early age?).

* As an only child, I was not averse to conversing with inanimate objects (such as those items in the wash). At other times I might talk to firewood that I was clearing of snow and taking into

our home to warm up in the fireplace, or perhaps explain to darts the importance of seeking out the bull's eye of the target as opposed to the wall surrounding same.

****

My first negative water experience occurred in the first year of occupancy in our second house. A heavy downpour lasting nearly two days exposed our roof to numerous leaks therein.

We had enough pots and pans situated under dripping spots in our limited-height attic to start a modern expansive kitchen. It was my task to crawl around the attic on my hands and knees, without poking a hole in the ceiling below me. (Just as I had been taught in school to always look up to our country's leaders, I had also thought one should look up to a ceiling; but, of course, I was proved wrong in both cases.)

I would pour accumulated water from the pots and pans into a bucket, which I then handed down to my mother to be dumped outside. While we were performing this interior function, my dad was out on the roof, attempting to patch holes causing the leaks.

The storm was supposedly one of those 100 year storms (that seem to come along every 25-30 years). I cannot imagine what Noah and his family felt like with 40 days of deluge, as I saw more rainfall in just those two days than I have ever seen, or desire to see, in such a time frame.

The dirt/gravel road to town had suffered enough ruts and gullies from the storm to make driving extremely difficult, if not downright dangerous. When the skies finally cleared and we ventured down the canyon, we discovered that some neighbors who lived a mile or two below us, had had a portion of their home's foundation washed away, with the resulting collapse of nearly half the building formerly resting thereon. The house was situated just to the left of the base of a draw, and while cozy and picturesque in normal circumstances, it had had no chance against the rushing waters careening down the formerly dry ravine.

This scene of major destruction provided me with a first hand example of the incredible force of water, and a much more realistic impression it was than I could ever have garnered from some Hollywood special effects on film. These were real people, not fictional characters from some movie.

****

Yet another event at the tender age of nine nearly kept me from attaining the ripe old age of ten.

I had been invited to spend the weekend with my friend, Stan, at his aunt and uncle's ranch adjacent to the Bitterroot River, near Lolo, Montana. (For those of you who utilize scenes from movies to act as a GPS locater of various places; this was roughly the location where the Brad Pitt character in the film, *A River Runs through It*, visited for gambling purposes. Does that help pinpoint it for you?)

Stan advised me that, when told he could spend the weekend at the ranch and invite a friend, he had requested, through his mother, that his Uncle Henry inflate a couple of the inner tubes that were kept in the barn, just in case the weather was such that we could go on a float trip down the river.

After a typical night of giggling, frequent farting and limited sleeping by nine year old boys about to commence an aquatic adventure, we arose to the aromas of an incredible breakfast, substantial enough for full-time ranch hands.

Once those healthy portions (if not healthy entrees) had been consumed by the two of us young whipper-snappers, we accompanied Stan's uncle, riding on his tractor while he hauled replacement poles for some fence repair. As we rode from one site to another, dropping poles, we began planning for our upcoming tubing experience.

Preparation for such an event, if occurring today, would include being covered with sun lotion from head to toe, just for openers, not to mention life vests, protective helmets, bug repellent and so much more. For us, it was simply, "Bye. See you later."

All these decades later in life, I consider it an amazing accomplishment to walk barefoot a mere twenty-five steps down our paved driveway to retrieve the morning newspaper without suffering pain from stepping on some minuscule piece of gravel. However, at the time in question, you'd have thought we were Huck Finn and Tom Sawyer, the way we started off, unencumbered by shoes, shirts or other superfluous attire and, of course, absent the pipe and tobacco.

Inner tubes over our shoulders, we hiked on up-stream from the ranch about half a mile, at which point we found the perfect sandy bank from which to begin our journey.

Although the water was cold, especially when contrasted to the sun's rays of warmth, we were hardy little boys, and therefore immune to the chilling liquid upon which we floated. Besides, we were not touching the water anywhere except our feet, hands and our juvenile little butts, as the rest of our bodies were safely separated from any moisture (other than intentional splashing) by our circular rubber rafts. Perhaps "safely" is not the correct adverb, as you will soon discover (and as did I).

If you have done any trout fishing on a river, you would be familiar with the swirling waters resulting from extremely sharp direction changes of that river, causing your grasshopper, fly, worm, or other tantalizingly tasty tidbit of interest, to go round and round, until either the current pulls your line and the attached bait downstream, or a hungry Rainbow takes the hook. Even if you are not into fishing, at one time or another you must have observed the whirlpool effect when draining a bathtub or flushing the stool.

As we navigated various combinations of curves, white water, protruding boulders, and overhanging branches, while spinning in circles on our inner tubes, I approached just such a whirlpool area about the same time that Stan hollered, "Hey, look over there!"

To this day I have absolutely no idea what it was that Stan felt I should observe. Just as I was attempting to twist around to make that observation, a nearly submerged evergreen branch caught the inside of my tube, flipping me backwards into the current.

I inadvertently gulped more water than air, as I was being submerged head first into and under an unusually deep cut bank. Filled with panic, and unaware of any sense of direction, I blindly reached out for something, anything, although just what, I had no idea.

My left hand brushed a solid object, which turned out to be a tree root, and which I then grasped with my right hand before I could be swept further away. Although my lungs seemed ready to burst, I pulled myself toward the friendly root and blindly felt for one of its neighboring limbs.

Once I successfully discovered one, and sensed that my body was situated such that my feet were below my head, I began sliding my hands up toward the trunk of the tree, whose legs I had shamelessly been fondling, and was able to pull myself back to the water's surface. I held myself at the river's edge, gasping for air, and realizing how close I had come to blacking out before emerging from underwater.

Stan had become aware that I was no longer atop my tube when he saw it floating, sans passenger, just beyond the curve where I had turned into a juvenile Captain Nemo. He was able to grab it and get to shore, albeit some thirty or forty yards downstream, about the same time I resurfaced. Leaving the tubes on a sand bar, he made his way back upstream until he noticed me clinging to the aforementioned tree at water's edge.

After I regained more normal breathing and had calmed down somewhat, I let go of my lifesaving bit of foliage and, half swimming, half allowing the current to carry me, made my way down to where Stan was. I described what had transpired, and after some discussion, we decided to continue our adventure, but to keep as "our secret" the close call I had experienced, once we returned to his aunt and uncle's place.

Yes, I know, such lack of supervision today by Stan's relatives would probably have landed them in the slammer, but in basketball vernacular, "No harm. No foul."

To this day (until now), I have not told anyone (other than Stan, who was on the scene) of this brush with death at such an impressionable age. I've heard all about how someone who has had such a near death experience sees his/her life flash by, but it didn't happen for me. Not in 3-D, not in Technicolor, nothing. Perhaps my inner movie projector failed to operate, or maybe I was on the wrong channel for proper viewing. But hey, I was just a little kid with hardly any life experiences to be flashed anyway, so no big deal.

****

Another incident with water, while not in any way life threatening, may be worthy of inclusion in this section, if only to demonstrate that while I might one day become a CPA, there was little chance that I might ever become an engineer.

I mentioned that we had a stream running behind our home in Pattee Canyon. During the spring and early summer's higher water flow, we actually had two streams, if you will. Just a hundred yards upstream from our property line, the creek divided, with the main part flowing on the south side of the resulting island, and a springtime only branch flowing on the north side. We also had a small vegetable garden adjacent to the seasonable branch.

I was the sole sidekick to my mother for all her extensive duties of keeping the place going while my dad was engaged in selling various products in every nook and cranny over a five state area (Montana, Idaho, Wyoming and the Dakotas).

When I wasn't helping with the wash as described earlier, I was supposed to weed and water the garden, so we could enjoy such home grown goodies as carrots, peas, beets and perhaps a few radishes. Filling a bucket from the deep, slow moving part of the stream just steps away from the garden was a snap. However, when that part of the stream dried up as summer arrived, the trek to and from the year around flow area required both more time and energy.

As that particular summer wore on, I decided that if someone could construct the Panama Canal a few hundred miles south of our location, then I owed it to mankind (or at least to my family) to replicate the feat (in a miniaturized version) right here in western Montana.

The next morning I dragged my dad's pick and one of his shovels to an area upstream, just beyond some trees and brush, which would serve to camouflage my project during the construction phase, yet still well within the boundaries of our property. I soon discovered why this part of the United States was identified as being in "The Rockies" as opposed to "The Sandy's," (although there is a small Montana town called Big Sandy, which seems like a contradiction).

As an adult, I have had numerous occasions to utilize a pick to extract large rocks, work through compacted clay, remove roots and more; but being the little tyke I was, it was all I could do to even lift this heavy tool. I may have been able to SING about "John Henry, the Steel Drivin' Man," but in no way could I replicate his physical skills.

In any event, with or without proper utilization of the pick, I began my digging project in earnest, figuring I would start with a shallow ditch which I could later deepen, widen or otherwise expand to accommodate the anticipated water flow from the still active channel over to the dried up one. Of course in the mind of a young lad, the definition of shallow is measured in inches, not feet, lest you think the folks down in China were beginning to become concerned about what all that digging noise was just below the surface.

I worked diligently during the week, but abandoned the project on weekends when my dad returned from his sales trips, so as to keep secret my progress to date (which was so minuscule as to be practically unnoticeable anyway).

Another two or three weeks passed in the same manner with very little return on my investment of labor, before I finally decided to share my results, thus far, with my dad the following weekend.

I'm sure it must have required great restraint on his part to refrain from laughing out loud, or at the very least, to keep a straight face, as I led him up around the protective foliage to observe what I had accomplished during the heat of summer. Instead he praised me for my efforts, using the utmost diplomacy in surveying my accomplishments, all the while nodding his head to reinforce his positive comments to me.

Although he never once recommended that I abandon further excavation, he tried to tactfully explain that, as the dry creek bed was situated on higher ground than that of the still running portion of the stream, there was always the chance I might not obtain the desired result of having water flow ("UPHILL, son? UPHILL?") over to the inactive channel.

Having determined that any career for his son in engineering or related fields was obviously out of the question, he chose that moment to suggest we play catch for a few minutes, and follow it with a nice, cold crème soda.

When speaking of a moving experience in one's life, several examples may come to mind, but I guess my attempt to defy the laws of gravity in this unsuccessful water project would have to be excluded. From time to time as an adult, I wonder if the subsequent owners of that property in Montana ever figured out what in the world was the purpose of that partially dug mini ditch.

****

A few years later, I happened to be spending part of the summer with various relatives in Iowa. During a week with an aunt and uncle, who had rented a cabin at Lake Okoboji, my cousin and I practically lived in the lake, exiting the water only for brief intakes of essential food or beverage and requisite nocturnal slumber.

Toward the end of our stay, I managed to contract an ear infection, which a doctor subsequently diagnosed as having resulted from my seemingly endless underwater swimming in possibly tainted water. Prior to that ailment, I could not only hold my breath for extended periods, but underwater depths seemed limitless.

The ear problem ended my time at Lake Okoboji, and it kept me relatively inactive with what seemed, to me, to be excruciating pain for several days afterward, while I stayed at my grandmother's home.

Never again, following that ear infection, have I been able to comfortably swim underwater more than eight to ten feet deep, although I continued to manage swimming the length of the local (Missoula) pool underwater without difficulty. Somewhere way back in my gene pool, there must have been a renegade guppy or some such creature.

****

One final reference to moving water involved not just me, but my trusting young wife.

Currently residing in the Denver area, following completion of my Navy obligation, we had returned to Montana for my ten year high school reunion. During my years in the Navy, she had acquired an interest in trout fishing, and having heard endless stories from me about the fishing on Rock Creek (southeast of

Missoula some twenty miles), almost insisted that I allow her to experience its famous waters for part of an afternoon.

Considering that it was MY high school reunion around which our trip was centered, it seemed only fair that I allow her some input as to how at least a small portion of our trip might be modified, so I acquiesced, and off we went to Rock Creek.

We found a convenient wide spot just off the gravel road adjacent to the river, parked our Buick station wagon, extracted our rods from the car and donned our hip boots. Just as grass always seems just a tad greener on the opposite side of some barbed wire, we quickly spotted the perfect fishing hole, which happened to be, of course, on the other side of the river.

Ever the cautious one, she suggested we could walk up the road a ways to see if a crossing to the other side might be available. Being a "guy," with as much patience for finding the long way around a situation as I have for, say, shopping, I said, "Let's just wade across here rather than waste all that time we could be fishing."

Although she gave me "the look," she consented to my suggestion, and we stepped into the rushing waters, which were far deeper than they at first appeared, due to the clarity with which the rocky bottom could be seen.

Just a couple of yards from shore, the river had already reached between knee and hip level (i.e. closer to my knee, but nearer my wife's hip, due to our height differences). Undaunted (my thoughts, not hers), I encouraged further progress towards our destination, advising her to take short steps, and to plant her mobile foot firmly before commencing the next step.

We attained the half way point in due course, albeit with water now nearly at my hip level and/or splashing over the top of our waders. At this point my lovely wife FROZE and gripped my hand so tightly that my wedding ring was cutting into adjacent fingers.

In words best left unsaid here, she suggested, if I may paraphrase, that we admit defeat and make every effort to reposition our posteriors to the original point of departure without succumbing to the raging currents, being dashed against the numerous boulders downstream, breaking assorted bones in the process, and in all likelihood, swallowing more water than would be prudent if we were to survive the ensuing moments of our all too young lives.

Without elaborating to any great extent on the tense time frame that followed, we remained upright, relatively dry from the waist up, and successful in returning to the comfort of the bank, even though exiting more than a few dozen paces downstream from where we had started. I made no further recommendations as to how to access additional trout havens. In fact, as I recall, I put my rod back in our vehicle, and volunteered to simply carry the net and the creel for her, for the duration of our Rock Creek visit.

To her great credit and in her understanding manner, while she has long since forgiven me for that little adventure, she has never forgotten it. More than once in the years since, she has reminded me that we could have made an orphan of our one year old child that day and "What was I thinking to have placed us in such a predicament?"

Of course, she tends to exaggerate just a little. Certainly at least ONE of us would have survived.

****

While water is an integral part of life, it is time to move along. If you crave still more of that sort of thing, swing by your local library and check out the original *Poseidon Adventure; The Perfect Storm; 20,000 Leagues under the Sea;* or *Titanic*, for all sorts of watchable water scenes.

Chapter 3

My Not Always Positive Experiences in Athletics

****

Sub-Chapter 3.1: Hunting Is for the Birds!

While my age could still be counted on far fewer than two full hands of fingers, my dad procured for me a .22 caliber rifle, cutting down the stock to better fit my small frame. Living far from neighbors as we did, there were numerous sites available for target practice without the concern of bothering anyone, let alone harming someone via ricochet or improper aim. I was taught to shoot from both a prone position and a standing one, and while no expert marksman, still managed to find the bull's eye on occasion.

When grouse season arrived one autumn, my dad advised me he felt I was ready to give it a shot (my pun, not his), so we headed up into the woods across the creek. My gun had in its chamber a single .22 birdshot cartridge, while my pockets contained ample follow up shells should the need arise.

Within the first half hour of our hunt, we came upon a grouse, which easily escaped my errant first shot. For openers, I had yet to attempt hitting a moving target. Furthermore, when the startling noise of the bird's wings, as it took off in flight, entered my thought processes, it must have injected a jolt of adrenalin sufficient to prevent me from hitting the proverbial barn from inside it. Finally, by the time I had pulled the cocking mechanism to allow me to fire, the grouse was far out of range of my weapon.

We flushed several more birds with no better result over the ensuing hour, but then my luck changed. I was roughly fifty yards away from my dad when a grouse I had previously flushed landed on a log within range of my .22. I slowly and quietly pulled back the pin and crept forward perhaps ten yards. Fearing I would again send my quarry out of sight, I placed the stock against my shoulder and my cheek along its side, aimed carefully, with the little protrusion at the end of the barrel perfectly aligned within the "v" of the sight and squeezed the trigger.

My dad encouragingly hollered to me to load up again and keep after that elusive bird, to which I excitedly replied, "I don't have to. I got him!" I was ecstatic, but I think my dad was, if possible, even more delighted for me.

By the time we completed this first hunting excursion perhaps another hour later, I had bagged my second grouse. Although my dad had carried his shotgun (to make it an official hunting trip), he never took a shot. He was there for guidance, support and protection, all of which I greatly appreciated. I'll give you three guesses as to what was on the menu at our house that evening (and of course, the first two don't count).

My First Grouse!

When my dad took this picture, he said I had earned the right to hold a real shotgun. I thought that since ballistics tests would show the cause of death was from my little .22 with its birdshot, I should use the smaller weapon, but "Father knows best."

******

Within a few years I graduated to a "410 single shot" shotgun, with a hammer to pull back to allow for firing. While this item of weaponry had more range and firepower than did my little .22 with its birdshot bullets, it was still quite limited when compared to my mother's 20 gage or my dad's 12 gage shotguns.

The bird hunters amongst you already know this, but grouse do not seem particularly intelligent at avoiding those hunting them. The Ring-necked Pheasant, by comparison, is a whole different breed of chicken. They can run nearly as fast as they can fly, and once flushed, are quite likely to fly the entire length of a cornfield before touching down again. They certainly do not pose on a log or sit on a low tree branch, waiting for some seven or eight year old beginner to use for target practice.

To compensate for the relatively abbreviated range of this upgraded gun, my dad emphasized the importance of shooting sooner, rather than later. To accomplish a degree of accuracy to partner with the suggested rapidity of trigger squeezing he was suggesting I develop, he and I would practice on clay pigeons.

We had a hand trap to throw the clay pigeons from the edge of our driveway out over the creek below us. He would toss one; I would aim and fire. If I was unsuccessful, he would be ready with his bigger shotgun, and would try to hit it before it fell to the ground. If, by chance, one of our targets was not shattered, either by one of our shots, or by hitting the ground, but instead landing in a bush, it was my duty to recover it following our practices for reuse at a future time.

Thanks to these repeated drills, I became fairly proficient at this quick aim and fire procedure. In fact, on pheasant hunting trips with my dad and some of his friends, I frequently had my quota of roosters before any of them did. (Perhaps they were just being considerate in allowing this youngster with the little popgun to get the first chance at a shot.)

I mentioned that it was necessary to manually pull back the hammer to allow me to shoot. Normally this was not a problem, but on particularly cold days, walking through the stubble fields, my thumb could become partially numb.

I recall vividly an occasion when I had started to pull back on the hammer just as I was about to raise the gun to my shoulder. My thumb did not entirely engage the hammer, slipping off before the shotgun was fully cocked. As the hammer came forward, it had sufficient force to cause the gun to fire into the ground a few feet in front of me.

While no canine or fellow hunting companion was injured as a result of my "slip," it was just fortunate that neither prairie dog nor gopher was nearby, as that very loud "Oops" of mine certainly disrupted the ground within the area of the shot pattern.

****

Despite that incident, my dad soon determined my shooting skills, and my size, had advanced to the stage that I was ready to try using my mother's 20 gage pump action shotgun. I had arrived! Once I excelled with her gun, I would be but a single step away from trying my dad's 12 gage pump, or, in my eyes, full maturity.

Looking back on this weaponry promotion, it turned out to be the beginning of the end, as related to my hunting prowess. Whereas previously I was efficient in all aspects of taking aim and firing with my little single shot 410, I now had the luxury of not one, but three shells at my disposal, each of whose range far exceeded those fired in my 410.

So I got lazy. No longer was I the first hunter to pull the trigger, nor even to have the gun tucked into my shoulder to take a shot. If I missed with the first shot, I'd just pump in another shell, and then a third, if needed. You guessed it, I missed with all three. That may have been an early example of the Peter Principle, as I had certainly risen to the level at which I was totally incompetent.

****

I suppose I could have overcome my newfound ineptitude in the use of a shotgun, but simultaneously at that point in my maturation, the first inklings of interest in members of the opposite sex began to cause my desire to be hunting "birds of a feather" to wane, in favor of other species of "birds."

However, before entirely moving beyond this hunting and shooting topic, a duck hunting adventure comes to mind from my high school days.

Two friends and I had decided to venture forth one Saturday morning to bag some ducks near a body of water south and east of Missoula. One of my compadres happened to have a speech impediment. Cliff was in several classes with me and my other friends, as well as playing on our basketball team, and we never gave his speech problem a thought, nor should we have.

Cliff had been bragging to us about this great hunting dog he had; it was partly to get to see this dog in action, that the other two of us had agreed to leave the comforts of home before dawn, traverse a slippery railroad trestle and suffer generally unpleasant conditions, while we awaited the hoped for arrival of a bunch of long-necked birds.

In the course of time our waiting was rewarded by the appearance of a small flock of Mallards. One of us managed to knock down a member of that flock, although, as we had fired almost simultaneously, none of us claimed to be "the man." Our prey landed in the water, about fifteen yards from the edge of the reservoir near which we had been standing.

Time for Fido to perform, right? By the way, Fido (or whatever his moniker may have been) was about the size of a cocker spaniel, although I don't recall the actual breed. Cliff led him to the water's edge, pointed toward the downed duck, and said "Fetch" or something similar. Fido looked up at Cliff as if to say, "Are you kidding me? That water looks not only wet, but cold!"

Cliff had his dog sit, and then he again gave the command to fetch, with the same response, or lack thereof. Cliff subsequently found a stick, tossed it in the direction of the floating bird, and attempted to have his star perform, but still to no avail.

Even without the benefit of exposure to any sun, Cliff's face had, by now, become beet red. He next reached down, picked up the featured member of our quartet, and tossed him about six feet out into the water, only to watch his animal perform a terrific dog paddle back to shore.

By this time, my other friend and I were cracking up, in contrast to Cliff, who was getting highly perturbed, or some similarly descriptive word. Finally, having bypassed any semblance of satisfaction with this canine's contribution to our hunting trip, he began yelling (with the aforementioned speech impediment), "DOD DAN DAWD!"

Apparently Cliff's animal had retrieved many a dry-land game bird without a hitch, but this had been his first opportunity to be "Aqua Dog," and he was having none of it.

We attempted, for about ten minutes, to wash the duck to shore by lobbing rocks just beyond it, but after having as many direct hits on top of the already lead-filled victim of our joint firepower as we did on the far side of it, we gave up, and unanimously adjourned to a popular café back in Missoula to discuss our adventure over burgers and shakes.

I do not recall that Fido received any treats that day.

****

Sub-Chapter 3.2: "Hoosiers"

(Or, Some Adventures with Hoops)

Basketball tends to be popular among both hunters and non-hunters, and regardless of where in those categories I might place myself, I am pleased Doctor Naismith and his peach baskets became an accepted piece of Americana.

Our driveway consisted of a 146.3 foot long (give or take about ten yards) entryway from the road, followed by a large circular area in which to turn around. At the uppermost point of that turning area was our sizeable woodpile, and just a few yards to the right of all that fireplace fodder was a basketball backboard and hoop, built and sturdily planted in the ground by my very own father.

The backboard was constructed from several 1x4 vertical pieces of wood nailed to some 2x4's, all connected to a tall 4x4 pole. (With all those "4's," one would think this might relate to golf rather than basketball, but it does not.) The height of the hoop could be generously described as being somewhere in the general vicinity of ten feet, which is to say, for comparison purposes, that a junior high school basketball team is similar to a junior college team in many ways.

Nevertheless, it was my hoop, and I was thrilled to have it. Other than on those rare occasions when my dad was home from his sales trips, and I wanted to show him my shooting skills, I don't recall that ANYONE ever set foot on my private court with basketball in mind. However, MY feet spent significant time thereon, as did each of my annual basketballs.

To clarify, the number one item on my Christmas list, beginning around the age of eight or nine, was a basketball; and while there were seldom more than two gifts for me under our tree, my first choice was usually there. If not, it became almost a lock that I would get one for my birthday.

All that bouncing around on the rocks and gravel of our driveway, plus that on the blacktop court at my grade school, normally brought to an end the short life of my frequent partner in crime, "Wilson."

(Spoiler alert-- here comes another film reference: No, I did not actually refer to my current basketball by name, as was done decades later by Tom Hanks, who had named his volleyball companion "Wilson" in the film *Castaway*, sometime after the turn of the century. Besides, in some years it may have been "Voit" or "Spalding" or some other brand.)

As mentioned in an earlier segment, having no siblings around with whom to converse, I sometimes substituted inanimate objects to be the recipients of my verbal outpourings, even if I did not actually provide names for them.

For example, when an errant shot (of which there were many) caused my rubber buddy to carom crazily off the rim or the top of the backboard, or to perhaps ricochet from a rock behind the basket following an air ball, said sphere would invariably make a beeline over the side and down towards the creek flowing below the driveway. I would then follow its general route down the hill to retrieve it from the water, or some shrub which sat along the bank.

Upon salvaging the basketball from its ill advised journey, I might then have a parent-like conversation with it (and, like many parent-child conversations, not anticipate any lucid response from the non-parent member). I would explain that, while I would always come to its rescue, we could have so much more quality time together if it would not keep impulsively dashing over the side of the hill.

Besides lecturing on such behavioral disappointments, I also became the voice of the players, the coach and the public address announcer during simulated games I would have with myself.

This is not unique, as I'm aware that many young lads have verbally described aloud, the pretended taking of a game's last second shot from long range. ("He crosses the half court line, puts up a desperation attempt and it's G-O-O-O-O-O-D!" or some such laudatory account.)

In my situation, in addition to vocalizing such game ending heroics, I would also have a running commentary for a full length game (perhaps thirty minutes of real time) interspersed with, in a different voice, of course, chanting from a fan or taunting from a defender.

Unlike the player in *Hoosiers* who sank shot after shot at his outdoor hoop, without the benefit of Hollywood special effects, I never did become particularly proficient in this sport, despite the hours on end spent with my series of basketballs. Perhaps too much of my time was absorbed chasing after the stupid ball, as it was drawn magnetically to the waiting waters of Pattee Canyon Creek.

****

We did not have either middle schools or junior high schools in Missoula at that time; just the eight elementary grades together (and no kindergarten either).

When I was in the sixth grade, I played on my first organized team, in a league sponsored by the local Kiwanis Club. Our team may not have been the worst possible collection of incompetents ever to play the game, but there is no question that we were somewhat lacking in experience, ability or any other basic requirement of a successful basketball team.

While there were referees for our games and uniforms (if you define that as having different colored t-shirts) to differentiate the teams, we had no coaches to recommend things like getting in position for a rebound, passing the ball, setting a screen etc. Lest you think we were at a disadvantage, simply because of our lack of coaching, none of the teams had coaches, so that was not our excuse.

Without going into all the sordid details, we lost our first seven games by such scores as: 27-2; 57-4; and 39-8. We did finish on a high note, winning our eighth and final game by something like 14-11. Great defense, right?

With a year of experience and the same basic roster the following year (nobody had chosen to skip further eligibility by signing with an agent and hoping for success in the draft), we had a much better record, winning seven of eight games and losing only to the league champions.

I cannot explain the turn around, unless the better players on the other teams had won spots on their regular elementary school teams, rather than playing in this Kiwanis League with losers like us.

Ah, but then along came the eighth grade. It was time for any of us older kids who had the desire to play on the so called "varsity" against other grade school teams, to have that opportunity. That is to say, even a mediocre eighth grader was generally given priority over a more talented member of the sixth or seventh grade, when it came to making the roster of whatever sport was involved.

As luck would have it, our school's seventh grade class happened to be loaded with athletic talent. Four players from that seventh grade class went on to start for our high school basketball team as sophomores or juniors; which was no small feat, in that some twelve elementary schools fed into the single high school. To take it a step further, two of those seventh graders wound up playing for the local Montana University basketball team, which, while certainly no Duke University, was still an accomplishment.

As a result, even though there was an unwritten rule that the majority of the twelve varsity players were to be eighth graders, we probably stretched the limits of the coach's adherence to this "given" with seven eighth graders making the team, including yours truly.

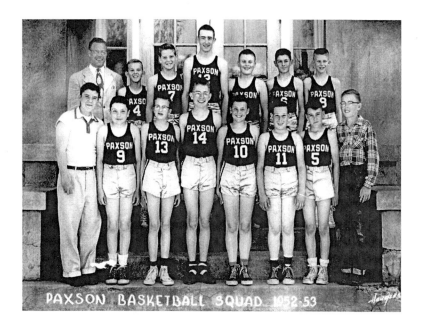

That's me in the front row, with

the number 10 on my jersey.

****

Not that you may care (and if you do not, simply skip to what follows the next series of "*******'s," which designate a new topic or a different slant on an old one), but just as in the numerous sport related novels I read at the time, I am now going to provide a few terribly enlightening details about some of the players on that team.

It seems only appropriate to focus on the tallest member, who was, quite naturally, our center. His name was Paul, and he towered over the rest of us (especially me) by several inches. His older brother, George, was a starter on the high school "B Squad" team at the time, and his younger brother, Jim, became an All-State

Honoree a few years later. However, the athletic gene somehow skipped over Paul.

While performing a simple layup during our warm-up period on the court, he could never seem to assimilate the hand and footwork coordination necessary for making this basic shot.

Even worse, when under the basket in a game or scrimmage, whereas rebounds would tend to fall into his hands with regularity, rather than simply taking one step out to allow him to make an easy put-back basket, Paul would just keep bouncing the ball off the bottom of the rim until some other player would eventually get possession of it. In other words, Paul was not exactly a scoring threat.

Two other eighth grade starters were fairly new to our school, with Wesley having enrolled at our school when his dad was transferred to Missoula to manage the local JC Penney store; while Roger moved to our school from across town when his parents chose to relocate to a different neighborhood. These fellows were our forwards. As you can readily see, our eighth grade's contribution to the team, even with the two recent additions, was minimal at best.

Our starting guards were both seventh graders, as were the first two subs off the bench. I was a second string guard, but saw very limited playing minutes in games, nearly all of which were in mop-up time, when the game was out of reach for our team.

OK, enough of preliminaries. It's time to move to what, in all the novels I had read, was the time the small school would upset the large one in the playoffs; or the slightly flawed hero got his act together to lead the team to victory; or the season long feud between two former friends was put aside for the big game, etcetera, etcetera, etcetera (yet another film reference, of course, as spoken by Yul Brynner in *The King and I*).

While the dramatic elements of MY story were not nearly at the level of those in my reading material, it WAS our final game of the season; although, win or lose, we were destined to finish with more losses than wins. Certainly, if you are one of those individuals who consider the opportunity to win even a game of "horse" to be critical at the time it is played, then you can understand that, as it was my final opportunity to ever suit up for a school's athletic team,

I was excited to be there, even if I spent the whole game on the bench.

Now whether it was the result of closer calls by the referees, or over aggressiveness by the players, we had lost a guard and both forwards to the personal foul limit early in the third quarter, with our top sub also fouling out before the fourth quarter began. If you do the math, you might expect that eventually my name would be called to report in for action, and you would be right.

Up to this point in the season, my scoring had been limited to a single free throw, placing me in a tie for next to last place in team scoring with Billy, another eighth grader. However I was right behind a seventh grader, Redge Martin, who had been given the nickname "Hook" after he threw a ball awkwardly over his head and shoulder as he was being guarded near half court at the end of an earlier blowout; and the ball miraculously hit nothing but net, giving him two points for the season (yes, it would definitely have qualified as a three pointer, had such a shot been part of the rules at that long ago time).

I entered the game with a few minutes left in the fourth quarter and managed to avoid making any errant passes, although doing nothing exemplary offensively to advance our cause. As the clock ticked down to a final buzzer, we faced a tie ballgame, with but two starters, one frequent sub, and two bench warmers remaining on the floor to begin our first and only overtime of the season.

Midway through the extra period, I managed to utilize a screen to break open momentarily, and someone passed me the ball. I was near the key and fired off a jump shot (well, I called it a jump shot, although my feet probably never cleared the floor by more than an inch or two at most). Much to my amazement (and, I'm sure, that of our coach), the ball swished through the net, giving us a one point lead.

We managed to hold that lead until just a minute remained, when our other basic bench warming sub fouled his player in the act of shooting. The shooter, who happened to be one of their top scorers, calmly sank both free throws, again putting us into a one point deficit.

As the opposition pressed us closely, our one remaining skilled guard drew a double teaming, leaving me open. He was able to get the ball to me via a crisp bounce pass; as I turned to take what I thought to be an open shot, their center suddenly was upon me as I released the ball.

Although he deflected my shot, he did so by clobbering my wrist, and was called for a shooting foul. With just seconds remaining, I was sent to the free throw line for two shots, and the opportunity to win the game.

At this time, allow me to inject a piece of information which affected my mindset at the time. As part of every one of our season long practices, each of us would spend some time shooting free throws (unlike what apparently NEVER occurred at practices for certain unnamed future Hall of Fame professional basketball players). As for me, although I was probably the shortest, and definitely the slowest, player on our team, the free throw required no jumping ability, speed or height. I had repeated the shot for hours outside of practice, and had a success ration of nearly 70 per cent, the best on our team. Thus, my mental outlook as I stepped to the line was that of complete confidence.

Then it happened. Our coach called "timeout."

Now we've all observed an opposing coach call a timeout to "ice" the kicker, just prior to a field goal, but this was OUR coach, for God's sake. For some reason, he had decided I might be nervous being in this clutch situation, having had such limited playing time all season. With the rest of my teammates gathered around me, he proceeded to tell me that I should just breathe normally, bend my knees and similar type comments, and above all to not be nervous. In other words, he was telling me not to think about elephants.

In those couple of minutes, my mental state flipped from complete confidence to that of panic, shaking arms, legs of rubber, and erratic breathing. I missed both free throws, and we lost the overtime game 32-31.

One year later, the movie On the Waterfront was released. It included the famous line by Marlon Brando, spoken to his brother, Charley, played by Rod Steiger: "I coulda been a contender. I coulda been somebody." I felt as if that quote had somehow originated from my youthful thought processes toward my coach that afternoon, when he unintentionally undermined every ounce of my self-confidence.

In retrospect, I fully realize that I'd never have gone on to any glory on the basketball floor, but oh how I'd love to have had a "do over" of those closing moments of that particular game.

****

In our high school of some 2,000 students, the best dozen players were on the varsity basketball team, another ten or eleven on the "Bombers" (junior varsity) and still another fifteen on the freshman squad. Having previously painted a reasonably accurate picture of my abilities, it would not surprise anyone that I was not among the 25-30 students selected to represent our high school in basketball games at any of its three levels.

However, during my junior and senior years, eight of us who wanted to play some form of organized ball, but were not on any of the high school sanctioned teams, found a sponsor and became an "independent team."

To clarify, the sponsor provided money for us to buy eight t-shirts, as well as some numbers to iron on to them, to identify who had scored or committed a foul. For this nominal investment, the sponsor would see its name in the sports page of the local newspaper, with an accompanying box score, as we would call in the results of any game we had played.

We competed against smaller high school teams from the valleys surrounding Missoula, who showed interest in substituting a practice game with someone else, in place of just another internal scrimmage. We also scheduled a couple of other independent teams similar to ours which had been formed for the same reason. Our team was victorious on occasion and tasted defeat on others, but we always enjoyed just having the opportunity to play.

Included in our basketball octet were three of us who had gone to school together from grade one (and ultimately, as it turned out, throughout college); a set of twins who had relocated from Renton, Washington, prior to the start of our sophomore year; and

Cliff, the hunting dog owner with the speech problem described earlier.

One of our players might be described under the category "gentle giant." Conrad was not really tall, measuring in at just over six feet and a fraction, but he had the ability to rise to the occasion, when a rebound was there for the taking. His problem was that he did not think of basketball as a contact sport.

That is to say, he might grab an early misfire from the midst of those battling for the ball, but knock an opponent away in the process. He seemed to feel he should apologize for his aggressiveness, and was often heard to say, "Sorry," after which he would be reluctant to repeat his "offensiveness" for the balance of the game.

Now if someone happened to send an elbow into his chin, sternum or other tender body part, he was not averse to retaliating, and he did so in the form of ripping off two or three rebounds in succession. As he was not generally the recipient of many such elbows, he was not really a significant factor in our games, but one couldn't ask for a better friend.

Cliff, a man of few words due to his speech impediment, let his quick hands perform their own sign language to the opposition. He could not only snatch away the ball from a dribbler before said individual realized he had lost possession, but his quick release on his own shots prevented most attempts at a block.

Doug, one of the twins, had a terrific hook shot! Let me restate that. Compared to a Lew Alcindor/Kareem Abdul Jabbar "sky hook," it may have been only moderately impressive. Well actually, when you come right down to it, I guess it wasn't even good enough to enable him to play for the high school varsity, either, but what the hell; to the rest of us it was poetry in motion, considering our level of play.

One of our games matched us against Florence-Carleton, a small high school situated in one of the valleys outside Missoula. The ceiling in their gymnasium seemed to be somewhat lower than any we'd ever seen, and its lack of height was definitely brought into play early in the game, when Doug, after a quick fake to his right, stepped away to let fly his normally accurate hook shot, only to see it bounce off the overhead tiles about one third of the way to the basket.

After one or two similar attempts with the same result, the normally unflappable Doug became completely frustrated, with his game being reduced to tip-ins, or jump shots from inside the paint. (Alright, for clarification, I would admit that in those early days, the only "paint" was the black line on either side of the basket and the line behind which the shooter stood for free throws, but it just seemed better to describe the close in shooting area in a manner to which today's round ball aficionados would relate.)

I have no doubt that the little school just described has long since replaced its vertically challenged gym with one to allow high arching three pointers, unknown at the time, as well as hook shots. Nevertheless, there is no question that their coach had schooled his players to prepare for the carom off the overhead before the shocked opponent realized what was happening. Talk about a home court advantage.

A week or two later, we had scheduled a game with another valley school on a frigid Saturday morning. We arrived at their gym, and noticed that both doors had been propped open with big blocks of wood, which seemed rather silly, since the current temperature was hovering just above fifteen degrees.

"I wonder who the idiot is inside that's attempting to heat the great outdoors!" questioned Wayne, the other member of our twin tandem.

"Probably some numb nuts administrator who already had plans for the day, who had to come in because the coach scheduled a weekend morning game" added Roger, our team's fastest, and most sarcastic, player.

We soon discovered that our initial observations were nearly polar opposites of the reality of the situation. As we entered the locker room to don our uniforms, we could see that the shower floors were covered with ice, with a warning in the form of a hand written "CAUTION" sign having been taped to the tile wall. Far from letting the interior heat escape into the sub-freezing outdoors, they were attempting, unsuccessfully, I might add, to entice some solar heat to enter the premises.

Despite the cold temperatures in the gym, most, if not all of the young men on the floor, had played more than a few times outdoors in equally chilly conditions, and at least there was no snow or ice with which to contend (at least until we hit the showers after the game, which, come to think of it, none of us was foolish enough to do).

There was just one other unusual predicament we faced during our season or two of independent ball. That little glitch took the form of one of the baskets being attached to a solid cement wall, thereby strongly diminishing the likelihood of an all out fast break layup attempt by whichever team was going in that direction. The hosts had tied a well padded tumbling mat from some ceiling support beams to prevent players from actually making direct contact with the concrete, but it still took some "getting used to" by us visitors.

Hey, at least we never had to play in an empty swimming pool, which I understand happened to the Harlem Globetrotters early in their travels.

****

Sub Chapter 3.3: "Three Strikes Are a Good Thing"

Maybe the shooting of a basketball toward an often netless hoop on a garage in some dusty alley, is simply "not up your alley," but on the other hand, you love rolling a somewhat heavier ball down a different type of alley. Yes, it's time to switch the focus to bowling.

As opposed to pickup games of basketball, softball or touch football, I knew very little about bowling, having never even touched this particular type of ball until this point in high school. Hey, I told you I had led a pretty sheltered life.

One snowy weekend afternoon, when other entertainment was in short supply, I reluctantly accompanied a few of my basketball teammates to a local bowling alley. Doug and Wayne, the twins, had each learned to bowl at a much younger age, and they insisted it was far less difficult than I seemed to view it.

"There's nothing to it. Just stick your thumb and two middle fingers in the ball, while holding it in front of your body. Use a five step approach toward the pins, while swinging the ball backwards; aim for a spot just to the right of the head pin; and let gravity bring the ball down to the release point. Once you get those basics down, we'll show you how to 'spot bowl' or how to throw a ball that will curve and all that good stuff. Now, go ahead and try it."

It sure sounded simple when phrased that way, so I acquiesced. I rented some shoes, after which my advisors helped me pick out a ball that would best fit my grip. Then I sat down to don my shoes and await the commencement of evaluating the results of their tutoring.

The alleys were elevated from the area housing the shoe counter, racks holding the rental balls, a refreshment stand, coat hooks and restrooms. With trepidation only slightly less, to me, than that of a condemned prisoner ascending a scaffold, I marched up the four steps to the alleys and took a deep breath, in anticipation of rolling a strike on my first ever ball.

As directed, I supported the ball, which now seemed to weigh well over 100 pounds, with my left hand, holding it just above the level of my belt, sighted the pins and began my approach. I swung the ball backwards in conjunction with my first step forward.

Somewhere in my grasp of instructions, I apparently missed the part where the bowler must maintain a tight grip with the thumb and two fingers during the backswing, because whereas I continued moving forward, my ball slipped off behind me, bounced down the stairs and rolled all the way across the carpeting to the door of the ladies restroom.

If I had been hoping to garner some attention by rolling a strike, I far exceeded my expectations with this initial ball, albeit not of the type I was seeking. After all, it could have been a boring old gutter ball.

I eventually regained my composure from that misfire and survived the next hour or so without further embarrassment, while making the conscious decision that I would not choose to pursue this activity for many years to come. As with many of life's momentary decisions, I did take up the activity again, during my two plus years stationed in Newfoundland while in the Navy, and managed to carry an average in the 165-175 range, but that has no bearing on this segment, so let's move along.

One afternoon a few weeks later, I had agreed to stop by that bowling facility to pick up one of my instructor friends, whose car was temporarily out of commission. Wayne had been called to fill in as a last minute sub for someone who couldn't make it for a recreational league match.

I had dropped off Wayne earlier, stopped at a music store to listen to several albums in which I had an interest, and ultimately returned to his match, anticipating that it should by then be nearly completed. When I arrived, the teams were about four frames from wrapping up, so I sat in a back row to see if I might pick up a few pointers, should I ever again become irrational to the point of stepping into that particular torture chamber.

During previous observations of Wayne's bowling technique, I had always been impressed by his exaggerated backswing, which resulted in the ball rising beyond a point directly above his head, before falling like a pendulum from the one o'clock side of high noon counterclockwise down past six o'clock to his release near four o'clock, with a follow through back to high noon. I had also noticed that all the other competitors brought the ball back, but seldom above shoulder level.

As Wayne led off the ninth frame, the scoreboard indicated his team was only a few pins down, while he was personally working on two strikes in a row. I had learned enough about scoring during my dismal initiation in the sport, to realize a strong finish could bring his team to victory.

The scoreboard hung directly over the alley. It reflected what someone sitting at the table just behind the alleys had written on a score sheet placed on a glass over a lamp, with the enlarged image appearing up on the board for observation by both bowlers and spectators.

Whether it was a jolt of adrenaline, or just the excitement of the moment, I do not know, but Wayne's backswing reached its apex at exactly the spot where the scoreboard was hanging down. His ball struck the edge of said board, raising it just enough to dislodge it from one of the hooks securing it. Although the scoreboard remained attached to the opposite side hook, the unsupported side dropped to the floor, causing quite a commotion, to say the least.

I thought to myself, once the initial alarm and ensuing laughter had subsided, "Ok, in the overall scheme of things, my previous antics could not hold a candle to Wayne's show stopper. Whereas my bowling future was open to debate, he'd definitely have a tough time surpassing that particular comedy sketch."

****

Sub Chapter 3.4: "Three Strikes Are a Bad Thing"

Abner Doubleday's sport of baseball first entered my psyche about 109 years after he allegedly invented the game. It was the autumn of 1948, and I happened to tune in to the Mutual Broadcasting System's World Series contest between the Cleveland Indians and the Boston Braves.

Although we had no professional teams locally, and this was years prior to any type of organized Little League program, I found the game to be interesting. The next day while in town with my mother, I happened upon a sporting magazine which had a story about the World Series, and included the picture of the Indians' mascot.

Montana had always had a sizeable population of Native Americans, and I had seen Lord only knows how many movie westerns on a Saturday afternoon, featuring mostly good cowboys and mostly (all too stereotypically) bad Indians.

Nevertheless, from that day on (until 1959, that is), I adopted the Cleveland Indians as my team, for the simple reasons that the name "Cleveland" sounded good and I loved their cute mascot. Not that it matters, but I have never ever been to Cleveland.

I finished listening to the remainder of that World Series, and by the next summer, I had begun memorizing names of the players on the Indians' roster. In the early 1950s when I spent several weeks with relatives in Iowa, my cousin and I began collecting baseball cards, and I was successful in accumulating them for most of my favorite Cleveland players.

Each summer I would enthusiastically follow pitchers Early Wynn, Bob Lemon and Mike Garcia, plus Bob Feller in the twilight of his career. Although each would win roughly twenty games, they always lost out to the hated Yankees with Vic Raschi, Allie Reynolds and Eddy Lopat, plus the up and coming "Whitey" Ford.

I knew the key stats for Luke Easter at first base, Bobby Avila at second, Ray Boone at short and Al Rosen at the hot corner. I had no idea, nor did I care, that Larry Doby was the first Negro to play in the American League. In fact, as we had no television, I had no idea he was any different from the other players. To take it a step further, even if I had known, he would still have been one of my favorites. (I was thrilled to get to see him play in an "Old Timer's Game" in Denver decades later.)

We may have had a total of three or four Negro families living in Missoula, none of whom I had ever met. I guess I was too young to have developed any prejudicial feelings, and if I had, they would have been more likely to be directed toward Indians rather than Negroes, due to all that scalping, arrows through the shoulders and blood curdling screams I had soaked up at the movies.

But I digress (and you might as well get used to my doing so).

You'll note that I said I was an avid Cleveland fan until 1959. So what changed? Did I feel the mascot was degrading to Native Americans? No. Was there now a local minor league team whose parent club changed my allegiance? Well, yes there was, but that was not the reason. So, what happened?

It was because of a Rocky and a rookie.

The rookie was Al Kaline, who jumped directly from high school to the Detroit Tigers in 1953. While I was a staunch Indians fan, I began to take an interest in Kaline, and the relatively unsuccessful Tigers, consistently a second division team during his first half dozen years on the roster.

Then in 1959, Rocky Colovito was traded to Detroit for Harvey Kuenn. Rocky was my current hero amongst all those

57

playing for Cleveland. I dropped the Indians like a hot rock and the Tigers became, and have remained to this day, my favorite of all the American League clubs. Oh, yes, I have never been to Detroit either.

****

You may have noted that I am saying far more about teams I followed in the newspaper, heard on the radio or, eventually, watched on television, as opposed to actually playing the game myself. Very astute on your part! I NEVER played in a baseball game; not for an inning, not even for a single pitch.

There was no Little League at that time in Missoula. I don't know whether or not I'd have signed up if there had been the opportunity, but it's a moot point. I had to be satisfied with being a spectator or a fan, rather than a participant.

There WAS the game of softball, however.

****

We had some relatively flat acreage just down canyon from our home which provided an area almost large enough in which to play this particular game. What we generally lacked was enough bodies to field a team. On a really successful day, with extensive preplanning and perhaps coinciding with my having invited a friend from town to stay overnight, we might have been able to scrape up as many as seven players. The age differences, as well as related skill levels for each age, ranged from as young as seven years to as old as thirteen.

We were limited to playing "workup," which, for those of you who didn't have to resort to this abbreviated form of the game, or may have forgotten doing so, consisted of having three batters, a pitcher, a first baseman and one or two outfielders, with one of the batters acting as a catcher.

Once the current batter had been retired via strikeout, being thrown out at first base or having his fly ball caught; he would move to the outfield and would work his way back to being a batter again via outs by the then batting players. He would move from, say, Outfielder #2 to Outfielder #1 to First Base to Pitcher and finally back to Batter.

If one of the bigger kids hit a deep ball toward what, except for the narrow width of this playing area, would have been referred to as left field, it was considered a home run. As soon as the fly ball headed in that direction, all hands would drop everything to begin a search over the side of the hill and/or in the ever present stream running there.

Few softball memories were created on that field, as very few opportunities to play came to pass. The unlikelihood of assembling enough kids, even for workup, shifted the site of significant softball play to those occasions when I stayed in town with a friend. In those instances it was easy to find a group of similarly aged youths choosing up sides for a game at the popular Bonner Park or some similar location.

****

During lunch hour at our grade school, there was always an expanded game of workup being played during springtime. If a student returned to school with perhaps a half hour remaining of his lunch hour, there were decent odds he might get up to bat. As the length of time diminished and the number of players increased, those odds dropped dramatically.

As you can imagine (or recall from memory, if you had similar experiences), with twenty or thirty boys in the infield-outfield area, the batter had little likelihood of getting beyond first base, even if he made it there safely. Still, one could seldom anticipate moving through the ranks of fielders to become a batter during the limited time remaining.

It should be noted that there was a form of discrimination among the eight age levels of students. No one from the first four grades was allowed to participate with the "big kids," and rarely did a fifth grader join in either. So we are basically talking about the top three years of students.

As I desired the opportunity to play as much as possible, I would wolf down whatever lunch I had brought and be amongst the first five or six players starting the game. That way I might get to bat at least two times before the masses arrived, and I'd be relegated to being a fielder for the balance of lunch hour.

While my abbreviated dining plan might lead you to believe I then experienced some sort of success in the batter's box, in reality, it typically meant nothing more than a couple of one hoppers to an infielder who would easily throw me out at first every time.

On one particular occasion as a sixth grader, I had finally succeeded in working my way up to becoming one of the four batters. As I was about to select a bat destined to give me a hit, an eighth grader, who had arrived late, approached me and suggested that he "pinch hit" for me, with me standing behind him and doing my own running.

Knowing he was one of the star athletes in our school, I figured this was a great idea, as he would quite likely get a safe hit and I would not be thrown out at first base for the millionth time.

I am well aware that no one has ever been overly impressed by my athletic skills, nor should they be. Conversely, the fact that I was not athletically proficient should not lead anyone to believe I made up for it with smarts, especially as I stood grinning safely at first base, following my pinch hitter's successful single.

The proud smile slowly disappeared from my face, as I realized that after all the time I had invested moving from being one of the numerous outfielders to the four infield positions and pitcher, to finally earn a turn at bat, I had freely and foolishly handed it over to a con artist, who had just arrived at the backstop, and effortlessly smooth talked me out of batting.

****

There was a spring ritual in the late 1940s and early 1950s involving local high school freshmen and the eighth graders at the various feeder schools. It involved the brief "kidnapping" of an eighth grade boy by a group of freshmen, aided by an older high school student with both a car and valid driver's license, during which the kidnapped student's head was shaved.

The rumor, amongst younger students, was that the high school kids used broken bottles to cut the hair, although in reality, they used electric razors. It was sort of a right of passage for the eighth grade boys, and while they always would run at the sight of a car full of high school kids, they exhibited their new hair style with pride for weeks to come. Sometimes it would be a Mohawk; at other times stripes, either side to side or front to back; or in yet other instances, just a bald cut.

The same older student who had stolen my batting opportunity a few weeks earlier, was again standing around the backstop, visiting with an assortment of students who had convened there, with roughly twenty minutes remaining before the bell would ring to commence afternoon classes.

He possessed what many considered to be "great hair," and had been observed laughing at his classmates when their locks were shorn, while bragging loudly that he could outrun any of those high school clowns who might try to capture him.

On the day in question, I had finally worked my way up to the position of pitcher, when I noticed two cars parked down the street, just out of view of those near the backstop. Whether my former pinch hitter was in the process of conning yet another unsuspecting underclassman out of his batting opportunity, or was simply sharing the latest joke with his admiring audience, he did not observe the arrival of those bent on his capture.

From the mound, I had the perfect observation post, watching innocently, as the visitors emerged from the assemblage of boys and girls, and cornered their prey by chasing him into the backstop before gang tackling him. He was carried yelling, twisting and squirming to one of the waiting cars.

About ten minutes later, he sheepishly wandered back to the school grounds, complete with not only a double circle of hair (visualize a mini donut placed inside a larger one) replacing his earlier wavy locks, but the remaining hair had been colored green, as well.

His was the most artistic of all the "shavings" I was to behold that year. Although I may sound as if I took pleasure in seeing this school hero get his comeuppance, he was really a pretty decent guy.

******

As I warned you earlier, here is one of those dreaded film references. Although it may take a couple of paragraphs to get there, it really does have a connection to the topic of softball. *The*

Ten Commandments starring Charleton Heston and a cast of thousands, would not be produced for another few years, so I had yet to see the laser-like printing from God onto the slates held by Moses in that movie.

Furthermore, our family seldom, if ever, attended church. But as a future CPA being predestined to be aware of critical details, I had somewhere along the way picked up a fuzzy awareness of the Old Testament's TOP TEN, and generally made a reasonably decent attempt at keeping them, at least to the limited extent of my understanding thereof.

For example, I may not have been aware that it was so specified in Item #3, but I did not take the Lord's name in vain, as I had not yet learned to swear. Sliding down another three slots on the tablet, I certainly had not killed anyone. Being somewhat unclear about #7, I gathered it was something that did not involve me, but instead related to adults and adulteresses only.

To sum it up, and no doubt, God would not have seen it this way, I felt moderately successful with having kept all the single digit precepts. However, good old #10 was the commandment which reared its ugly head, and completely overwhelmed me, during one particular experience in grade school.

****

I have no recollection of the first glove I used when I initially began playing catch and/or getting involved in some form of softball games in grade school. It was probably one my dad had picked out for me as a birthday gift. I just do not remember.

On the other hand, one Monday, when a classmate arrived at school with a particular new glove, I recall vividly how I immediately lusted after that item something awful, thereby committing the "sin of covetousness" in spades.

Unlike any other mitt I had ever used, this one had just the perfect feel on my hand. It may not sound like it makes sense, but in addition to the thumb and webbing, there were only three "fingers" on the glove, resulting in having one's two middle digits cozily ensconced in the center compartment.

When my friend thoughtfully allowed me to try it out while he was batting, it seemed like it had been grafted to my hand.

Suddenly balls which had been bouncing over or under my own glove were drawn, as if by a magnet, into this new glove's webbing. To get to the point, I had to have one just like it.

I inquired about where it had been purchased, and for how much money. He replied that Montgomery Ward was the place, and he also told me what had been the retail price of it.

That night I checked my porcelain bank which, I think, was in the shape of a kitten or a dog. No, we were not Jewish or anything, I just wasn't into pigs. The contents added up to nearly what I needed for the glove, but not quite enough. Montana did not then have a sales tax, and may still be one of the few states without one. Therefore I knew to the penny the amount that I was short.

I then went about seeking extra chores around the house for which I might be paid; along with a one week advance on my allowance, which had just recently been increased from twenty to twenty-five cents, I quickly accumulated the funds needed for my greatly anticipated acquisition of this perfect glove.

Now I just had to work out how I could arrange for a shopping trip to Montgomery Ward. That may sound like no big deal, until you consider that we lived some four or five miles southeast of my grade school, whereas the Wards store was two miles to the north in downtown Missoula. My transportation to and from Paxson Elementary was provided by the school system, not my parents, so I could not just happen to miss the bus, unless I wished to cause big time conflicts with my mother, who would have to make an unplanned trip to town to bring me home.

Although I had no choice but to wait patiently, that Friday my mother advised that she had to come to town for groceries and some other items, and would be picking me up after school. When I hopped into the car, I sweet talked her into taking a slight detour and dropping me off at Wards, while she took care of her errands.

I entered the store and practically ran down the stairs to the sporting goods department. Arriving at the section which displayed baseball and softball equipment, I began searching diligently for you know what. But it was nowhere to be found!

Despite having full confidence that I could pick that exact glove from a large pile of such objects by feel alone, I had foolishly not bothered to notice either the brand name or model number of it, when allowed to use it during that earlier afternoon. I simply never considered that it wouldn't just be sitting there like a puppy at a pet store, waiting for me to lovingly take it into my possession.

I was in a quandary to say the least. There was no way I could wait until the following Monday to obtain the needed details from my classmate, as the next trip to town could be another week or two, and I just had to acquire that glove!

Gathering up my courage, I began looking for a clerk to assist me with my problem. Being somewhat small in stature, I probably failed to impress whoever was on the floor, that I was a prospective big spender worthy of his attention. Eventually I found someone to help me; but how was I to explain my enigma? ("Hi there, I'm looking for a particular softball glove, the manufacturer and model of which I have no clue. Can you help me?")

I decided to pose my query as follows: "Excuse me, sir. I have a friend at school who told me his new glove came from Montgomery Ward, but I can't find one like it on display. My friend's name is Alan Strom. Would your records be able to indicate the type of glove he got here?"

Bear in mind that Missoula, at the time, had a population of perhaps 25,000-30,000 people, and also consider that cash was really the only media of exchange. Credit cards were not even a twinkle in some bank corporation executive's eye, and store charge accounts were seldom, if ever, utilized.

Thus the records of any purchase would have been a single line on a cash register tape, which would long since have been rolled up, secured with a rubber band, and set aside in a box somewhere (perhaps for some bright eyed rookie CPA to review?).

The clerk politely excused himself and walked upstairs. A few minutes later he returned, walked over to a side doorway, through which he then entered. Shortly afterward, he exited with ....MY GLOVE!

Grinning to the point that my face might have split open, I thanked him profusely, although I did not know the meaning of that word at the time, and pulled out my resources to pay the ransom on this new family member, before walking up the stairs to await my mother's arrival.

Had I realized at the time how utterly ridiculous, outlandish or just plain hopeless, had been my request of this clerk, I would definitely have been impressed beyond words, with his successful discovery of the previously unfound piece of softball equipment. Instead, being the ignorant youth that I was, I simply considered him to be one of the more helpful employees that I had encountered within the retail establishment, but not really a "superstar," or anything of the kind.

If you are familiar with Paul Harvey's *The Rest of the Story* clips on the radio; in a similar vein, you will now discover the "story behind my story" as to how the ingenious clerk was able to provide me with the desired glove.

Using another film reference, I am reminded of the line from *Casablanca* spoken by Rick (Humphrey Bogart) when his former lover, Ilsa (Ingred Bergman) wanders into his bar: "Of all the gin joints in all the towns in all the world, she walks into mine."

While my incident and its resolution were not nearly as improbable as in that movie situation, there are some similarities. For example, had I walked into JC Penney, or any of the other possible outlets carrying softball equipment, and asked the same question I had posed to that specific clerk, I'd have been dismissed as the dimwitted delinquent I was.

What I did not know at the time of my request, however, was the fact that my school friend's father just happened to be the store manager of our local Montgomery Ward. My clerk had simply walked up to the manager's office, or had found him on the main floor somewhere, and told him some kid was looking for the same glove that he, the manager, had given his son.

Mister Strom had then told him a new shipment was in the storeroom, awaiting the arrival of the high school receiving clerk to check it in. He was to leave a note on the open case, indicating that one of the gloves had been removed, and why, and then to make the sale to his customer. Riddle solved, customer satisfied, end of story.

****

Sub Chapter 3.5: Footballs Sure Bounce Funny

In an area between one quarter and one half mile down the canyon from my cozy abode, there were located four homes, constructed in what could be described as a valley within a canyon, or at least a wide spot on either side of the road. One of these residences housed the local university's current head football coach, Ted Shipkey, along with his wife and three sons.

While Jimmy, the youngest of these siblings, was my age, and became a reasonably close friend during the relatively short time of his father's stay at the university, the two older brothers generally avoided any contact with us young pups.

One day, however, the stars conspired to bring together the three of them, two other boys who lived in that same four house neighborhood, a friend spending the weekend with me and, obviously, me.

The reason for this assemblage of mostly unskilled athletes or jock wanna be's, was to have a game of touch football on Ely's Pasture, a sizeable chunk of grazing land belonging to an old couple named Ely, who, in addition to the pasture and their one small house, had constructed two huge red barns. That may not seem unusual; until you consider that the sum total of livestock they owned at the time consisted of three cows.

Don't ask me why such a strange ratio of animals to structures, as I have no clue. Perhaps they had planned on more bovines before business bombed. Or perhaps the health of one or the other of them had declined. It doesn't really matter, except to make it clear that we did not have to worry about dodging dangerous "dogies," or their droppings, to any extent.

Tom, the coach's middle son, had a horse he was learning to ride. He also acquired a motorbike the following year, which he deemed essential in order to deliver the local newspaper to the moderately few residents of the canyon, although he dropped the route before the cold weather hit. I guess he kept the bike, but that has nothing to do with this incident anyway, so let's just drop it, OK?

In any event, Tom chose to ride his horse the equivalent of an entire couple of blocks, from his house to the pasture. He then removed the saddle and tied the animal to some shrubs.

The bigger kids didn't go all out against those of us who were lacking in size, but somehow during one convoluted play, Jimmy got his leg caught in an awkward pileup. When the dust cleared and the rest of us were getting to our feet in anticipation of the next pass or pitchout, he was still on the ground.

Tears were flowing freely to accentuate his cries of "Ow! Oh boy! My leg, it really hurts!" or some such expressions of discomfort. Remember, this was before children adopted the language of a thumb smashing carpenter, certain truck drivers or longshoremen.

Inasmuch as none of us present had gone to medical school, it was still our combined considered opinion that we might well have a broken leg with which to deal, and that someone should probably go to the coach's house for help. In the first place, it was the closest home of any of the participants in our game, and, more importantly, the injured player's mother was there.

Had it been my decision, I'd have taken off running as fast as my chubby little legs would carry me in the direction of the closest responsible adult. However, Ted, the oldest of the three brothers, told Tom to "go get mom while I look after Jimmy." Rather than relying on his two human legs, Tom determined that a jockey had better odds than a jogger of reaching the desired destination in the shortest timeframe.

I visualized how my Saturday matinee cowboy heroes would have grabbed the reins of "Lightning," "Trigger," "Champion" or some other equine of Hollywood fame, leapt on its back, and galloped off to bring the posse, or whatever the mission was.

Instead, Tom (very slowly and deliberately, in my opinion) walked to where his blanket and saddle lay. He carried them over to his mount, placed them on the animal's back, cinched everything up quite properly and, finally, inserted his shoe into the stirrup, pulled himself into the saddle, and began the short ride to his house for help.

I have placed this incident in the category of "football related recollections" even though I've not provided any description of the football game.

Truth be told, I have never had a love of horses, especially when it comes to having to "ride" them, an activity which I have tried to avoid at all costs. Therefore, in order to include something for all you horse lovers; this was my best shot, other than an incident occurring in Yellowstone Park which, like the Grizzly Bear adventure, will appear further on in the book.

As an epilogue of sorts:

- Jimmy's leg was, in fact, broken. He had to wear a cast for several months, but he fully recovered.
- The horse in question may have deposited its rider at his residence that afternoon a few seconds earlier than such arrival could have been attained on foot, but just barely. I have no idea what sort of future that brave steed had.
- We never again played football in Ely's Pasture.
- The coach shortly thereafter departed to take another college position somewhere in California.
- The old couple never did expand the size of their livestock holdings.

****

Unlike our independent basketball team, which provided realistic game-like competition, there was nothing comparable for the game of football.

Doug and Wayne lived in a home situated at the edge of the university campus, 542 Eddy Avenue, to be specific, for those of you who may ever have driven around the town of Missoula. Diagonally across the street from them was the "Clover Bowl," a grass field one block wide and a much longer block long.

It was the practice field for the university's marching band, as well as the site of multiple fraternity touch football games during the fall, and softball games in the spring. But on Saturday afternoons it was available for slugs like us to use at our discretion.

For instance, we might practice kicking field goals over one of the six goal posts, and compare our leg strength (distance) and accuracy to that of the current high school team's kicker, whom we all felt had won his position on the varsity team by default.

If there were at least six of us, we might play a "pass only" game of touch football, sort of a precursor to what was later made famous by the Kennedy family in their sizeable yard. If only three or four of us were present, we might take turns being quarterback while others ran pass patterns, hoping that some additional people driving past might observe us, and stop to join us in an actual game.

One night, six of us had congregated at the twins' home after having gone to a movie. We all seemed in the mood to play the role of tough guys, due in part to just having seen the original *Ransom*, in which we had watched Glenn Ford kick the baddies' butts in their failed kidnapping attempt. (Yes, the film was later remade with the much more aggressive Mel Gibson, but at the time, Glenn Ford seemed plenty tough to us.)

It was too early to call it a night, but not so late that we'd upset neighbors by doing something over on the Clover Bowl. Hmm. What to do? It was far too dark to pass around the ball; but one of our sextet suggested we could play a modified game of tackle, with the ball carrier lining up directly behind the center so as not to get a running start.

Not that anyone was watching us, but had they been, our activity may have looked similar to a scrum in rugby. At the time, none of us had heard of rugby, and thought we had discovered a great new activity. It was really just a lot of pushing and shoving, with nobody sure who had the ball, but determined to block or tackle as appropriate. The entire game may have taken place within all of ten yards of the field. Great fun! Of course, maybe it's just a "guy thing."

****

Sub Chapter 3.6: It Takes Balls to Play this Game

Whereas swimming had been the only sport in which, to this point, I had ever displayed even minimal talent, near the end of my junior year of high school, I was the recipient of a tennis racquet for my birthday. For several years we had enjoyed a regulation size badminton court set up on a flat area just below our Pattee Canyon home; much like working my way up from a .22 birdshot rifle to a pump shotgun for hunting, my folks must have figured it was time for me to move up from badminton to tennis.

My friend, John Wertz, had gotten into tennis a year or two earlier, and one afternoon he offered to give me some pointers, but without much success. For openers, he was left-handed; so it seemed I had to reverse whatever he told me before attempting it. Then, he would have me repeat boring things like tossing the ball in the air for the serve for extended periods, when what I wanted to do was to try hitting the ball back and forth. I don't know whether teacher or student first tired of the "lessons" that day, but we soon abandoned them for more productive activities.

I joined the high school tennis club my senior year. Under the watchful eye of a faculty advisor, our club was allowed to practice hitting ground strokes against the wall of the girls' gym after school a couple afternoons per week during the winter. I was beginning to feel comfortable hitting a forehand, but while attempting to similarly improve my backhand stroke, managed to break seven separate window panes located high up on the second floor of the building within about a fifteen minute time span. I was basically presented with a "cease and desist order" by the teacher in charge, and was summarily banned from future indoor practice sessions.

Several of my close high school friends, including Doug Baldwin, became skilled enough at the sport to compete in the State Interscholastic Games in May of that senior year, but I was not amongst them.

The Megerth family lived next door to the Wertz's, and their son, Roger, had honed his own tennis skills earlier in life such that he not only competed in the annual state tourney, but became the, at the time unprecedented, four time Montana High School State Champion. Although he was three years older than were we, he was always very friendly when he saw John and me tossing a baseball back and forth in the street in front of the two houses or shooting hoops on the Wertz driveway next door.

Later, as a college sophomore, I signed up for a tennis class for P.E. Much to my delight, the instructor was none other than Roger Megerth. He had gone to Pamona College for his undergraduate degree, playing for their varsity tennis team, but had returned to Missoula to obtain his Masters. In case you hadn't figured it out by now, Roger was my tennis idol.

On our first day of class, after warming up by hitting a few basic ground strokes, he had each of us move to the base line to serve from both the ad and deuce positions, in order to get a feel for what level of experience we might have developed for that aspect of the game.

While playing during the previous two summers with Doug, John and others, I had somehow managed to pick up a potentially potent serve. It was pretty fast, with some real pop on it. Perhaps I should clarify that just a tad. It could be considered a "wild serve" to the receiver, as he couldn't tell from my toss and racquet motion, just where it was going. Unfortunately, neither could I.

When it was my turn to serve, Roger acknowledged that he remembered me from my friendship with his next door neighbor years earlier, and said something along the lines of "Show me what you've got."

Had I been given twelve balls to serve, in lieu of just the two, I would probably have hit ten of them either long or into the net. To everyone's amazement, I not only managed to get both serves into the service box, but neither of them was returnable. My first serve blazed directly into Roger's body, all but handcuffing him in his attempt to return it. My second serve to the ad court hit several feet short of the back of the box and hopped well wide of his lunging swing.

He tapped his racquet strings against his opposite hand in the accepted manner of indicating "Well done!" and moved on to the next student. To say that I was ecstatic would be an understatement, and under the circumstances, I felt it best not to tell Roger or anyone else in the class that my intent had been to hit the first shot out wide and the second one into the body.

As the class progressed over following weeks, Roger took me under his wing and gave me numerous pointers to improve my overall playing ability. Over the next year, my game improved to the point that I entered the All Fraternity Tennis Tournament on a doubles team with a fraternity brother. We lost in the semi-finals. The next year I teamed up with another SAE, Wayne "Tink" Hinrichs, and we won the doubles championship. (I still have the belt buckles given as the prize for winning.)

Other than three or four required classes I had missed due to scheduling conflicts, I had completed everything needed to graduate with a Business Degree within four years. Since I was currently in the process of applying for Navy Officer Candidate School, I decided to remain in school for another year, taking various elective classes of interest along with the few required ones. One such elective was Varsity Tennis.

Montana was a member of the eight-team Skyline Conference, although generally considered the weak link in all conference athletic team competitions. In years past, the tennis team might have included no more than one or two scholarship players. Just a year earlier they had two, Mike Hogarty and Don Hubbard (the latter yet another SAE). However this year there were none.

We did not have a coach, either. A returning player from the prior year's varsity team volunteered to be a player-coach. We were initially assigned a ranking on the varsity team by drawing numbers, and proceeded to challenge each other during our daily practices for the chance to move up in position. I managed to latch on to position number six out of the eleven on the team by the time our first traveling trip commenced.

Fortunately for me, the fellow in the number two slot was also in Law School studying for the State Boards, and was therefore unable to travel, or even play in many of the home matches, leaving me as the fifth and final member of the traveling team, plus occasional home matches. Still another player, ranked near the bottom, dropped the course and left the team.

Our mode of transportation was a Chevy Corvair, into which was squeezed our five players and a graduate assistant faculty advisor, with our gear similarly crammed in the trunk. As both the lowest ranking and one of the smaller players on the team, I got to "ride the hump" in the back seat at all times.

Our first road trip took us to Utah to play the three conference schools in that state (Utah, BYU and Utah State). Utah had been reigning conference tennis champs for several years running. Whereas we had zero players on scholarship, they probably had at least 15-18 of them.

Just prior to the first match, our player coach advised us that while we probably had no hope of winning anyway, he was going to juggle the team such that our #1, #2 and #3 players would play at positions #3, #4 and #5; with our #5 (that would be me) playing against Utah's #1 and our #4 playing their #2. That would be called "improperly aligning one's team," even in the best light, but we were so highly outclassed, I doubt that Utah's players even noticed.

We lost each and every match on that road trip, and fared no better in our following home matches against the same three schools. Our player-coach continued to stay with the "stacked team" approach, which made me feel like little more than a sacrificial lamb every time.

As the season was winding down, we were on a non-conference road trip to Washington and Idaho. Our final match of the trip was in Spokane against Gonzaga. Although I had chosen not to say anything regarding our positioning during the season, lest I sound like a whiner, two other players on the team convinced the coach to play this match "straight up."

Because only four courts were available that day on which to play our matches, my #5 singles match was delayed until the top four matches were completed. I had walked from court to court, watching as we split the four singles matches, winning at first and fourth singles while losing at #'s two and three. Then while our top four singles players were converted into two doubles teams, I finally commenced my #5 singles match.

Much to my delight, I was managing to stay even with my opponent, winning the second set after dropping the first. By now, our doubles teams had quickly completed their matches, winning one and losing the other. Thus as I began my third set, our two teams were deadlocked at three wins each.

I'll not dramatize things any further, but simply say that I somehow squeaked out a 7-5 third set victory, propelling our Montana squad to its first (and, as it turned out, only) team win of the season.

Montana University's 1962 Varsity Tennis Team.

As you analyze me in the photo (second from left, standing) you'll note not only that I'm getting a jump start on a receding hairline, but also my goofy smile which seems to say "Please, please, please. Don't awaken me to ask what I'm doing posing with actual bona fide athletes."

It was quite a thrill for me to have had the opportunity to be playing a varsity sport for my college, even if I was in that situation, for all intents and purposes, by default. Whether a result of my winning that Gonzaga match, or due to having played in slightly over half of all scheduled matches, I was one of five players qualified to receive a letter jacket, an item of apparel which I wore proudly during my last summer in Yellowstone and years following.

Over subsequent decades, when reconnecting with either of the Baldwin twins, or Con or others from that close circle of friends from high school/college, it never fails to come up in conversation about the absurdity of the guy with the least athletic credentials of any of us, being the only one to wind up with an "M Club" jacket.

****

Ok, enough of this sport related stuff. Even naïve little kids ultimately grow up; hormones take charge and life just keeps getting better (eventually).

****

Chapter 4

Breasts and other Pleasant Surprises

Perhaps it was the naiveté of the Eisenhower 50s; possibly the propaganda of family television shows such as *Leave It To Beaver* and *Father Knows Best*; or maybe it was simply being in a small-town Montana environment; but its younger residents inevitably seemed a bit behind the times in both clothing and hair styles, as well as the latest products, none of which had climbed over the mountains or crossed the prairies from either coast into our protected little Shangri La. Sexual enlightenment might also be included.

Oh, we had our share of young people who knew what "it" was all about, but there were many who were no more knowledgeable than was I. Now to proceed:

Allow me to start with some background on my parents. Neither of them were "believers." They did not attend church, even for Easter or Christmas services. They felt that everything started and ended with whatever happened right here on earth. No afterlife, no heaven or hell. When it ends, it ends. Period, lights out, the party's over, crossed the finish line, end of story. Those are not my beliefs, but they were theirs.

This is not meant to imply that they were self-centered, greedy or anything of the kind. They were the epitome of what are considered to be "good people," always willing to lend a hand when needed. They served in various capacities of clubs, civic groups, PTA, Cub Scouts and the like.

They once took into our home a boy, slightly younger than I was, and cared for him over an eighteen month time frame, while his mother was painfully dying of cancer. He lived with us during that period without any financial remuneration from the boy's father, who was already financially strapped, due to his wife's medical expenses.

Young Jimmy, who stayed with us during his mother's cancer battle, posing with me (and two of those female versions of people) in front of the historic "Freedom Train" which toured the then 48 states in the late 1940s.

Jimmy and I; keeping the peace in the wintry wild west.

Even had the lad's father tried to buy groceries, or in some other way attempted to lessen the financial burden taken on by my parents' free foster care (long before there was such a term), my folks would have politely, but firmly, declined such an offer.

In other words, they were pretty decent types, all things considered, for those who think "good works" get one into heaven; although since they didn't believe in heaven, it wasn't a factor. Just like in that Christmas song regarding Santa, they were "good for goodness sake."

Although of merely average stature, and in no way appearing muscular, to my way of thinking; there was nothing of which my dad was afraid, or from which he would back down. He had been in the company of numerous unsavory (i.e. dangerous) shipmates, first on a tanker, and later on a freighter destined for Glasgow, Scotland, while not yet twenty years of age. Despite his earlier association with obviously rough speaking shipmates, and considering that he was in no way religious, I never recall hearing him use any vulgar language in my presence.

Yes, if he stubbed his toe, he would probably utter a "Damn it!" If he got really upset about something, he might expand it to "Damn it to hell." As an exclamation of amazement, he could be quoted to have said "Lord God Almighty," even while professing no belief in an almighty being. Other than those, or similar exceptions, he never used any of what today, might be parenthetically described as "expletive deleted" in one of our current family newspapers.

Of course, ladies NEVER used coarse language, at least in public; and as my mother was quite a lady, I never heard her lips convey such things either.

As a result, any crude references to body parts or bodily functions were unknown to me as a youngster; when they did begin to seep into my thought process, they came not from my home life, but from whatever my various companions provided me.

For example, when describing bathroom related activity, I didn't learn pee and poop, wee-wee and doo-doo, number one and number two, or even the more formal urination and defecation. I definitely never heard piss and shit. What I was taught was "big and little."

I have never heard anyone else use those references, but it apparently worked satisfactorily in developing my toilet training. Still, such references could leave me appearing somewhat lacking in understanding in certain circumstances. For example, during a summer when I spent time with my grandmother in Iowa, she kept asking me about my "BMs," and while I always replied "OK," I had no idea what she was talking about, until much later, when I learned she had been inquiring about the status of my bowel movements.

Anyhow, with that extended preface, although I considered my father to be afraid of no one or no thing, when it eventually came time for him to discuss with his young son the "Facts of Life," my dad's otherwise fearless reputation was in a world of trouble!

****

Although my father was frequently away from home, involved in the selling of a variety of products throughout a five state area, every now and then, he had to cover Missoula and the surrounding small towns. Such sales calls could occupy several days.

During one of these timeframes, my mother had decided he should drive me to school in the mornings, rather than have me utilize transportation provided by the county. He could then use this togetherness time to cover the popular "birds and bees" topic with me.

While I do not recall precisely how he attempted to initiate this phase of my education, I do remember that it involved drawing pictures on the very dusty dash of his car. The span of time covering the departure from our driveway until our arrival at my elementary school approximated some fifteen to twenty minutes, and we made absolutely no progress on the first of our four scheduled mornings, simply because he spent it telling me what he was GOING to talk about, rather than actually talking about it.

The second morning he drew a big circle in the dust. He then explained that the circle represented an egg carried inside the female body, which, by itself, could not become a baby; but if it was fertilized by things called spermatozoa, that a baby could certainly be the result of such fertilization.

Obviously he had to keep his eyes on the road, as the canyon was a series of blind curves; therefore his artwork did not have as much time to be adequately developed as might have been the case, had we been covering this topic at the kitchen table over milk and cookies. As a result, we had arrived at school long before I had the opportunity to learn just what these spermatozoa looked like. I would never try to give an opinion about the age old question of which came first, the chicken or the egg; but for this particular lesson, the egg was definitely the starting point.

On morning three we progressed to a picture of little wormy things on the dashboard, and their apparent plan to somehow break through the shell of yesterday's still present egg drawing. These worm-like creatures turned out to be the previously described spermatozoa. Many of them apparently got involved in searching out the single most likely point of entry in the egg, but, unlikely as it might seem, it took only one such successful entry to enable the egg to fulfill its role of becoming a baby.

The final morning of these art lessons (he had to leave earlier on Friday to set up some sort of demo) centered on the development of this successful sperm and egg growth into an actual baby. He drew tiny arms and legs, to go with a large head, and explained that it continued developing over a nine month period until the mother gave birth.

He then asked if I had any questions about what we had covered over the four days. I replied that it seemed pretty clear, and I exited the car to start another day of school.

Of course I had absolutely no clue about what my mother had actually wanted him to discuss with me. Although covering in great detail how the sperm fertilized the egg and the nine month period of gestation leading up to childbirth, he had failed to mention the source of these spermatozoa, or how they managed to get on the same playing field with the egg.

Furthermore, while stating that the baby remained in the mother's stomach for all that time, which might explain why some women seemed to have a large tummy, he didn't expand further.

Nor did he explain how the baby was relocated from inside the mother's stomach into a baby crib.

In other words, I remained as ignorant after those four sessions as I had been before them. I didn't tell him, but I'd much rather have talked about the next hunting or fishing trip we might be taking.

If I seem to be poking fun at my father, let me turn the finger back at myself, as I don't recall giving even the "dusty drawing on the dash" presentation to either of our two fine sons. Somehow or other, they must have learned the basics, as both are now parents of some mighty wonderful offspring, our grandchildren. In my defense, there was just so much more information available for young people our sons' ages, than there had been for me at the same relative age, thereby reducing the need for a lot of input on my part. Or another way of putting it, "A poor excuse is better than none at all."

****

While I was far from knowledgeable concerning members of the opposite sex, and how they differed from boys, beyond the "Sugar and spice and everything nice" versus "Snakes and snails and puppy dog tails" rhymes, my eyesight was twenty-twenty, so there were a few things I could discern without parental assistance.

Furthermore, I was able to sense the presence of certain protrusions in the chest area by touch as well as by sight. To clarify and eliminate any confusion, I'm not referring to the use of my hands or fingers at this point. I'm definitely not saying that such touching ever brought about thoughts related to anything of an erotic nature.

For example, when I received hugs from my grandmother, or females of a similar age, I often felt buried in the softness of their ample breasts, which tended to hit me at head level. While intended as a loving gesture, the experience was obviously about as far away from being in any way sensual as one could imagine.

On the other end of the spectrum were girls my age. The Episcopal Church, attended by the families of a couple of my buddies, sponsored (or at least, allowed use of their basement for) a dance class for seventh graders. Though our family was not affiliated with the church, I was allowed to participate in the classes; perhaps because my young friends' parents vouched for me.

Dear old Mrs. Lester (probably all of 32-33 years of age at the time) would literally pound out the beat on the piano, so that even had I been deaf, I could have followed it via vibration alone. We novice Arthur and Kathryn Murray "wanna be's" would then struggle to learn the box step, or whatever else we were directed to do.

In any event, while all dancing tended to be conducted at arms length in these classes, there were situations when our upper bodies made brief contact. On these occasions, I felt nowhere nearly as uncomfortable as I did when in the grasp of my grandmother. Perhaps it was just the fact that the size, or lack thereof, of the mammary glands of a seventh grader, was not as intimidating as those of a fully mature woman, but I think not.

****

In the eighth grade, the curves of my female classmates seemed to have become slightly more defined.

On wintertime Saturday mornings at our school, under the supervision of one of the male teachers, the boys were allowed to use the gym to play basketball; while the girls could practice cheerleading, cartwheels or related activities on the floor of the balcony overlooking the gym.

One of the related activities in which the girls were involved was practicing the "jitterbug" with each other. While they were all becoming quite proficient in the steps, swings and twists involved in this upbeat type of dancing, the boys, as usual, were totally clueless.

During a break in the basketball action, necessitated by the presence of more than ten boys on the court, requiring the excess to sit out, a couple of us clueless lads walked upstairs to observe these dancing darlings. The fact that we may have been covered in sweat at the time, never gave us pause. You know how guys can be.

Observing the bewildered looks on our faces, a couple of these young ladies offered to teach us the steps. I happened to be paired with Judy, who was one of our cheerleaders. (If you were to scan back a few pages to the photo of four kids in front of the Freedom Train, Judy is the taller of the two girls shown.)

My good fortune may have been pure chance, or more likely that our mothers had long been friends. Then again, it may have been that she felt sorry for me and my two left feet. She was a far better teacher than I was a student, but I eventually began to pick it up.

On succeeding Saturday mornings, despite my enjoyment of playing basketball, I looked forward to the times I had to sit out, so I could rejoin the dance practices up on the balcony, hopefully once again with Judy as my instructor/partner.

Whenever, in the course of certain dance twirls, she would follow the pull of my right hand, and spin into me, with my right arm encircling her; or as my eyes locked in on her perfectly moving hips, I considered this activity to be well worth my temporary absence from the basketball floor.

I was not yet ready to abandon games of male competition, with some form of ball involved; or to renounce the thrill of landing a battling trout with my fly rod; or to relinquish the challenge of trying to take down via shotgun, a fast moving pheasant. However, I was certainly willing to allow these previously uninteresting and unnecessary members of humanity to at least have an entry on my list of topics of interest.

****

As a freshman enrolled in a Social Studies class, I had an assignment early in the school year to interview the manager of a local business. The business to which I was assigned was the Sprouse Reitz Variety Store.

If that name does not sound familiar to someone, it might be thought of as a less popular version of Woolworths (aka the "Dime Store" or the "Five and Dime"), right down to the red signing over the front of the store.

Timing, as they say, is everything. During my interview with the store manager, he asked me if I had any interest in a part-time job, as he had an immediate opening. His stock boy had quit the previous week, and he was about to lose one of his female clerks as well. She had graduated from high school a few months earlier, and was moving back east with her family. The manager was planning to combine some duties of both positions until just prior to Christmas, since business had, as usual, declined following the first month of school.

I had previously labored in such fluctuating (as related to revenue generating) business enterprises as lawn mowing and newspaper delivery. The idea of working a set number of hours per week for a guaranteed hourly rate, without the need to battle the elements of rain, wind, snow, plus unfriendly dogs and slow paying customers, sounded too good to pass up, and I quickly accepted his offer.

My daily responsibilities at the store included pushing a wide dry mop, sprayed with some sort of coating, up and down the aisles to remove dirt and other objects without raising dust. In addition I was to sweep the sidewalks in front of the store; or if it had snowed, to shovel away the white stuff. I was taught how to cut pieces of glass into various lengths for displays of small items on the counters, and, as the new stock boy, to check in all merchandise received.

This last element of the job involved signing for deliveries, opening and verifying the product, affixing price tags to each unit, and finally, advising the manager when items were ready to place on the floor for sale.

Upon receipt of shipments, I carried the packages down some rather flimsy stairs to the basement to perform the balance of my duties. The basement wasn't really a backup storeroom, as seldom were there sizeable quantities of product ordered which might require storage. Most products were acquired for a limited sale period, as opposed to a drug store, which had standard products on hand at all times. There were a couple of rows of boxes stacked in the middle area of the room, plus a few shelves along one wall of the basement for what limited storage might be required.

One product which was always maintained in storage was bulk candy, and it was stored on the main floor on shelves directly behind the back wall of the sales floor. It was kept there to provide easy access by sales clerks, the store manager, or me. Such availability was necessary to allow for replenishing the covered displays at the front of the store adjacent to the two cash registers.

The display cases had a sloping glass in the front, with a mirrored back, a couple of inches behind it. The candy was stocked from the top and behind the counter. This process allowed little kids to press their often runny noses against the glass, while they begged their mothers to buy them some chocolates, lemon drops, red hots, or whatever their little hearts desired, without at the same time contaminating anything.

When a customer selected a product for purchase, the clerk would use a scoop to gather the ounces or pounds requested, place the candy in a metal container on a scale and, once the proper acknowledgement had been received from the customer, to pour the contents into a paper bag and ring up the sale.

I had previously experienced the joy of nibbling candy samples, during the year or two that my father had worked for the Sweets Candy Company; but currently he was employed by MJB Coffee, Tea and Rice. Because the former sweet samples were no longer available to me at home, having ready access to all these candy varieties was quite appealing to this short, chubby high school freshman.

One of the perks of my job was that I was authorized to sample any (or all) of the candy I cared to eat from the supplies in the back room. As you might imagine, such a temptation proved to be more than anyone, especially me, could resist. I indulged in more than a reasonable volume of the chocolates one afternoon, early in my period of employment. While I did not become physically ill, the desirability of further excessive indulgence diminished dramatically from that point forward.

Another function of my position was to deliver the daily deposit of receipts to the bank each afternoon. At the time there were no armored cars utilized, unlike the situation today.

Once the manager had counted, balanced and otherwise completed whatever reports he had to assemble, he would give me the cash and checks for deposit in the bank. He would place the deposit in a canvas bag with a zipper on top (no lock) and then put the bag inside a paper sack, which might suggest that it was nothing more than school supplies or some other incidental purchase.

The bank was approximately the equivalent of six blocks from the store, two of which were the Higgins Avenue Bridge over the Clark Fork River. I was instructed to be very nonchalant in carrying the deposit. (I doubt that the manager used that term with an uneducated little freshman, but I got the idea.) I was to tell no one of that aspect of my job, both for my own protection, and to avoid the loss of any deposits via robbery.

I never experienced a negative incident performing this function, but looking back on it, the entire process seems absurd. Even in quiet, safe Missoula, someone with far less banking knowledge than, say "Butch and Sundance," would have noticed a pattern, and could have easily lightened my load. The liability of entrusting someone so young with such deposits, and placing him in danger, should someone decide to relieve him of the funds, would be unthinkable today. But that was then, and it somehow worked out satisfactorily.

I mentioned that one of the store's female clerks had given her two-week notice, which, at least in part, precipitated my hiring. She had a very outgoing manner, was always smiling and was quite attractive. Whereas I could best be described as a short, shy, nondescript new entrant to the high school population, she had apparently been very popular. Her class involvements had included student government and Pep Club, among other activities.

In spite of such contrasts in character, she did not avoid talking to me at work. She taught me how to load the above described candy counter racks, had helped me build one of my few window displays, and always said "Hi" when I reported to work after school.

One afternoon during my second week of employment, I was in the basement, deeply engrossed in documenting a sizeable order of fuzzy stuffed animals that had just arrived; a product which the manager had advised he wanted to get out on the sales floor sooner, rather than later.

I sensed someone behind me (probably my earlier "grouse stalking skills" asserting themselves). I figured it was the manager, checking on my progress. I was wrong.

Instead, it was the female clerk, whom I'll call "Miss Robinson" for a couple of reasons. One is that I just do not remember her real name. The second will become evident in due course.

She told me it was slow up on the floor, and she'd been sent down to see if I needed any help. I replied that I was almost finished, but perhaps she could help me carry some of the stuffed animals up the stairs in a few minutes.

She mentioned that it was her last day at the store; that she was leaving for Boston in a couple more days; and how she would really miss being in Missoula, with all the friends she had made during her six years here. I think I mumbled something about how I'd miss her, too, and all her encouragement on this, my first regular job.

As I stood up from affixing the last price tag to the final furry fox, she stepped right in front of me and said, "How about giving me a goodbye hug?"

I would like to say that I came up with a bit of witty repartee, but I'm afraid my response was more along the lines of "Um. Ok, I guess." (The ultimate in suave, right?)

She then moved against me, as I stood with my back to the counter, which contained invoices, pens, box cutters and other paraphernalia, but no PANIC BUTTON; something for which I immediately felt an urgent need.

"C'mon, put your arms around me. Haven't you ever hugged a girl before? Don't be so nervous!"

As she mouthed these and similar words, she placed her arms around my neck and pulled herself even closer to me. Although she was four years my senior, she was relatively short. Thus, in spite of being vertically challenged myself, we were nearly eye to eye as we (mostly she) embraced.

This brings me back to the topic of breasts. As to whether Miss Robinson's particular pair were just naturally incredible, youthful and firm; or whether she had supplemented what God had given her, with the enhancement of some solid foam padding, I had no way of knowing. They were not what one might call mammoth, but they certainly did make an impression on (or, better stated, a depression in) my chest. In other words, these were not my grandmother's bosoms.

At some point, having sufficiently embarrassed me, she released me from my agony (and my ecstasy). The total elapsed passage of time for this embrace may have been as little as a few seconds, or as long as a minute; but for however long it lasted, the event made an indelible imprint on this young lad in that dime store basement.

Whether she had already forgotten about it before the end of the day, or had laughingly shared her mini-seduction with future girl friends over ensuing weeks or months, I, of course, have no idea. Obviously, the memory of those moments have remained with this long since fully grown version of the young lad in that basement, along with an "If I'd known then what I know now; WOW!" insert.

Before closing this segment, I must admit that this relatively harmless prank of hers came no where near that of "Mrs. Robinson" nearly fifteen years later in the film *The Graduate*. On the other hand, the Dustin Hoffman character, Benjamin, was a college graduate, not a naïve young freshman in high school. So in relative terms, I got every bit as much of an education, even absent inappropriate touching by either of us, as did Benjamin in that movie.

****

About a year later, one of the big films of the season was *Picnic*, starring William Holden and Kim Novak. Other than the famous dance sequence between the two main characters, which I still consider today to have been one of the more sensual few moments on film, the movie itself was not particularly memorable. Having again seen it, on DVD this time around, the overacting by the majority of the characters is rather pronounced.

At the time, however, I had eyes only for Miss Novak, and those eyes were often focused on her chest area. As it happened, the theatre was filled to capacity the evening I went to see it; and the only available seats were in the very front row. Needless to say, her already healthy lung protectors were even more amplified from such a vantage point.

I innocently considered that said attributes were intended to be seen, not touched. My first contradiction to that point of view came quite by accident, believe it or not.

I was enrolled in a swimming class called Water Safety Instruction. It was a coed class for advanced level swimmers, focusing on the skills necessary to become a lifeguard.

Our instructor, Bob Oswald, was sort of a white version of Charles Barkley, if the latter could be reduced to six feet in height without much loss of girth. Mr. Oswald would demonstrate to the class, on dry land, a particular movement to be utilized when approaching a drowning victim; after which he would portray said victim in deep water, and have one of us try it on him. The thought process seemed to be that if Oswald could be rescued, then we could rescue anyone. Following the enactment would be a critique, both by fellow class members and by Oswald.

We were then to team up with a classmate and attempt to perfect the rescuer's moves. To avoid any near drowning by accident, he told us that if we happened to get into trouble underwater with insufficient air, to simply "tap" our partner; the partner was then to cease struggling and allow the winded classmate to surface, take in oxygen, and try it again.

We had to take our final exam a few weeks later, involving both oral answers and the performance of various skills learned throughout the course. Example: Oswald described a situation in which the rescuer had turned into the victim, as a result of the panicky reactions of the one initially being rescued. He called upon a student in the class who, while perhaps the strongest swimmer, was not the most focused on the subject matter. To Oswald's query of how to escape the grasp of the panicked victim, he responded with a completely straight face, "Tap him." I guess he must have been listening in class at least part of the time.

Now getting back to my "look, but don't touch" theory; one of the rescue skills we were to perfect, was the "Cross Chest Carry," which involved bringing to safety a non-active victim in deep water.

We were to place the immobilized party on his/her back while we were treading water. Then, placing our armpit over the shoulder of the other person, we were to reach across and down, grasping (now don't get ahead of me here) the area just below the rib cage. We could then carry the victim to shore, utilizing the side stroke. Pretty basic, simple stuff, as compared to what might be required with a more active victim.

I was normally teamed up with another guy for performing the various "in the water" skills; but on this occasion, my partner happened to be a girl named Annette. Oswald instructed her to jump into the deep end of the pool to await my rescue. I dived from the shallow end, quickly and efficiently swimming to her location.

Calmly, I told her to simply relax, while I shifted her onto her back. I slid behind her, with my elbow placed exactly over her shoulder, such that my forearm and hand crossed over her body, and I grasped her SOFT AND LOVELY BREAST.

For a moment, we floated there on the surface of the deep end of the pool; then she shrieked briefly and began giggling, as did I, and we both promptly sank to the bottom of the pool.

Being the gentleman I was, I may well have let go of that particular piece of her anatomy before we hit the bottom, but I wouldn't swear to it. Be that as it may, short of breath, we quickly kicked our way back to the surface. Our faces were quite red, as we emerged from the depths.

I apologized profusely, once I regained normal breathing, for having made that one small error of placing, not my "armpit," but my "elbow," over her shoulder. (As it is said, the devil is in the details.) It was only my virtuous (at least up to that point) reputation that prevented her from accusing me of using any excuse to "cop a feel."

****

Little boys seem to have an inborn fascination with their penises. Some of them never outgrow it.

Whether writing words or drawing circles in the snow, trying to hit a moving ant or insect in the dirt, or aiming at a bull's eye decorated deodorizer in a urinal; there is no question that the act of urinating contains far more pleasure for the male of the species than it does for the female.

****

Being a fan of time travel, I'm now going to step back a few years.

It seems that one of my elementary school companions had an interesting "twist" when it came to penises. Now I had never conducted an extensive study of this portion of the male anatomy, nor had I spent an inordinate period of time comparing such body parts among my prepubescent associates.

However, while changing clothes following an afternoon at the local swimming pool, a natural youthful curiosity brought to my attention, and that of two others in the afternoon's quartet, that the fourth member's "member" seemed to possess a curve near its tip, a characteristic which the remainder of us lacked.

We were at an age when we had yet to learn restraint when it came to asking questions of a personal nature, and certainly lacked the political correctness so prevalent today. As a result, one of us (no, not me) pointed at the subject matter and blurted out, "How come your dick is bent at the end?"

A second boy asked if the bending allowed him to pee around a corner.

I suppose it was now my turn to make some comment, as I had been silent up to this point, but I deferred.

None of us asked then, what might have immediately come to mind just a few years later; namely whether its configuration was modified when in a state of arousal.

I cannot speculate as to the level of knowledge, regarding things of a sexual nature, possessed by my companions. As for me, I could name a few states in addition to Montana, but "arousal" was a state of which I was totally unaware.

Enough of this detour from the topic; it is time to refocus on little boys and their various urinating habits, techniques and other pastimes (or is it piss times?).

****

Two little lads could impulsively start a pissing contest; the winner might be determined either by the strength of stream and the related distance attainable thereby, or by the accuracy of one's aim.

On another occasion, they might instead have a piss fight with one another. This event required both digital dexterity and the ability to shift position rapidly, to avoid being hit; all the while trying to carefully ration available ammunition to continue the battle. Trust me when I tell you how difficult it is to maintain a high level of such skills, while simultaneously giggling to the point of hysterics.

Those two examples of peeing activities have probably been performed with greater or lesser frequency, depending on whether a boy lived in the city or the country, along with other factors. However, one which seems to extend into the teen years and beyond is the apparent exhilaration derived from simply spraying one's stream from a higher elevation to a lower one.

Maybe it is simply an extension of the victorious gunfighter pissing on the grave of his adversary, to reflect dominance.

Why would a guy pee from a bridge, deep down into some abyss? It could well be, like the old joke about why a dog licks his testicles; because he can.

Then there is the fellow who chooses to pee from the back window of a fast moving station wagon. He may try it simply because he has to go, and the driver is not willing to stop the car. Be advised: this would be a big mistake. It would make "pissing in the wind" (by either gender) seem elementary by comparison, with the consequence of being totally unsuccessful in attempting to refrain from wetting one's pants.

My favorite recollection of peeing from some high position to a lower one occurred early in my elementary school career.

Another boy and I had gone for a hike in the mountains, across the road and a mile down canyon from our home. We had filled canteens of water and packed a lunch. It was our intent to ascend to the top of the ridge and claim it for ourselves by planting a flag, a piece of red flannel material tied to a stick, much like what was done years later by the first men on the moon.

We eventually reached a level generally above the timber line and determined we had reached our destination. There happened to be a solitary old Ponderosa Pine standing within the open area, seemingly beckoning us to climb it. And we did.

I wouldn't pretend that the future screenwriters of the film *Titanic* were eavesdropping on us, hoping to come up with a quotable line of dialog for Leo DiCaprio to utter, as he and Kate Winslet leaned out over the bow of their doomed vessel. However I do recall vividly the two of us hollering at the top of our lungs, from a point far too high in the tree for our own safety, "We rule the world!" as we extracted our woeful little wieners from our jeans to pee on all that was below us. Of course, it was "juvenile." That's what we were at the time.

In retrospect, I feel no qualms about having enjoyed such frivolous bladder emptying activity in my youth. Now, in my declining (decaying?) years, hampered by an enlarged prostate, the flow of my "stream" is significantly diminished; or you could say that my tinkle has become but a trickle.

****

Lest you think such behavior in little boys has changed dramatically in the decades since I surrendered my own youth, may I inject a comment made by our own grandson, when he was just shy of reaching the age of ten years?

Josh and his family were spending a Labor Day Weekend with us at our mountain cabin. The building sits on a steep slope and contains a sizeable deck, which extends a dozen or more feet beyond the cabin itself. When standing at the railing, one overlooks from on high, all sorts of photogenic real estate.

Out of the blue one afternoon, Josh asked politely, "Nanna, is it alright with you if I pee off your deck?" His two older sisters rolled their eyes, while Ashley, the elder of the pair, commented, "Gross!"

I guess such actions are just something in our male DNA, over which we seemingly have no control. Sorry ladies.

****

Chapter 5

A Two Step Plan to Become Brilliant

Stephen Covey, of "7 Habits" fame, is just one of any number of writers or motivational speakers to present a pathway to success. I hereby present my own such pathway, based on a far more basic two-step plan:

***Step One-Learn from your mistakes.

***Step Two-Make a lot of mistakes.

Having tried to focus on step one, all the while considering the unplanned emphasis placed on step two, I have every reason to feel that I ought to rank well into the upper echelon of well-educated individuals.

My learning opportunities were admittedly not the type that make newspaper headlines, or provide joke material for a late night talk show host's monologue. That is to say, I was not the guy who happened to hit the "activate button" for a massive fireworks display one day early; nor did I accidentally turn up the thermostat in an ice sculpture viewing room while substituting for the head custodian. I did, however, intertwine my share of goofs throughout my years of growing up; while I was attempting to make a buck in the process of doing so.

Whether from poor business decisions, lack of planning, pure ignorance on my part, or simply outside influences over which I had no control; I suffered through countless situations resulting in a personal financial setback, or at the very least, my being portrayed as quite the fool.

Through these experiences, I have ultimately learned what NOT to do. A couple of well known phrases come to mind in that regard. One is "Too soon old, too late smart." The other one would be "Fool me once, shame on you. Fool me twice, shame on me." In no particular sequence, here are some of those lessons:

****

Sub Chapter 5.1: "Beware 20th Century Fox! There's a New Kid in Town"

There have been numerous comedy teams over the years. Laurel and Hardy, Burns and Allen, or Martin and Lewis may quickly come to mind, as well they should.

As a child, my favorites had to be Bud Abbott and Lou Costello, hands down. Not a Saturday showing of one of their movies would escape me and my hard earned assortment of coins. But I did not stop with catching their antics on the big screen.

One year, I saved up sufficient scratch to acquire a 78rpm phonograph recording of their famous "Who's on First?" routine. The following year, since my family had an old movie projector, I purchased, over the course of the summer, three eight-millimeter versions of the comedians' films from the local camera store.

There was no sound with them, just words on the screen, similar to subtitles for foreign films, depicting what was being said in the original theatre version. Each film consisted of a few clips, excerpted from a feature length show, all compiled into a 50 foot roll of silent celluloid. The titles of these shortened versions related to the action taking place on such clips.

One was called "Cowboys and Indians." The second was "Oysters and Muscles" (which dealt with Lou finding a live creature in his soup, and later having to fight Lon Chaney in a wrestling match). The third one escapes me.

I would estimate that I had close to six hard-earned dollars invested in both the record and the three films. In the late 1940s such a sum equated to at least a year's worth of my weekly allowance, my annual birthday gift of a silver dollar from my Iowa grandmother, and any nickel or dime bonuses I might receive for having performed some special assistance around the house. In other words, the majority of my net worth was tied up in this comedy team.

Included amongst the two or three gifts awaiting me that year under our Christmas tree, was a printing set. More specifically, it consisted of a box containing an ink pad; a wooden handled device with adjustable inserts; and some rubber numbers, letters and pictures.

While this device did not exactly place our kitchen table on a par with the New York Times' Press Room, kids do have great imaginations. A young playmate and I could spend the better part of an afternoon printing small one-page newspapers, containing advertisements for auto dealerships, furniture stores and the like.

During an afternoon stay at the home of my friend, Stan, I had brought along my printing set. We were, as usual, getting our fingers covered in ink, while assembling the necessary letters and pictures for a theatre ad.

Just then it hit me, and I said, "Hey, let's not just print an ad for some pretend theatre, but make up a real ad for one of our own."

"What are you talking about?" Stan replied.

"Look, I've got some Abbott and Costello films; a projector and screen; and that phonograph record you listened to at my house. If your mom would let us use your basement for our theatre, we could set up a bunch of chairs and block out the windows with blankets to make it dark while we show the movies. Maybe she'd even let us make popcorn and Kool-Aid to sell for refreshments. We could charge neighborhood kids admission and everything, and take the money we make to buy some more movies, and do this all summer!"

OK, so this may sound too much like one of those old Judy Garland films in which the farm is in desperate financial condition, when suddenly she bumps into Mickey Rooney (or later, Gene Kelly); whereupon they look into each other's eyes and proclaim, "Hey, let's put on a show."

Yes, I saw that movie and others like it over the course of my youth, but at the time, this was a truly original thought being verbalized so exuberantly from my normally quiet mouth. It also seemed to have reasonable money-making potential, as it was long before television made its way into the generally "ten years behind the rest of the country" State of Montana.

A few days later we had completed preparations for the grand opening of the Eagle Theatre. Neither of us were bird watchers or anything like that, but one of the little rubber pictures in my printing set was an eagle, and none of the other designs seemed to go with "Theatre," so Eagle Theatre it was.

We had distributed our "Now Showing" advertisement to neighborhood kids and set up the basement, using not only his mom's kitchen chairs, but also some folding ones we borrowed from another neighbor lady, who had seemed quite interested (amused?) at our business venture.

We had selected "Cowboys and Indians" for the initiation of our weekly showings, to be preceded by the playing of the incredibly funny, to us at least, "Who's on First?" record, in lieu of a cartoon.

We planned to also run about thirty seconds of one of the other two films as sort of a "Previews of Coming Attractions" for the next week. If we could make enough money from our Grand Opening, we were considering purchasing an actual cartoon to go with the next week's film. Then we'd add some sort of western, such as Hopalong Cassidy, from the second week's income, just to mix up the genre of available viewing choices.

(Ok, let's be realistic. I had never even heard or seen the word "genre." Nor would I have had any idea what in the hell "genre" meant, and would have difficulty, even today, using it in a sentence without cringing; but as an adult, I've listened to Roger Ebert use it on his movie review television show so frequently, I thought I'd just toss it in at no charge. You're welcome.)

To say that our audience that afternoon was somewhat below our expectations would be an understatement. We had set up seating for around twenty kids. Even at the bargain price of five cents admission, as compared to the going rate at a real movie theater of twenty cents, for children twelve or under, we had, at best, three fourths of our seating unoccupied. Admittedly, that theatrical entrance fee of twenty cents covered movies more than fifty feet in length, and they did have sound.

We sold a small bag of popcorn, or a paper cup of Kool-Aid, for three cents; or both for a nickel. Stan's mother had not only consented to the rent-free use of her basement for our venture, but she also provided the popcorn, drinks and cups to us at absolutely no charge. Even with our limited number of customers, we felt success was ours for the taking.

Such was not to be.

Whereas I could hardly contain my laughter when listening to poor Lou, struggling with the names of the players on Bud's baseball team, the tastes of our paying clientele were evidently quite different. Before the record was even one third completed, one of the kids said, "This is boring. Let's start the movie."

I tried to counter with some sort of "Just give it another minute and you'll really like it." However another customer voiced that he had heard it before and it was just stupid.

Having picked up somewhere that the customer is always right, I asked if the entire audience felt the same as those two more outspoken critics did, and when they mumbled their agreement, I stopped the record, and proceeded to show the movie.

I was encouraged when a member of the audience laughed during the scene in which Bud and Lou are in an old car, being chased by Indians; Bud tells Lou to "Take off the brake!"; so Lou hands him the emergency brake handle.

However, rather than having responded to the humor on the screen, this young fellow was apparently being tickled by the boy next to him. Although he had laughed, he also responded by punching the tickler, the result of which was that both of their cups of sticky liquid spilled on the floor, along with most of their popcorn.

All too soon, our 50 foot long feature film reached its conclusion. While I commenced the rewinding process of our film, we asked if anyone cared for more refreshments. The more vocal individual amongst our paying customers complained that he didn't like that flavor of Kool-Aid, and that it didn't have enough sugar anyway.

As quickly as my stubby little fingers could accomplish the task, I removed the now rewound reel of film, and had the second one threaded up, down and around the necessary sprockets in order to show the trailer for the next week.

When I stopped the projector just over a minute into the new film, someone asked me what I was doing. I tried to explain that these were previews for what would be showing the following week, along with a cartoon. My explanation was far from satisfactory, and he insisted that we show the rest of the movie, or give them their money back.

I reluctantly completed the remainder of the movie, after which our audience began to depart. As they were doing so, someone's foot caught on the extension cord into which I had plugged the portable record player. The cord somehow kept the actual machine dangling from the table, rather than crashing to the floor. Less fortunate was my prized "Who's on First" record, which popped off the turntable, hit the concrete floor and broke into three jagged pieces. (If only it had landed on some of the spilled, but relatively soft, popcorn, it might have survived to take its rightful place in my present vinyl record library.)

The unaudited results (just a sampling of CPA terminology for you) of our unsuccessful "movie empire in the making" were heavily skewed into the negative category.

We then weighed all factors involved from our day: Our tally from admissions and refreshments was less than fifty cents; my broken record, purchased originally for just over a dollar, was now worthless; we had a very sticky and popcorn-littered floor to clean. It was probably not the time to seek out the level of interest of potential investors in our business venture.

My business associate graciously offered to donate his share of our insufficient gross proceeds, to help cover the loss of my single audio asset, but I rejected his offer.

Ever resilient, a difficult lesson from the cruel business world now a part of our experience, yet with youthful optimism on our side, we gathered up the compiled coins and headed off to bury our initiation into the School of Hard Knocks, by taking in the latest double feature at the more established Roxy Theatre.

****

Sub Chapter 5.2:

"Now Just Where All Does This Route Cover?"

Undaunted, despite the negativity associated with my earlier business failure related to my newspaper printing set; when another young friend, John Wertz, suggested the two of us ought to get a newspaper route, I jumped at the idea. Apples and oranges, right?

We both had bicycles on which we already spent endless hours transporting ourselves to and from such diverse geographic locations as the swimming pool, softball fields at Bonner Park, the Dairy Queen and so forth. It only made sense to utilize them as a means of enhancing our financial needs.

Missoula had both a morning and an evening newspaper, published by the same company. On Sunday, there was just the single, typically voluminous edition. The route for which there was an opening was for the afternoon paper.

The man who interviewed us for the delivery job explained that it seemed ideal for the two of us, although it would need to be under just one name. The reason for the single ownership was, that upon completion of one full year of delivering papers, and assuming no serious customer complaints, the owner of the route would be given a savings bond.

I don't recall whether the bond was of the $25, $50 or $100 variety (which actually meant they paid $18.75, $37.50 or $75.00 and in ten years it would be worth face value). It didn't really matter to us anyway, since we had already told him we planned to operate the route for only five months, May through September. Being in an exceptionally generous mood at the time, and considering it had been his idea in the first place, I suggested they put the route in John's name.

The interviewer advised us that we would have only around forty customers, as they limited the number to what one carrier could reasonably handle without having to return to his home, or the newspaper office, to pick up additional copies. While there were two carriers involved, technically it was still a one person route.

He further said it was the perfect route for the two of us, as it covered an area on the south side of town; based on John's home address, it was practically right in his neighborhood.

Perhaps the enthusiasm of the gentleman to sell US on the route, as opposed to us trying to sell ourselves to HIM, should have been a clue. However, we were just so eager to latch onto our first ever entrance into the job market, that we did not bother to request a few more details. As it happened, we more than likely signed ourselves up for the newspaper route with the very lowest "cpm," by which I mean "customers per mile."

Were you to drive it today, the area covering what had been our route some sixty years ago would reflect a typical suburban layout of wall-to-wall homes, with an interspersed strip mall, grocery store or gas station. However, prior to 1950, the residents of all that acreage consisted mainly of prairie dogs.

Most, if not all routes for the Daily Missoulian, were in fully developed, relatively high density areas. The distance from the newspaper building, on the northern end of Higgins Avenue, to any given route, other than ours, was from as little as a single block, to as much as three miles.

From my friend's home to the first house on our route was only two miles, so no reason to whine; other than the fact that we had to first ride our bikes nearly two miles to the Missoulian Building to pick up our papers. As I was destined to someday become a CPA, I had little difficulty determining that we would have logged some six miles prior to ever lightening our load by a single paper. (Decades later, when our two sons had paper routes of their own in the Denver area, trucks dropped the assigned number of papers at the delivery person's home. Man, did our kids have it soft!)

Ah, the excitement of our first day on the job! We reported to the back door of the Missoulian Building; identified ourselves; were handed our allotment of the day's edition; and sat on the concrete floor with all the other carriers, as we learned how to fold said papers.

While engaged in such preparation of our "Daily Missoulians," our counterparts exchanged tales of being chased by barking dogs; the interrupting of excessive yelling and screaming at certain homes while making collections; and being splashed by fast moving cars during deliveries. As we were obviously the new kids on the block, I'm sure much of what we were hearing was said to intentionally make us apprehensive, and it worked. A quick visual survey confirmed that we were quite likely the youngest members of this brotherhood.

You'll recall I spoke of "folding" the newspapers. Our Denver Post currently comes to us rolled with a rubber band around it, or placed inside a plastic bag during inclement conditions. But at the time, everything had to be folded, not rolled. Don't ask me why; I'm just repeating what we were told to do. (Perhaps Kenny Rogers was, himself, a newspaper delivery boy in his youth; and he came up with the lyrics to his "Know when to hold 'em, know when to fold 'em" song while preparing his papers for delivery.)

There were two folding methods, one for the more voluminous Sunday edition, with a different way for the other six days.

Sunday required just two folds, with the right side inserted into the left side, resulting in a long, bulky, but basically flat product for delivery. For other days, the procedure began the same way, with the paper facing you, and folding first the right side and then the left, but adding two more folds from bottom to top. The top was then tucked into the bottom, leaving a package somewhat rectangular in shape, which was supposedly (with enough practice) easy to toss onto a porch from the street, without having to dismount one's bike. Now if that explanation was too confusing, find a book about an engineer who had a paper route, instead of this poor old CPA. But hey, if little kids could figure it out, how tough was it?

Our first three or four customers resided within a single city block, but then things spread out; it was the equivalent of a couple more blocks to the next recipient. For the balance of the route we experienced far more exercise for our legs than we did for our throwing arms.

The majority of the houses had numbers visible from the road. For those lacking such identity, it was necessary to somehow verify that we were leaving a paper at the proper location.

Option one was trying to find someone at home, and that generally meant the female member of the family; as the male tended to be employed outside the household, while the lady of the house was up to her eyeballs caring for kids, washing clothes and dishes, preparing meals, cleaning the house, ironing and all that fun stuff. Even with such a workload, there was no guarantee that she would be at home when we attempted to verify an address.

Option two could be to ask a nearby neighbor, if there was one.

Option three might involve backtracking to the previous house; checking that address, say 543 Jasper Street; comparing it with our unidentified customer, whose address was 672 Jasper, to see on which side of the street and roughly how close it should be; then proceeding to the next house that did have an address, say 712 Jasper, to confirm that, by default, the residence with no number showing must be our hard-to-locate customer.

If that tactic was not successful, option four was to skip that paper and continue the route, doubling back afterward to hopefully find someone at home to confirm that we had the correct location.

Once we had determined the proper place, we made notes (Smith-1174 Mount Ave-green bldg with red pickup out back on blocks) to avoid repeating the sequence the next day. Hopefully they didn't repaint the house and move the truck before we had memorized the location.

Delivering was the easy part, compared to collecting. Whereas rain, sleet, wind or attacking dogs never kept us from providing each of our clients with their daily headlines, athletic contest results, comics and ads; it was surprising, to us novice businessmen, how frequently our efforts failed to be rewarded with a smile, a "Thank you" and the monthly payment of probably less than two dollars (and maybe, just maybe, a small tip added on.)

There were addresses where we knew someone was home, because we had seen an individual in the yard or through a window, but they would not come to the door. Others would apologize, while saying they did not have any change with them; or that we would have to wait until the husband got home; or if he was already home, that he didn't get paid but every other Wednesday, so we'd have to wait until next week.

Then there was always some clown who would pull out a twenty dollar bill, give us a phony smile, and tell us that was the smallest he had at the time. Still others would grumble about the paper being all wet one day, so they were thinking of possibly dropping their subscription, or in some similar way try to belittle us, even while paying for our previous month's labors.

On the brighter side, there was one customer for whom we were very grateful. It was a restaurant, more specifically a steak house; the manager always had a kind word for us, paid immediately upon request, and never failed to include a nice tip.

On collection days, we would return to John's house to add up our money, and determine whether or not we had sufficient funds to pay for the papers we had delivered over the past month.

I cannot recall exactly how the financial aspects worked, but it was something along the lines of us paying three and a half cents for each paper being delivered. Each edition had a printed "newsstand price" of five cents; to entice customers to subscribe for a full month, a discount of ten percent, reducing their cost to four and a half cents per paper, was provided. That would equate to a one penny per paper differential, between our costs and our anticipated revenue.

Thirty papers per average month, times forty customers, times one copper penny per paper, would equate to $12 of glorious profit per month, not counting tips, if any. Ah, the motivation of capitalism!

For those who may not be aware, Montana utilized silver dollars, not paper dollar bills, at the time. While holding a single silver dollar in your hand is no big deal, a substantial accumulation of these coins tends to be not only bulky, but fairly heavy as well.

Consider that some forty customers were paying $1.35 per month (30 papers times four and a half cents); and that more than a few of them gave us two silver dollars, for which we had to have the correct change. Between the change we had to carry with us and the silver dollars we were given during collection (discounting for a moment those who might choose to stiff us temporarily, as they usually made up for it the following month), you can understand that we could both be carrying thirty silver dollars in each of our relatively small pockets in our blue jeans.

(Do you suppose that was the real reason, just a few years later on, that boys' jeans seemed to hang down so very low on, or below, their hips? Nah, neither do I.)

Despite working through the occasional cold or sore throat, facing inclement (rainy) weather, surviving a couple of mean dog incidents, and having to deal with something short of a stable full of ideal customers; we did persevere with our route for the originally agreed to time frame, although forfeiting the savings bond by not keeping the route for a full year.

While we had been given the most time consuming and geographically spread-out assignment available, and were frequently teased about it by some of our older and wiser carriers, we did succeed in coming out ahead financially at the end of the five months. It also helped us to develop a solid work ethic, which benefitted both of us in later years.

Nevertheless, it caused each of us to be just a tad more inquisitive, when it came to checking the details (aka: the small print) before simply accepting some smooth sales pitch.

****

Sub Chapter 5.3: "When Is a Golf Club Not a Golf Club?"

Having failed miserably in the movie business, and then succeeding, albeit on a very minimal per hour basis, in the newspaper delivery field; I moved on to a moderately successful couple of summers mowing lawns, while still in elementary school.

As related elsewhere, I obtained my first actual wage-paying job with Sprouse Reitz Variety Store as a freshman in high school. Due to after school involvement in various clubs, student government and other activities during my sophomore year, I was unable to provide the required hours to my dime store employer, and reluctantly tendered my resignation.

Living in a college town, the availability of any job, regardless of how menial it might be, was hard to come by; and for a high school student with an extremely abbreviated résumé, it was especially difficult to be walking away from the job I had fallen into almost entirely by chance.

Fortunately for me, the father of my close friend, Conrad, just happened to be the manager of the sporting goods department in our town's largest emporium, the Mercantile. While he apparently considered it inappropriate to place his own son on the store's payroll, raising the ugly nepotism flag by so doing, he seemed to have no such qualms filling an opening in his department the following summer with none other than little old me.

I was technically a stock boy, rather than a retail clerk. However, when one or both of the full time men who normally waited on customers were at lunch, on break or otherwise not on the floor, I was not only authorized, but expected, to assist anyone needing shopping assistance, or to ring up a sale.

Merchandise available for sale in our department ranged from fishing hooks to motor boats, sling shots to shotguns, and more. The likelihood of someone asking me to assist in the purchase of an Evinrude Engine to propel his craft, or to determine the best boat for water skiing was remote, to say the least.

Nevertheless, a young kid like me could certainly handle a horseshoe sale; give recommendations on the type of dry fly most likely to "bag the big one" on the Blackfoot River; or properly complete the paperwork for the purchase of hunting and/or fishing licenses.

One of my first bits of instruction by Dale and Claude, the two long-time clerks manning the sales floor (one of whom probably had sold me my first fly rod years earlier), related to the status of someone seeking a license for either hunting or fishing.

Facial recognition of long time customers was generally sufficient to bypass the requesting of a driver's license or other form of identification. However, if there was any doubt, we were required by the Montana State Fish and Game to ascertain that

ONLY MONTANA RESIDENTS were to obtain the less expensive "Resident License." Not having sold licenses to many of the same people year after year, as was the case with Dale and Claude, it was more than likely that I would necessarily have to ask for identification.

You'll recall my mentioning that silver dollars were the standard media of exchange in Montana for smaller purchases. My learned supervisors advised me that a dead giveaway by someone claiming, fraudulently, to be from Montana, in order to avoid the higher price of a non-resident license, was his ultimate payment for the license with paper dollar bills.

Without exception, the utilization of paper dollars triggered a request for identification. Even during my limited floor time, I did have two individuals who were caught by not using silver in payment for a license.

As a fairly typical youth, I had personally utilized most, if not all, of the items of sporting equipment and paraphernalia available for sale in the department, including golf clubs. I had caddied at the local country club course on occasion, and had even played a few holes with some other caddies on grounds maintenance days, when the club was closed to the public for watering, mowing or the moving of holes.

Despite that exposure, I was not then, nor have I ever become, particularly interested in or knowledgeable about the sport of golf. (I am a long-time member of that small segment of the populace who considers golf to be an unpleasant interruption to an otherwise pleasant walk.) This lack of expertise brought about my only serious chewing out during that summer's employment.

Included in our department's advertised products for the week was a "Golf Club Sale Spectacular." I do not recall the specific sale price for the clubs, but for sake of argument, let's say it was "ONLY $5 PER CLUB!"

Claude was not due at work for another hour, and just moments after Dale had gone on break, several upper classmen from high school entered the premises and approached me about the sale items in our ad. I led them to the area displaying golfing equipment, remaining nearby to answer any questions they might have. I recognized one of them as our high school's top golfer, and figured he was far better equipped to provide assistance than was I.

I suppose I should have been just a little bit suspicious, when our local Ben Hogan type asked me, "Does this ad cover woods, putters AND irons?" (His emphasis made it sound as if he doubted that such a great deal would be extended to irons, too.) I replied in the affirmative, after which he whispered something to his two buddies.

Moments later, I was ringing up a big sale; consisting of two putters, six woods and a single nine iron. As most of the individual sales in my retail career to date had been well under twenty dollars, I was pretty impressed with myself concerning this just completed forty-five dollar transaction.

When Dale returned from break, I was alone in the department. He asked if I'd had any customers in his absence; I proudly recounted my spectacular sales acumen in the golfing equipment sale to the high school students.

Rather than complimenting me, he proceeded to explain that the sale related to irons only, and that I had probably been successful in wiping out any profit that the department had hoped to realize from the golf ad.

He said the intention of the ad was to attract customers to the sale items, which were priced very close to cost; while in the buying mood, they might also select a new putter or become enamored of a shiny new driver to replace the beat up one currently being utilized. None of these more expensively priced items were on sale.

I knew enough not to make some smart-ass response ("Well, we may have lost money on each club, but we made it up in volume."); instead, with head hanging, shoulders slumped and demeanor downtrodden, I accepted my dressing down without comment.

****

Sub Chapter 5.4: Drug Trafficking, Bogus Markdowns and Late Lunches

Having broken my wrist in the spring of my junior year, my only job of that summer, as described previously, was to paint our house. However, following my senior year, I successfully gained employment in a locally owned drugstore.

Yes, I was back in the retail business once again, and this time without any golf clubs to mess up my performance reviews. No, I'm kidding. Back then nobody gave such reviews to employees, especially stock boys making the grand total of $37.50 per forty hour week, before taxes.

Stoick Drug Store was, at the time, one of the most highly respected outlets in the area. I had heard commercials for them as far back as I could recall, always referring to good old brothers, Rhynie and Jack.

Rhynie was no longer amongst the living, and Jack was nearing retirement, when I first grabbed a bucket of hot sudsy water, a pole mounted sponge, and a squeegee, to facilitate the removal of dirt particles from the display windows at the front of the store.

Jack's son, Bob, was the heir apparent to running the store; Rhynie's son, Jerry, was currently one of the store's pharmacists, but had no long term plans to remain in the family business as the "junior cousin."

Jerry subsequently relocated in Sandpoint, Idaho for a few years before purchasing his own drugstore in Kalispell, Montana. His store near Flathead Lake not only survived the arrival of bigger box stores with pharmacies, but thrived; he was later joined by his children and a granddaughter as pharmacists, making for four generations in the profession.

Let's get back to Bob. He was very outgoing and personable, and was frequently named in the newspaper as having been on this civic committee or that charitable fundraising team. He had a charming wife and well-mannered children. My initial impression of this man was nothing short of exemplary.

110

Very early during my summer working in the drug store, however, that impression began to reflect a little rust around the edges. (Bob did nothing illegal, to my knowledge, although I heard various negative sounding rumors after I had departed the state of Montana; in any event, this branch of Stoick Drug was no longer in business when I visited Missoula several years later.)

I suppose "deceptive business practices" would be a valid description of what I am describing. Follow along to see if you concur.

I was in the process of unpacking cases of new merchandise, not currently available for sale in the store. My instructions were to utilize two sets of stickers when pricing each item.

The first (white) sticker included both a cost and a retail price. The cost price was necessary for inventory purposes (yup, another of those cool accounting terms). It was reflected by substituting the numbers 1 through 0 for the letters in "stoickdrug" with "s" being 1, "t" being 2, and so on. Amazingly workable, wouldn't you say? A retail price was also printed on the sticker in easily understood numbers, e.g. $7.99.

I was instructed to carefully mark out the white sticker, making it still readable, even if no longer "valid" to the eye of the customer. I was then to prepare a yellow "Reduced Price" sticker, reflecting a somewhat lower price, which still happened to be well above cost.

Ok, this procedure might not fall into the category of being out of step with "Truth in Advertising," but it would probably qualify as "sneaky." But then, I was little more than a rookie in this retailing game, so what did I know?

****

It didn't take a geography whiz kid to realize that we were not very far from the Canadian border, and that more than a few of our daily shoppers were either from Canada, or had recently vacationed there.

At the time, the exchange rate placed a premium on Canadian money over that from the United States. As I recall, a dollar of their money was worth about a nickel more than was ours.

This was not something I knew intuitively, nor had I suddenly begun perusing the various currency exchange rate tables in the business news.

I initially became aware of this differential when I was called out to the retail floor to cover for one of the two ladies who normally rang up sales. I was told to never give out Canadian money as change, unless specifically requested to do so by someone paying with Canadian bills of a larger denomination. Instead, I was to place any Canadian currency underneath the cash drawer after the completion of the transaction with the customer.

There were two or three occasions during the summer, during which the sole pharmacist in the store was also the management person, who would otherwise have taken the daily deposit of receipts to the bank. You guessed it. I was asked to make the deposit, even though they had no knowledge of my earlier banking experience of a few years earlier.

I was specifically told to make certain to exchange the separate bundle of Canadian currency for U.S. at the current exchange rate. Again nothing illegal had taken place, but it didn't pass the smell test. I guess if it helps out the old bottom line, it can't be all bad, can it? Or is this where the "slippery slope" comes into play in management's approach to things?

****

Enough pot shots at those calling the shots; it's time to once again point the finger at yours truly.

As a youth, sleeping was sort of taken for granted. I played hard, ate well, and it was decades prior to the prostate problems that now interrupt a night's sleep with frequent bathroom visits.

I was familiar with the location of all the sleep medications sold by Stoick Drug. While they consisted of numerous brand names, there were two obvious types: one to help you go to sleep and another to keep you awake.

Among the various brands available were: SleepEze and Sominex in the former category and No-Doz in the latter. They were located on shelves directly over or under each other, depending on your point of view, neither of which makes any sense.

One day a customer stopped me, while I was stocking some other products just down the aisle from her; she wondered if I had any recommendations for something to keep her awake without any negative side effects. She advised that she had never taken any of these types of products, but she didn't like coffee and needed something to avoid drowsiness. Holding in her hand a container of Sominex, she asked, "What have you heard about this product?"

I should have readily confessed that, not only had I never allowed coffee to pass my lips, but I also had no familiarity whatsoever with any of the popular brands of medications available on our shelves.

But no, I had to exhibit the value of having graduated from high school weeks earlier. Not wanting to appear unwilling to assist, I volunteered that I had heard some very good things about Sominex, which was true.

Unfortunately, the comments I had overheard were taken completely out of context, from another lady who had been telling her friend how Sominex had really helped her. What I had not heard from her conversation was that it had helped her overcome her inability to get a good night's sleep.

To mentally back up my recommendation, I also reached back to my Latin classes, trying to come up with the root word involved. I thought perhaps it came from "somnolent," which I recalled meant extremely drowsy; then if I added the "ex" at the end, it logically had to mean "without drowsiness." Sort of like kids today who say, "Terrific job. NOT."

I never saw the poor lady again. I certainly hope she had not been planning an extended driving trip after accepting my pathetic advice.

****

I wouldn't want you to think that I spent my entire summer in the drug store either questioning the business ethics of my employer, or providing totally invalid and possibly damaging advice to customers of that establishment. Therefore I'll terminate any further such comments, and instead relate some activities and/or observations made during that summer.

Nearly every other city block seemed to contain a drug store in the then small town of Missoula, prior to the arrival of the big chain drugstores we have today.

As for some examples: there was a long time Missoula family named Peterson, who operated the Peterson Drugstore; the brothers Stoick and family gave Missoula Stoick Drugs; an individual named Palmer started Palmer's Drug; and yet another individual named Lud Polich, who, for some reason unknown to me at the time, chose not to include his name on his store, instead naming it Smith Drug. How interesting. Do you suppose, no, let's not go there.

From time to time each of these various pharmacies would run out of certain medications; and they would borrow needed quantities from other drug stores in order to fill a given prescription. A quick phone call would determine if another location had sufficient product to allow for such a loan.

Along with my other assignments, I was the employee designated to walk with reasonable haste from our store to the drugstore with sufficient product, and to transport the needed medication back to our pharmacy. I guess that made me one of the earliest "drug runners," long before such a description came to the forefront.

****

Today's newspapers, magazines, billboards and television programs contain ads for every conceivable sort of personal product from tampons to condoms to cures for erectile dysfunction; large displays of such products are prevalent throughout most stores.

To say the least, such products were not as blatantly displayed back in the days of the Eisenhower Administration. For example, Kotex sanitary napkins were disguised to the point that one would consider them to be in the witness protection program of packaging. Lots of floral print in pastel colors, but certainly no embarrassing lettering that would indicate what in the world the product might be. Exactly how to find this essential, but unidentifiable, product in a store was probably a key segment included in special mother-daughter conversations that took place behind closed doors.

Condoms were available only from the pharmacist, rather than being exhibited for the prurient public's potential purchase. That is to say, a package of Trojans was just not one of those impulse purchases, as might be a candy bar, a magazine or a tube of lipstick, which one might pass while approaching the checkout counter.

Naturally, as a lowly stock boy, I was never allowed inside the confines of the pharmacy portion of the store, and so was never involved in dispensing any sort of birth control device. Nevertheless, being observant of the behavior of various individuals, I did pick up on the fact that women purchasing such products, or any other items of a more personal nature, would tend to stall, when approaching the checkout area, until I had departed, in order to avoid embarrassment.

****

When it came to lunch break, I was given great flexibility concerning its timing. My overall workday ran from 8 a.m. to 5 p.m. and I could spend my leisurely hour for lunch whenever I might choose.

I had the philosophy then, as now, of completing the more difficult part of anything sooner, rather than later; thus I would frequently delay taking my lunch break until as late as 2:45 p.m. which left me with a very easy to accept afternoon of slightly over an hour.

A couple of doors east from the drugstore was a combination café, bar and gathering place; at the very back of this establishment could be found the following: a tickertape machine; a large green chalkboard; and an old chair, occupied by an even older appearing occupant. This elderly man seemed, from my perspective (of course I had just completed high school) to be but one foot removed from the grave; dangling from his lips, or between his shaking fingers, was an ever present cigarette.

Permanently printed on the green chalkboard were a series of boxes, laid out like a nine inning baseball score box, in which had been listed the names of various major league baseball teams.

With head bowed and smoke clouding his eyes, and as ashes miraculously defied gravity by hanging on to the end of his cigarette, this ancient gentleman would feed the latest bits of tickertape through his yellowed fingers; his purpose was to ascertain the inning by inning events of each afternoon ballgame then in progress.

Flicking the amazing accumulation of ashes, he would reach for a piece of what appeared to be a wet stick of chalk, and transcribe the most recently completed inning on the board. It appeared that he had written the latest numbers in invisible ink, or more accurately, invisible chalk. As if by magic, about fifteen seconds later, the figures would boldly appear to those observers standing nearby.

Please do not ask why he did not simply use regular blackboard chalk, as was used in all schools. I have no clue, unless it was to keep the chalk powder from mixing with his cigarette smoke, to make for a "really deadly" air mixture.

There were, in the mid 1950s, but sixteen major league teams, eight in each league; so it was fairly simple to track the games being played, even though a far greater number were played during the daytime than is the case currently.

Although I mentioned earlier that I was initially a Cleveland fan, and later switched to Detroit, during that particular summer, the Milwaukee Braves in the National League and the "Damn Yankees" in the American were the elite teams. The Pirates, on the other hand, ranked amongst the worst, despite having on their roster future superstar Roberto Clemente, and just a few years earlier a pitcher (Murry Dickson), who had won 20 games for that last place team. I tended to root for the underdog, so I kept close tabs on the lowly Pirates.

I would spend many of those late afternoon lunch breaks keeping track of the various games, pitchers of record, and who had hit home runs; dreaming of one day having the opportunity to watch a real major league ballgame in person.

By the way, while there were numerous employment opportunities I may have considered during my lifetime, replacing that scorekeeper with the invisible chalk was not one of them.

****

Missoula had just recently obtained a minor league baseball team, playing in the old Pioneer League. If classified today, this league would probably be labeled as an "A", with the next level being "AA", then "AAA" and finally the majors.

Since this was prior to the establishment of "Everyone is a winner" mentality, which pervades society today, our league was simply designated as "Class C." As I recall, if a player was demoted by Missoula, his only option remaining was to play for the Class D team in Elmira, NY.

You don't want me to get on my soapbox and tell you my opinion of teachers who hand out "participation certificates" for art, music, or athletic competition; or reading about schools which have nine valedictorians, for crying out loud. There is a reason to keep score in all such matters. Receiving such meaningless recognition for effort expended would be the equivalent of some poor soul hoping for a word of greeting from an old friend, but who settles for receiving a piece of mail addressed to "Occupant."

Back to our baseball team, I think roughly a third of the players assigned to us were from Cuba or Puerto Rico, and spoke no English whatsoever. Another third or more might speak acceptable English, but could neither hit, nor field, well enough that anyone would care to converse with them anyway. A very small percentage of them had any real potential, and a couple actually made it to the majors eventually. One such individual, Jim Kaat, who was a pitcher of some renown a few years later, broke into professional baseball in Missoula.

There were a lot of characters on the Timberjacks. (I'll explain the origin of that moniker elsewhere, but for now, please just accept it.)

Start with our shortstop, Carlos Espinosa. Although he'd be unable to say "Timberjacks" even in his wildest dreams, he had somewhere managed to pick up the phrase "Hubba-Hubba Baby" as part of his infield chatter. Because of his extensive overuse of that expression, it soon became his nickname.

Our player-manager was Jack McKeon, who much later in his career became a successful major league skipper. While managing Missoula's team, he also played the position of catcher. It was generally viewed that as a batter, McKeon would hit either a single or a home run, as he was too rotund to ever get to second or third base on any ball staying inside the fences. Despite such an apparent lack of speed, it was all but miraculous how he could practically beat the runner to first base, when jumping out of his catcher's crouch to back up the first baseman.

Speaking of first basemen, ours (and I'm sorry that I cannot recall his name) was lusted over by nearly all ladies in attendance. He might be described as the Robert Redford of that generation, only slightly taller. Blond, broad shouldered, and possessing a smile that melted female hearts, his ability to stretch (nearly doing the splits) to corral a low throw made him a crowd favorite. Unfortunately his hitting prowess did not match his other attributes, and I don't think he ever advanced beyond the "AA" level.

Although he didn't play for the team until the early 1960s, another Timberjack who later became famous (albeit not in baseball) was country singer Charlie Pride; he also worked part time in a smelter, as well as singing the National Anthem for local ballgames on occasion.

Yet another member of the Timberjacks' cast of characters was a pitcher who probably weighed in at around 170, but at some 6'8" in height, looked like an elongated scarecrow when standing on the elevated mound, looking in for a sign from the catcher. I had seen newspaper and magazine photos of a pitcher for Cincinnati named Ewell Blackwell. Nicknamed "the Whip," he was 6'6" and was comparable in stature to our local boy, but there any similarities ended.

Getting back to my drug store lunch breaks, one day the Timberjacks were in town, but not scheduled to play until that evening. I was walking along the sidewalk in front of Monkey Wards (or Montgomery Ward and Company if you want to get all formal about it), when I noticed the lanky pitcher in question holding a bamboo pole out over Higgins Avenue, the main street of town.

When an auto would approach and slow down, he would lift the device, only to lower it again after the car passed, similar to the moveable metal arm one might see in today's parking lots. Because of his already beanpole like appearance, the addition of the bamboo extension gave him the look of a praying mantis.

Whether because of his celebrity status as a professional athlete (albeit entry level at best) or just that the local arm of the law had more critical items on its agenda at the time, he continued this harmless activity for the few minutes I was able to observe him, prior to returning to my lucrative drug related duties. Hey, at least I was actively employed.

****

Stalling out a furniture delivery truck smack dab in the middle of the busiest intersection of Missoula; dropping a case of toilet paper from the highest shelf of a Denver grocery warehouse by having hit the wrong lever of a fork lift; nearly slipping from the top of a slippery jet fuel storage tank during a New Years Eve midnight inventory of the Frontier Refining Company facility in Cheyenne, Wyoming; oh sure, I could continue with detailed examples of poor decisions, errors of judgment, or just plain and simple goof-ups I survived during my working lifetime, but you've suffered enough, so let us move along to the next segment.

****

Chapter 6

"Psst! The Greek Sent Me."

****

While not as football crazy as towns our size in Texas, a Friday night home game to watch the Missoula Spartans take on squads from Billings, Butte, Great Falls or other locales was always a fun family event.

One of the local high school heroes while I was still in elementary school was Dino Damaskos, considered to be one of the fastest kids in the state.

Several years later when I was in high school, one of my classmates was Dino's brother, Frank, who played halfback for the Spartans and also excelled in track. He was nicknamed "The Flying Greek" after setting records in the 440 and other middle distance races, breaking those of his older brother in the process.

Another classmate, John Datsopoulos, was our Student Body President, as well as running track and playing forward for the basketball team. John was known as "The Galloping Greek."

I was a member of Key Club, sponsored by Kiwanis International, as was John. The club scheduled board meetings twice monthly, hosted by various members in their homes. Over the course of three plus years in Key Club, I had occasion to visit John's home several times. His mother always provided home made refreshments for us, which had introduced me to a variety of Greek dessert items.

Add in the fact that still another classmate in elementary school was of Greek ancestry, and I thought I knew pretty much all there was to know about Greeks by the time I was ready to commence college life.

****

Included in the assortment of groups handing out materials from tables at college registration, was one jointly sponsored by the Inter Fraternity Council and Pan Hellenic Council; their purpose was to provide details about "Rush" (no, not Mr. Limbaugh; he came along much later).

The sign hanging from their table made reference to the "Greek System." Call me naïve (if you haven't already), but this aspect of college life was something of which I had no knowledge whatsoever.

Oh sure, I had heard the song "The Sweetheart of Sigma Chi" at some point earlier. I also recalled that, as a nine year old, I was among a sizeable group of children who were hosted to a very impressive Halloween Party, put on for area fourth graders by something called the Sigma Nu Fraternity. They had hung sheets which had converted large rooms into haunting mazes; filled big tubs for bobbing for apples; tape recorded sounds of scary creatures; and organized other well planned Halloween activities. I recalled having been very impressed with that evening's events, put on by these young college men.

Nevertheless, I had no true understanding of fraternity or sorority activities, as neither of my parents had belonged to such a group, nor had older siblings of friends with whom I associated in my pre-college days. Because it sounded as if it might be interesting, I signed up for Rush Week, along with Doug, my close friend from Missoula. His twin brother, Wayne, had opted to get his military obligation out of the way before starting college, and was currently at Army Reserve Boot Camp.

I'm sure this event may differ from state to state, and has probably evolved in the decades since I was involved, but I rated the week as having been quite enjoyable. As a lowly freshman, I'd never anticipated the ego enhancing pleasure of being eagerly wined and dined by all these dignified and mature college students. (At the time, alcoholic beverages were not officially sanctioned in fraternity houses, so the "wined" part in that last sentence may have been a misnomer. Sorry about that.)

In subsequent years, as an active member of my fraternity, I was involved in learning details about prospective pledges who were going through Rush Week, in order to know how best to impress them with our house, as compared to others they would be visiting. However, I was completely snowed by these smooth talking college men when I participated as a "rushee" myself.

For example, if a fraternity had members who had attended the same high school as did the guest, those members acted like long lost buddies when introduced, even if they had totally snubbed him during high school. If the fellow being rushed had been a jock in high school, he might be approached by a varsity athlete who belonged to the fraternity; if a musician, then by someone involved in similar college activities.

Rush Week consisted of brief visits to each of the houses. At the time, there were nine fraternities on campus, along with six sororities for the fairer set. The visit included a tour of the physical structure, some light refreshments, and visiting with someone with whom the guest might feel some rapport.

Next, he was to select his two top choices for a follow up visit, with the first choice providing a meal, excluding dessert, and the second choice providing that dessert. The fraternities could limit the number of attendees, and in the process, effectively scratch any "undesirables" from being included. Yes, that sounds tacky, and it was, but that's how things worked.

I discovered later, as an actual member of the fraternity, that some of those being rushed were considered to be "pocket pledges." Such a description was given to someone participating in Rush Week, who had secretly been locked-in as a new pledge, based on his close ties with an existing member of the fraternity. While siblings or cousins would be the most frequent such situation, often long time friendships might also be the cause.

A pocket pledge might intentionally attend a different house for his first choice; while there, he would zero in some highly desired rushee, and confidentially mention that "the more I think about it, the more I'm leaning towards XYZ Fraternity" or similar comments. Talk about unethical business practices!

The typical sequence of events, following the initial visits, dinners and desserts, was that participants in Rush Week would then return to some central location to sign up for the fraternity to which they most desired to pledge. At about the same time, the fraternities prepared their own list of rushees to whom they wished to offer membership.

The listing of students interested in pledging a particular fraternity was then forwarded to the respective house. If the name appearing on the sheet coincided with one on the list of students desired by the fraternity, the selected student was again contacted to attend yet another dinner for new pledges, at which time he would formally pledge to become a member of that fraternity.

Somewhere in this overall process, Doug and I had decided to "sleep" on our final decision, prior to committing to any particular fraternity. In addition, we were considering whether or not we had sufficient funds to cover not only tuition, books and so on, but also fraternity expenses.

My dad, who by then had left behind his traveling salesman role, was now a licensed realtor in Missoula. To add another wrinkle to our big decision, he had made the two of us aware of a small bowling alley which was available for sale. We had sat down with him to crunch numbers, and were wavering between becoming small business entrepreneurs versus trying to make it through college (and joining a fraternity) without additional financial resources.

Within about ten days, Doug and I made our decision: we had our entire lives to work, so we should enjoy college and all it had to offer, including fraternity life. Now our thoughts turned to which of the various houses was our top choice. We had decided that, unless one of us had some significant negative vibe about a particular fraternity with which the other party strongly disagreed, we would pledge the same house.

We drove to the "93 Stop and Go," a favorite drive-in burger place located, as you might guess, on Highway 93. As we devoured one of their specialties, with onions of course, we compared notes from our visits to all the fraternities, and quickly determined that Sigma Alpha Epsilon was the one for us.

Half an hour later, we pulled up to 1120 Gerald Avenue, parked the car, walked up the sidewalk, and rang the doorbell of the SAE House.

The place was nearly empty. It was about 7:30 on a typically beautiful Montana September evening; no mid-terms or other class work had yet invaded the lives of students; and most of the residents were out on dates, taking in a movie or otherwise socializing away from the house. One of the few men present answered the door, and asked if he could help us. We replied that we had come to pledge SAE.

The poor guy couldn't have been more befuddled if the two of us had been Mormon Missionaries, attempting to convert him.

First of all, he did not know either of us. Of perhaps greater significance, rush had been over for nearly two weeks, and he had moved on to other matters. Most importantly, Doug and I had not gone through the wrap up of Rush Week, and therefore were unaware of the sign up sheets and offers of pledgeship from any of the fraternities. We had not stopped to consider that one or both of us might not have been on the list of desired pledges voted on by the active members at the conclusion of Rush Week.

Talk about naivety on our part; or stated another way, what egotistical self-confidence we possessed, to assume that OF COURSE they would want two such amazing young men as we had been told we were by every insincere glad hander, at each house we had visited weeks earlier. (Fortunately, as it turned out, we had both been on their final list of students to whom they had offered pledgeship; even though we were not aware such a list even existed.)

Our greeter had us wait in the big living room, while he tracked down someone else in the house who knew where the "list" was, and ultimately found both our names included thereon. These two men then gathered the few other brothers who were available, to welcome us to the brotherhood, give us pledge pins, and set up a time for us to return for additional information about what we needed to know about joining the latest pledge class.

****

There are certain elements of any fraternity which are not to be shared with anyone other than active members, and I am confident that nothing included in the following pages would violate such confidence. I must say that I have, in no way, ever regretted my decision to join this fraternity. While I did not agree with everything that took place, I think that overall, the environment helps most students adapt to life beyond high school.

I have many fraternity brothers with whom I have kept contact over the decades following college. I have extensive fond memories of activities related to the house and its brothers. As you will read elsewhere in this book if you keep at it, I have one of the brothers to thank for getting me a job in Yellowstone Park, which brought about meeting my future (now current) wife and love of my life.

That being said, I did not push either of our sons into fraternities when they headed off to college. They both developed their own close friendships during their years at Colorado State University, completely outside the Greek system.

Fraternities have bounced around from being "in" when I was in college, to becoming nearly defunct, and more recently making a comeback.

There have been deaths of young men and women related to their fraternities/sororities and the drinking involved. There have been hazing situations causing death. Had any of these deaths taken place in dorms or private housing, it would have been just as tragic, but when it hits the media, somehow the fraternity connections make for better copy.

For me, the Greek life seemed to be the logical way to go, although not everything mandated made sense to me at the time.

For example, all pledges were required to attend "study table" three nights per week. Somewhere along the way, I had picked up the idea that, having graduated from high school, I was now in the process of becoming responsible for myself. I was paying, or taking advantage of a partial academic scholarship, for the privilege of learning subjects of my own choosing, so why would I want to jeopardize that opportunity by not making my grades?

Because I still lived at home during my first quarter, I was given a partial exemption from driving back down to campus for study table beyond once per week, with the proviso that if I failed to make my grades that quarter, I would not only have that exemption rescinded in the future, but could well lose my pledgeship as well.

My 3.47 G.P.A. for that initial quarter made the whole thing moot; but I often think that had I been pushed on the matter, I might well have dropped my association with the fraternity. In addition, the whole study table thing seemed more like an extended bull session, and several of those pledges who spent the full three nights per week there still failed to make their grades.

Each pledge class was supposed to perform a Pledge Sneak or Pledge Prank. Ours had something to do with arriving at the house around 3:00 a.m.; taking every eating utensil, dish, cup, glass, pot and pan from the kitchen; dipping each item in flour; and making trails all over the house, up and down the stairs, across the piano, into and out of each room (the brothers all slept in a common area on the top floor, not in their individual rooms at the time), down the front porch steps and around the lawn.

Now just what that experience was supposed to teach us, I've never figured out. Naturally after the whole thing was over, we had to vacuum the flour covered carpets, mop the linoleum, wash all the kitchen items and finally prepare breakfast for the actives. Other than the preparation of breakfast, I thought the prank was ridiculous at the time, and have yet to think otherwise.

One rather contradictory (at least to me) aspect of the fraternity became evident during the ceremony in which the pledge becomes an active member of the brotherhood. I'll not divulge any secrets of this solemn event; but with candles providing the only light, and actives attired in special robes, there was a moment when one of them began describing to us initiates, what makes a "True Gentleman."

Included in his devout homily, to which we listened with much reverence, were the words, "These lips from guile be free." Without a doubt, this description of what would be expected of us as true gentlemen of the fraternity would make perfect sense, were it not for the fact that its application to daily life in the fraternity was totally inconsistent.

Point in fact: just a day earlier, during "Hell Week," pledges had been required to assume the position of a dog, lifting a leg as if to pee on the andiron in the fireplace of the living room, while yelling at the top of his lungs, "Rah, rah, rah, shit, piss, fuck!"

I'm not pointing fingers, as I'm not proud to admit that I probably had one of the more foul mouths in the house in those foolish days of youth. However, it did seem more than a little bit contrary to the behavior of a true gentleman; not unlike some church leader who reverts to embezzlement, adultery or other sinful acts when "in the world."

In adhering to full disclosure, I must admit that one member of our pledge class had far greater moral character than did I. Either that or he was determined to show he might have to succumb to the letter of the active member's command, but he would still maintain his independence in so doing. While carrying out the order to assume the position near the fireplace, he avoided the crude verbal aspects of his act by modifying it to "Rah, rah, rah, defecation, urination, fornication!"

Ok, so I had to stretch a bit to find something less than positive about my fraternity years. I really did enjoy my time as a Greek. Among many fond memories, looking back from my older and wiser position in life were the following tidbits.

****

Sub Chapter 6.1: Hell Week

For those individuals who had made their grades, and had otherwise fulfilled the requirements to become an active member of the fraternity, one final obstacle stood in the way. A pledge had to survive Hell Week. While there was no water boarding or physical abuse involved, there was a great deal of harassment perpetrated by the active members of the house (see the "rah, rah, rah" incident mentioned above). We were also required to memorize the full names of each active and to sound off when asked, "What's my name, pledge?"

Half a century later, I can still rapidly call to mind those full names; this knowledge makes it nearly foolproof when trying to select the correct Tom Johnson or Bill Smith in a phone book, while traveling around the country, and trying to look up a former classmate, all thanks to that memorized middle name or initial.

To help our pledge class learn to work together, the active body prepared a wonderful spaghetti dinner during our Hell Week, complete with rolls, salad and (non-alcoholic) beverages, all served to us as a group in the dining room. We had been diligently taught earlier in our pledge period: the correct fork or spoon to use for certain courses of a meal; how to place a napkin on our lap; how to use that napkin to wipe one's face, to avoid having an errant food particle cause discomfort to a table partner; how to enter the chair from the left and exit from the right; and various other bits of dining etiquette.

The actives in charge of this activity did impose one small handicap to our enjoyment of their wonderfully prepared meal. There were fourteen of us seated for dining, seven on each side of the table. Next, a twenty foot long "two by four" (actually, two twelve footers taped together) was tied around our left hands, while we placed our right on our laps. We then were told to dine in unison, so to speak.

If you think a bite of pasta or a sip of water using one's typically non-dominant hand, taken in conjunction with similar functions by a half dozen other pledges of varying height was not an interesting experience; trust me, it was.

I have always had difficulty keeping a straight face when something strikes me as other than serious. For example, marching in ROTC during college (and later at Navy OCS), when I observed people getting out of step or turning the wrong way in close order drills, it nearly always brought a huge smile to my face; I was frequently chastised for such lack of décor, or for not appreciating the seriousness of the moment.

During Hell Week, all sorts of things seemed to bring one of those smiles to the forefront. We had been warned at the beginning of the week that this was serious business, and at no time did they want to see anyone smiling. The punishment for allowing the smile to come out was to wipe it off on the floor, followed by a few pushups.

Apparently via some sort of divine intervention, all fatal viruses must have relocated to somewhere else that week; as my lips kissed the linoleum with such frequency that I'd have caught every disease known to man at the time, had such germs been present.

****

Sub Chapter 6.2: Living in the House

Each active was required to live in the house at least one of the three quarters of every school year; summer quarter did not count as part of this requirement. Rooms were assigned in September, using some sort of seniority system, as a result of which the less desirable locations went to underclassmen.

As new residents, we were told we had to paint our rooms, but could select, within reason, the color to be used. One of my roommates had a massive selection of phonograph records, and he suggested our painting project would seem to go faster if performed to music. He selected "Stan Kenton in Hi Fi" (which included "Peanut Vendor") to start things off; and while I was previously unfamiliar with Kenton, I became a full-fledged fan long before we finished the paint job.

As mentioned earlier, all residents were relegated to the top floor of the house for sleeping, in an area lovingly known as "Siberia."

Rows of bunk beds were placed in every available bit of square footage, with most having electric blanket cords wound around bed posts and plugged into assorted extension cords, which themselves eventually found their way to electrical outlets, in a manner which would never pass the most lax safety code imaginable.

There were perhaps a half-dozen window openings in Siberia, none of which contained any glass. Actually the windows themselves had long since been removed to allow the free flow of air from outside. Such airflow was intended to remove any unhealthy germs which a sick resident may otherwise have breathed on an unsuspecting brother, plus the noxious odors resulting from thirty or so freely-farting fellows like us.

One drawback of the windowless room became all too apparent during inclement weather. Rain was bad enough, although infrequent, but during a snowstorm, when combined with the vicious Hellgate winds, it was not unusual for several beds to be covered with the white stuff. For those unfamiliar with Missoula, one traveling on Interstate Highway 90 will pass through Hellgate Canyon when entering the town from the east; fairly strong winds are known to frequently sweep through its boundaries and into Missoula as well.

During my junior year, one of my classmates had a final exam in an 8:00 class; he had specified an early hour "Wake up Call" to the pledge assigned such duty for the week. Each resident wishing to be awakened at a particular time was listed on the pledge's roster, and said pledge was to ensure the active had his feet on the floor, before assuming his obligation had been satisfied.

When the pledge arrived at the active's bunk on the morning in question, he saw only a huge mound of snow, so he figured the active had already arisen and was on his way to class.

Unfortunately, the student was simply buried inside a mummy type sleeping bag under the deep blanket of snow, and he missed the exam, thereby flunking the class. Whether his professor listened to this version of "My dog ate my homework" excuse and gave him the opportunity to retake the exam, I do not recall.

****

Sub Chapter 6.3: "Do, Re, Mi, Fa"

Our fraternity was referred to as the "Singing Fraternity" (along with several other less complimentary nicknames). We had several talented musicians in our house, and one of them led us in a weekly song practice. This dedication to practice resulted in our fraternity winning various awards at campus skit nights and other musical performance events, but it also prepared us for serenades.

Upon becoming initiated into active membership in the fraternity, an individual received an SAE pin. On the back of the pin was imprinted a number indicating where he ranked in the overall life of the fraternity's listing of membership. For example, my pin number is 100137; that number would not only enable me to identify that I had the grabbed the correct item from a box containing the pins of several roommates, along with cuff links, car keys and breath mints, but it would also identify me as having been the "one hundred thousand, one hundred thirty seventh member" activated into the fraternity.

When one of our fraternity members gave his "pin" to a young lady (something short of becoming engaged, but more than just going steady), a serenade was arranged between our fraternity and the residence of the young lady. This was typically staged at a sorority house, but could also be at one of the dorms.

The brothers would march quietly from our house to the girl's house, where she would be standing in a second floor window, surrounded by candlelight. The brother who had become pinned stepped forward to a point just beneath the window, while the rest of us serenaded the couple with two or three fraternity songs expressing love, cherished feelings and the like. It was quite an impressive time.

These musical events had to be arranged well in advance, as other fraternities performed similar activities, and it would never do to have competing serenades going on at the same sorority house.

Another event related to the pinning, which required very little advanced planning, was the handing out of cigars by the lucky guy to all the brothers. Now there are cigars, and there are CIGARS. Almost without exception, the ones given out on these occasions were "Crooks Wine Soaked Cigars" which probably ranked at the very bottom as far as quality, aroma and price (the latter being the reason for their popularity).

On an evening when such a pinning and cigar distribution occurred, the house turned blue from the smoke. Everyone was expected to at least light up and take one puff to honor the brother; but most of us smoked the entire rotten thing as we stood around congratulating our benefactor.

****

Chapter 6.4: Activities with the Fairer Set

Not everyone graduated from high school with fully refined social graces, and not all had attended "The Prom" during those years. To help bridge that gap for those feeling less than fully comfortable with members of the opposite sex, fraternities and sororities would hold "exchanges" from time to time.

These evenings (typically during the week, to avoid conflicts with weekend activities, sporting events and the like) would be similar to today's cocktail parties, minus the fancy hors d'oeuvres and alcohol. (You may be thinking "No food, no booze, NO WAY!" However such events were considered practically mandatory, so attendance was maximized.)

Conversations typically consisted of mundane topics such as "So where are you from?" or "What is your major?" or "Did you see that movie, concert, ballgame etc.?" Sometimes a youthful looking senior girl would get paired up with a more mature looking, but not necessarily mature acting, freshman, which was unfortunate all the way around. But more often, people who knew each other from common classes, or who had dated each other in the past, would introduce someone from their house to one or more members of the other house, such that a connection might be made leading to a subsequent date, thereby acting as a step in the right (social) direction.

*** Shut the door? What door? ***

Pledge classes sometimes pulled pranks on sororities, such as the night our class decided to steal the front door of the Kappa Alpha Theta Sorority. Somehow we had obtained information that the sorority was on an exchange with another fraternity. Therefore, while the ladies were away, we mice absconded with their door, and placed it in our basement.

After numerous phone calls from the returning Thetas to everyone they could consider, our house president was confronted; he admitted to the larceny of his pledges. By then, it was around midnight; we returned and reinstalled the door under the watchful eyes of their scowling-faced house mother.

*** May I mention the unmentionables? ***

One night we conducted a panty raid. If you have no idea what in the world that means, go ask your grandparents (or great grandparents).

All I can recall of the entire event was one young lady member of the Alpha Phi Sorority; she was standing at the top of the porch steps in her robe, crying out "You bastards, you bastards!" even though we had not bothered to enter her particular room to pilfer anything from her personal panty drawer.

Perhaps she was simply upset that we didn't consider her intimate apparel to be worthy of our wicked wantonness.

*** Hey darlin'; you doing anything Saturday? ***

Each fraternity typically held one or two major social events per school year, with the winter quarter normally including a more formal affair. For us, this night of nights was the *Violet Ball*. While other fraternities also went the extra mile to make their comparable dinner dances special, there were not very many coeds on campus who would not jump at the opportunity to be invited to our shindig.

Despite the positive opinions of the fairer sex concerning our winter formal, female companionship was not likely to simply appear out of the mist. Each of us in the house still had to take some sort of action in order to obtain a date for the evening in question. For those with steady girl friends, it was simply a matter of clearing the particular day on the calendar. For the rest of us, it meant picking up the phone, calling a sorority or dorm, and asking for a certain young lady to come to the phone.

Looking back from the present, and with the benefit of having made numerous phone calls over the years to schedule job interviews, coordinate car pools for kids' activities, obtain subs for league tennis matches, or organize teams for neighborhood clean up sessions; I would consider such an exercise to be no big deal.

Today's methods of communication are far different from what they were a half century ago, what with texting, email and more; so there may be no way to compare the two periods. Still, there must be at least a tad of trepidation in the mind of a young man, when making the initial contact with a comparably aged lady from whom he would request the honor of attending an event of this magnitude.

If, say, the formal is to take place on February 24th, how soon is too soon to make the call? Two weeks, a month, the first day of the winter quarter, the day before heading home following final exams the previous quarter?

If you call too early, hoping to avoid the reply, "Gee, I'd love to go, but I already have plans for that evening; but thanks for asking!" you may come off as a hopeless or desperate guy, who knows he doesn't deserve a positive response.

If, on the other hand, you wait until just ten days prior to the event, you may be forcing the girl to respond in the negative; simply because by waiting so late, she may think of herself as the last gal standing, in a long line of unsuccessful phone calls that preceded the one you made to her. Or she may feel offended that you waited until so late to call, because you figured no one else would ask her out.

By my sophomore year and those that followed, I had become slightly less: (a) awkward, (b) clumsy, (c) inept or (d) all of the above; but as a freshman involved in attempting to obtain a date to our winter formal, I was about to display my version of a "triple threat": grieve, grimace and gag.

There were but two telephone lines for the entire house (you'll recall, this was long before the advent of cell phones); one of them was situated in a built-in phone booth on the main floor, with a door that closed to provide ample privacy for its user. The other sat in the second floor library, and while more than adequate for such calls as ordering a pizza, checking with another fraternity regarding making up a ballgame that had been rained out, or contacting one of the members living off campus; it was fully susceptible to eavesdropping, harassing comments from passersby, and even the occasional utterance of inappropriate language, if you can imagine such a thing.

I recall sitting in the living room, on the big couch next to the piano, waiting for the nice, private phone booth to become available; As I waited, I was also trying to build up my courage to such a level that I could actually dial the numbers I had scribbled on a piece of paper, currently being grasped in my very sweaty hands.

It was some three weeks prior to our formal, which seemed to be within the range acceptable for seeking a date. I had a trio of names and related phone numbers for potential companionship at the event; any one of which would thrill me no end if the response was in the affirmative, with no preferred ranking amongst the three, from my perspective.

Crunch time arrived; the booth was finally available. I entered, sat down and closed the door. I took a few deep breaths, though not enough to hyperventilate, and placed the receiver against my ear. I dialed the number of the lady behind door number one, so to speak.

The person answering the phone said she didn't know if Daphne was around, but that she would be happy to check for me. (No, Daphne was not the real name of the person I was asking out, but since I can't recall the name, I had to make up something for you, dear reader.) A minute or so later, I was advised that she didn't seem to be there, but I could leave a message if I so desired. I declined.

A few more inhalations of oxygen, and I dialed candidate number two. She was a very attractive and outgoing girl with whom I had played several hands of an impromptu game of Bridge at the student lodge between classes one morning. She politely declined my invitation to the ball, telling me she had just started going steady with a fellow from the Phi Delt house, but would really have loved going with me, were it not for her recent involvement.

(I never did date this particular gal, but would bump into her from time to time on campus. She continued to be quite popular, and seemingly upbeat, throughout her school years. I mention this only because I subsequently learned that, while in her late thirties, she committed suicide. There is no "joke" here, as I can think of nothing more tragic than someone taking his/her own life, especially at such a young age.)

Now I was dialing what I hoped to be one of those "third time's the charm" happenings. Of all things, Diane (again, not her real name) answered the phone herself, which was just a little bit discomforting; I asked to speak to "Diane Whatever," and when she said "Speaking," I found myself stammering, as I had not anticipated such immediate contact.

In any event, when I popped the question, she replied, "You won't believe this, but I just got off the phone with Fred Olness (a fellow member of my own pledge class) asking me to go with him. If you had called just five minutes sooner, I could have said yes. I guess I was destined to go to your formal one way or another."

I mumbled something along the lines of "Well, Fred's a great guy, so I know you'll have a good time. I'll probably see you there, and maybe we can share a trek around the dance floor or something." (Great impromptu response, you may be thinking; when what I was internally verbalizing was "Damn, damn, double damn" or words to that effect.) Apparently, while I was sitting in the phone booth trying to get my act together, Fred had walked into the library, picked up the phone and made his call.

*** Might you be Heather? ***

Following the "miracles happen every day" train of thought, I did eventually get a date for our Violet Ball; Doug and I decided to share transportation costs and make it a double date. He had been set up with a "blind date," with the assistance of one of the actives. Although Doug had not met her in person, he had spoken to her over the phone to set up details for the evening.

Both of our dates lived in the same girls' dormitory at the time, and following standard routine, we checked in at the desk in the waiting area of the dorm. The person manning the desk called up to the respective floors to advise our dates that we were there to pick them up.

My date came down the stairs first, looking perfectly radiant and beautiful. As we knew each other, at least somewhat, she recognized me and approached the two of us. I introduced her to Doug; we then wandered off to talk about the upcoming evening, while Doug continued to wait near the bottom of the stairs.

When his date did begin descending the stairway, he fully intended to acknowledge her arrival by saying, "I'm Doug; are you

Heather?" (Or whatever her name was). However, being socially challenged at the time, much like me, he instead looked up at her and said, "Who are you?"

While I have long since forgotten who his date was that evening, whenever he and I have reconnected in the decades subsequent to that night, I always find a way to remind him of his initial goofy greeting on that long ago double date.

This picture does NOT depict the double date just described, but was taken at yet another "Violet Ball" during our college days. The reason for including it is to "maim two birds with one photo" by showing you Doug's appearance. As the twins are all but identical, I now have no need to include a photo of Wayne elsewhere, even if I could find one, which I could not. Most people who know them would say that Wayne is, by far, the better looking of the two. As for the ladies; in order for my date to consent to accompanying me to this event, I had to sign a notarized document stating that should I live until I was in my 70s and subsequently decide to write a memoir, I must never divulge her name, nor that of Doug's date, in order to protect their reputations. So I shall comply.

Sub Chapter 6.5: Spring Break

Spring break, for college folks east of the Mississippi, generally translated into a trek to Fort Lauderdale; but for those of us in cold, dreary Montana, it meant anywhere in California.

For two years running, five of us would pile into a car following the completion of whomever's final exam was the last one scheduled, and drive through the night in a southwesterly direction. In each instance, one of those in the vehicle had their origins in California; this game plan provided the rest of us (all from Montana) with a place to hang out rent-free for a week, as well as having a native of the area to point out all the highlights we would not want to miss.

As was the case for most students during final week, none of us had experienced what might be thought of as a decent night of sleep for a few days. We would take shifts behind the wheel, with at least one other member of the group assigned to remain awake, and make certain the driver did the same.

Wayne, the twin who had gone into the Army Reserves while the rest of us were starting our first quarter of college classes, was now a fellow student once again. As he had a part-time job as a disc jockey at a local radio station, often working the late night stint (and tending to be a night owl even when not working), he volunteered for a middle of the night shift behind the wheel. To utilize the line by Julia Roberts in *Pretty Woman*, "BIG MISTAKE!" It turned out that Wayne was a completely different person behind the wheel, than he was behind the microphone at the radio station. Just moments into his scheduled two hour shift, he was already yawning with gusto, and readily surrendered the wheel to me, after admitting he was having difficulty keeping focused on the highway.

Our target that spring break was Santa Barbara, and we reached our destination safe and sound, although thoroughly exhausted, just prior to lunch time. We unpacked the car, depositing our limited luggage in the Baker residence. (Michael Clement Baker was our Californian of record.)

To straighten out the kinks from our extended drive time confined to the car, we decided to shoot some hoops in his driveway. In contrast to the cold we had left behind in Montana, we basked in the welcome sunshine, while enjoying the rare treat of juicy, sweet oranges, direct from the tree growing adjacent to the driveway.

After devouring a wonderful lunch Mike's mom had prepared, we decided a little shuteye was in order, such that we would be well rested for the upcoming week in this sunny paradise. We ended the much needed period of slumber a few hours later, and began plotting activities for the following few days to provide for maximum intake of the sun, which had been in such short supply back in the Treasure State.

Whereas the day of our arrival could not have been better from a weather standpoint (aka Chamber of Commerce perfection), unfortunately the next five days brought extended periods of rain. Yes, we had slept away the best hours of the entire week. In so doing, we had blown our opportunity to observe any cute young ladies scampering around in shorts or other warm weather attire. In fact, the closest thing to contact with members of the opposite sex during our stay, turned out to be the playing of various board games with Mike's little sister (elementary school age). Although we maintained hope that each ensuing day would bring the return of sunshine and blue skies, such improving conditions never materialized.

Lessons: Eat dessert first. If stated in the form of a commandment, "Thou shalt not procrastinate." Or simply the phrase "You snooze, you lose." Finally, from a more recent book title, "I'll Sleep When I'm Dead."

****

On another of our California spring breaks, our host, Bob Carlberg, was from the Sacramento area. Some of you may recall a popular teen heartthrob singer named Ricky (subsequently modified to Rick, to sound more mature or some such thing) Nelson. He was the son of Ozzie and Harriet Nelson for you "really old" folks. Brother Bob was about as close to being a dead ringer for Ricky Nelson as someone could be, although he couldn't sing a lick.

Bob had numerous friends of the female persuasion still living in the area; he arranged to have a bunch of us attend a dance together on our first night there. From that point forward, it was up to us to follow up; as he had more serious plans for his week back home, and his own vehicle in which to help carry them out.

Doug and I asked two of the girls at the dance if they'd care to go to a movie; and somehow it worked out that we had access to the set of wheels in which we had driven down from Montana.

We had a fun time, and one of the gals seemed to have more than a passing interest in Doug, so she set up yet a third evening together for the four of us. Doug and I were to pick up the other girl, with all three of us to then drive to the home of our hostess for dinner. Our meal was to be followed by some swimming in their pool, weather permitting, and finally some pool of the green felt and corner pocket variety in their basement.

The mother of the girl organizing things had a very nice spread prepared for us; she and her husband both went out of their way to make us feel welcome, both in California overall, and to their home in particular.

Following dinner, Doug excused himself to "go to the restroom," while the rest of us made small talk. Such conversation was suddenly drowned out by the frantic exclamations, "Oh, no! Oh my God, stop!" coming from Doug's location.

The bathroom door opened, and a very red faced Doug began apologizing, as we all stood in the hallway nearby. It seemed that the toilet had become totally clogged, and both water and disgusting looking bodily waste were spilling onto the bathroom floor. The parents were very gracious about everything, and tried to assure Doug that he was not at fault; but everyone present was extremely embarrassed about the situation.

Not that a brief series of three dates, between a guy on spring break and this young lady, would ever have gone beyond the "If you're ever in Montana, we'll have to get together" stage; but had anything someday materialized, Doug would forever have been the brunt of jokes from his prospective in-laws when describing their first meeting with their son-in-law.

****

Over time, things change. Black and white silent films are replaced by Cinemascope, Technicolor and Stereophonic Sound. Radio's *Suspense* or *Inner Sanctum Mysteries* become television's *Lost* or *Criminal Minds*. Basketball's two-handed set shots are shoved aside by the NBA's dunks. Montgomery Ward and Woolworth's popularity disappear and are replaced by Wal Mart or Target. A much smaller change might be exemplified by the relationship between fraternities and alcohol.

When Noble Leslie DeVotie founded the SAE Fraternity in Tuscaloosa, Alabama; I doubt that his primary intention was to create an environment in which young men, many of whom would have been underage, could congregate for the purpose of consuming excessive quantities of liquor and generally making complete fools of themselves. Nevertheless, to pretend that beer and spirits have never darkened the doors of an SAE house, or any other fraternity, would be absurd.

On a return visit to my alma mater for Homecoming one year, I stopped by the SAE house to observe changes that had taken place in the many years since I had graduated. Among other evident deviations was a bar that had been built in the basement, from which beer was readily available to residents and/or guests (after showing valid ID, I am sure). This modification had apparently been authorized by the powers that be in the university administration, as there was certainly no attempt to hide anything.

In contrast to this very visible bar, the possession, let alone consumption, of alcohol was not permitted in the house when I was an active member. That did not mean the brothers did not imbibe. Far from it! There were keg parties practically every weekend; just not in the house. Prior to social events, certain brothers felt the need to get a jump-start on the evening's activities by attending a pre-party at the home of someone living off campus, or perhaps just having a few drinks in their cars.

I was never what one might consider to be a heavy drinker in college. In fact, at one point, someone referred to me as "Cork Cooper," with the implication that simply sniffing the cork from a bottle of wine was sufficient to put me in a stupor. I was not alone in this low tolerance to alcohol.

One weekend, Doug, Wayne, Conrad and I decided to have a private little drinking party at a small hunting cabin located near Nine Pipes Reservoir, midway between Missoula and Flathead Lake. Con's father had a multiple-year lease on the cabin, and knowing what fine upstanding young men we were, he graciously gave us the keys to the place. I don't recall anyone mentioning to him that alcohol would be included in our provisions for the weekend.

We also managed to have an older member of the fraternity purchase a case of beer for us. Yes, you read that correctly, I said a SINGLE CASE, or two dozen individual cans, to get really specific.

Also included in our supplies was a tape recorder; we had decided to treat the weekend as not only a relaxing retreat from the rigors of college studies, but also as an experiment to gauge the effect of limited consumption of alcohol on four normal, well-rounded, sensible (albeit underage) male Caucasians.

We arrived at the cabin just before dark on a Friday evening. After dining on whatever it was that we had brought for that purpose, and walking around the premises to familiarize ourselves with the place, we plugged in the tape recorder (one of those reel-to-reel models for those of you into antiques). We then began the experiment by identifying those present, the date, the location, and our intention to determine whether or not twenty-four cans of beer, divided more or less equally amongst the four of us, would modify our behavior, and if so, to what extent.

We placed the microphone next to each beer can, in order to catch the unique sound as it was being opened. We then described the taste of that initial gulp of the ice cold malt beverage being consumed, as well as our surroundings in the cabin, just to provide sufficient information to make our study sound scientific.

We had brought along some decks of cards, so Wayne and I played solitaire, while Doug read a magazine. Conrad kept busy observing where everything was situated, in order to ensure that things were put back identically to how they had been upon our arrival.

Rather than chug-a-lug, like some animalistic Neanderthals from *Animal House*, we waited until all four of us had finished our first beer before opening our second one. We turned the recorder on and off, depending upon whether someone had something profound to contribute to our study.

After all of our second containers had been consumed, we each took a turn with the mike as we opened our third can. Actually, not all of us had completed can number two. Conrad was barely into his second one, wishing to maintain a sense of sobriety in the event one or more of the rest of us failed to do so. He told us to continue at whatever pace we chose, and he would catch up with us eventually.

Feeling confident that we were in no way functioning at diminished capacity, we quickly saw through Conrad's script, and conspired to help him catch up a bit more quickly. While Doug caused a distraction by asking about the bed arrangement in the sleeping area, Wayne and I poured out a portion of Conrad's beer and replaced it with an equal amount of hard liquor we had discovered beneath the sink. When Conrad took his next tiny sip, he commented about the strange taste, and we all assured him it must be getting flat; once he cracked open his ice cold can number three, the true taste would return. Do you think he was convinced? No, I don't either.

Rather than drag things out any further, here is a recap of our scientific study:

Conrad, who had barely begun his third beer by evening's end, advised us he had found a fascinating article in some magazine which he really wanted to finish (while covertly keeping a watchful eye on the rest of us).

Doug, following his fifth beer, said he was sleepy and was going to bed.

I was roughly half-way through my sixth brewski, when I mentioned to anyone who may have been listening that I thought I'd go for a walk in the rain, which had started an hour earlier. When I failed to return shortly thereafter, Conrad ventured outside and discovered me lying in some mud; as raindrops fell on my smiling face, I kept mumbling about how rain was such a cleansing substance. Conrad awakened Doug, and together they managed to get me back inside and into a chair, where they encouraged me to change into some dry clothes.

That brings us to Wayne, the only real party animal of the group. When I described the cabin as being situated near Nine Pipes Reservoir, you probably guessed that its name had some sort of Native American origin. If so, please proceed to the head of the class.

All the small towns nearby (Arlee, Ronan, Ravalli) were inhabited in great part by Indians. I know that what follows is a great example of political incorrectness (although that phrase had yet to be introduced into mainstream vocabulary at the time), but I'm simply describing what took place.

Wayne had obviously been consuming beverages at a slightly faster pace than the rest of us; somewhere into his sixth beer, he advised us that he was going to go find a squaw and have sex with her. As he drained the last drops of number seven, he began tossing shoes around the room, while becoming even more vocal about finding a squaw.

We told him he was in no condition to drive anywhere, but he was still insistent about having sex with Pocahontas or one of her kin. He then proposed the following: if he could consume two more beers AND begin acting sober in the process, would we provide the driving to allow him to pursue his impulses?

As it appeared he was about to pass out anyway, we agreed to assist him by driving to a nearby bar. Sure enough, within ten minutes he was zonked out in his big soft chair. (This portion of the evening was completed shortly before I had decided to venture out into the rain.)

The following morning we prepared a huge breakfast, and tried to listen to the tape we had made from the night before. I jokingly asked if anyone cared for a beer before breakfast, to which all responded with a series of groans. We replayed the tape, making comments about the increasing volume and slurring of the spoken word by each voice thereon. At some point it became nothing but incoherent shouting, so we shut it off.

Having dedicated ourselves to this scientific study, and determining that it probably had very little value to add to the outside world, we packed up our belongings, spruced up the cabin and headed back to campus. Ah, the rigorous life of the scientist.

Chapter 7

The Yellowstone Years

A couple of hundred years ago, famed mountain man, John Colter, was literally running for his life (bare-ass naked at the time) in the area now known as Yellowstone National Park. I doubt that he was thinking ahead to the present day; when millions of tourists would be visiting the multitudes of geysers, steaming hot pools, waterfalls, caverns, paint pots and the wide variety of wild animals wandering in and around such wonders of nature. His focus was entirely on the Indians pursuing him.

I'm positive he never envisioned that a future CPA would basically pay for his college education (not to mention meeting, and ultimately marrying, the girl of his dreams) while working summers amongst all the beautiful aspects of Yellowstone. For that matter, he probably never imagined that there would ever even BE a creature called a "CPA."

Nevertheless, for five glorious summers, I labored in what I probably considered then, and most assuredly do now, in retrospect, the best possible working environment that existed for a young man in my situation. What was so fantastic about this particular bit of summer employment, you may ask?

Start with the pay scale. I had most recently been in the employ of a local drug store, between the summer of my high school graduation and the beginning of college, for the welcome (at the time) wage of $37.50 per week. In contrast, my starting rate of pay with the National Park Service was a whopping $1.71 per hour, or a substantial raise of over $.77 for the same sixty minute time frame.

Opening, checking in, and pricing cases of merchandise in the dingy, dusty backroom of a drugstore could NEVER hold a candle to hiking around in the great outdoors of Yellowstone, regardless of the remuneration associated with performing either activity.

As for broadening the knowledge of a young man not yet out of his teens, this was definitely the place to be. Expanding my vocabulary; building my stamina and overall body strength; observing up close and personal the natural wonders, as well as wild animals, of Yellowstone (many of which were not accessible to the general public); sexual awakening; learning to reside with fellow workers in extremely close living quarters, which allowed me to learn all sorts of good stuff; and picking up a limited introduction to botany; these are just a small sampling of the opportunities which were made available to me during those summers.

****

Sub Chapter 7.1: A Hand of Bridge
That Definitely Shaped My Life

There are all sorts of jobs in a national park. For example, a charming young lady (who, three years later, was to become my wife) ventured west from a small Indiana town to work as a "savage." That nom de guerre was given to employees of a lodge, hotel or general store who performed the duties of cabin maid, waitress, bus boy, clerk, etc. There were also a number of government positions covering the gamut from forest ranger through road maintenance, post offices, trail crews, and sanitation engineers, plus a few other categories. My job fit into that "other category."

The savages were grossly underpaid, from a monetary standpoint; however if one did not require funds for college to be earned from such employment, the time could be compared to a three-month summer camp, without the merit badges to show for various accomplishments.

Incredible sunsets; fabulous fishing; no "hours" in the dorms, as one had back at college at the time; healthy hiking challenges; swimming in the Firehole River; nightly dances at various locations throughout the park; enough "Kodak Moments" to fill several dozen photo albums; the opportunity, if so desired, to experience the thrill of losing one's virginity, back when that was

148

not already considered a "given" by the time one graduated high school, as seems the norm today. These were but a few of the desirable aspects of working in Yellowstone, and generally of far more value to the average savage, than the size of the paycheck.

The more highly compensated government positions tended to result from appointments by Congressmen, Senators and the like. As our family had not been particularly active in either political party, it was hardly likely I would ever land such a coveted slot, and had therefore never even considered having the opportunity to work in the summer paradise of a National Park.

Unlike at least a sizeable portion of the savages, I definitely did not fit in the category of comfortably well-off college student. No, I would require a much more financially lucrative position to cover a multitude of expenses which included college tuition; books, board, room and fraternity expenses; gas and maintenance for my auto, including roughly one quart of oil with every ten gallons of petrol; and an occasional movie or other form of entertainment.

Having earned a partial academic scholarship for my freshman year, which would extend to my sophomore year if I maintained a certain grade point average; and having saved most of my paltry earnings from my drug store labors, I had temporarily suspended my concerns about how to pay for college, and had even joined a fraternity.

During any given week in our fraternity house, it was fairly typical that at least a couple of Bridge foursomes would be in progress, both prior to lunch, as well as immediately afterward. I happened to be in just such a foursome following the noon meal, trying to decide whether or not I still had time to make it to my one o'clock class, if I left immediately and really hoofed it the six blocks to campus.

I don't recall the name of the class, only that it was not all that interesting. I do remember deciding that I could probably afford a "cut" without endangering my current grade; besides, after several totally unbiddable hands, I finally had been dealt some decent cards and had a chance to make a risky four heart bid. I bagged the class and opted to complete the Bridge game.

Now I certainly do not advocate such callous behavior for excelling in college; however my decision to cut that class and finish the hand literally changed my life from who knows what it might have been.

Just about the time I had finessed my way to a successful making of the bid, an upperclassman named Bud Edwards wandered into the large room where we were playing and said, "I just got off the phone with my dad, and he said he could place up to seven guys with work for the summer. Does anybody in here need a job?"

I immediately responded in the positive, without even knowing what it paid, where it was, or if I was qualified. It turned out that Bud's dad happened to be the Assistant Superintendent of Yellowstone National Park, and as such, had some discretionary hiring available to him. He easily found seven "takers" including yours truly.

A few short months later, I had completed my freshman year of college and was about to learn all the inner secrets of "Ribes Eradication Related to White Pine Blister Rust Control." (How's that for a mouthful?)

You may have noted a subtle shift from all the heavily slanted accounting related subject matter, to topics more generally associated with botany. You botanists out there may begin to get that special tingle, even feelings of arousal, associated with reading such material; but don't get your hopes up too much.

Yes, I'll attempt to provide some slight satisfaction to those botanists who might quickly leaf through the next few pages searching for one or two erotic botanical passages; the focal point will be "ribes," and I hope it will make for a juicy chapter.

To be totally accurate, ribes could be utilized to actually make juice, I suppose, as the term ribes encompasses the various species of wild gooseberries and currants, something your mother may have made into more than a few pies, jams or jellies.

Several hours of our first day at the Blister Rust Control Camp, situated near Canyon Village in Yellowstone Park, were spent looking at slides of the seven species of ribes which could be found in the park, along with scenes of the devastation of Blister Rust on the White Pine Tree.

For you enthusiastic botanists in the audience, Blister Rust is a fungus disease that attacks and kills the White Pine; but said disease cannot spread from tree-to-tree. Instead it must pass through a host plant, which was the ribes family.

Paraphrasing the words from that great television show commencing in the late 60s, *Mission Impossible*, our job, should we choose to accept it, was to eradicate those ribes, such that for lifetimes to come, the tourists coming to Yellowstone would be able to view White Pine Trees in all their majesty and glory; or so was the sales pitch we were given that first morning.

For historical purposes, it should be noted that the *Ribes Eradication Project* in Yellowstone commenced around 1947, and was abandoned as another useless government endeavor, around 1968. Fortunately for me, and my "college needs" bank account, my time working on Blister Rust Control covered the period 1958-1962.

While there were seven species of these dreaded ribes available for our eradication efforts, there is no truth to the rumor that the highly successful Yul Brynner-Steve McQueen film, *The Magnificent Seven* in 1960 had its origins in the mind of some future film maker who had spent an earlier summer working on such a Blister Rust Control crew.

Ribes grew in diverse locations, ranging from swampy marshlands to rocky mountaintops, plus everything in between. Over five decades later, I may be walking through the woods of Colorado, and come upon one of my former arch enemies, say the "ribes montigenum," simply smiling as I pass it by; much as a tourist today might visit Japan or Germany, with no World War II related thoughts. Nevertheless, our primary objective at the time was to stamp out those evil gooseberries and currants.

****

There were three methods utilized to eliminate said shrubs from the vast terrain of Yellowstone Park. The least employed of these was via the High Fog Gun, used in areas with a heavy concentration of ribes, but lacking access to water. The gun consisted of a three-pronged metal head attached to an 18 inch tube, with a faucet like handle on the other end, all of which was connected to a tank. The tank, carried on a back-pack, was filled with a highly concentrated chemical.

The gunslinger, for lack of a better name, would use the prongs to remove soil, until the crown of the plant was exposed; he would then scratch the crown to tear away portions of the protective outer skin and give a quick turn of the nozzle to spray chemical on the unprotected crown. The chemical caused the plant to grow at such a rapid rate that it could not sustain such growth, and it would die.

A second, but somewhat similar method was practiced where water was readily available. In this instance, two large trash cans would be filled with water from a nearby stream. The aforementioned chemical was then added to these containers, in a less concentrated form than in the high fog guns; a gas operated pump would send the resulting mixture through hoses leading from the trash barrels.

Crews, consisting of four to six members, would locate, scratch and spray ribes in an area roughly fifty yards to either side of the stream; they could fully saturate the crown area with the diluted chemical, rather than just applying a quick spray, as with the high fog guns.

To provide a better description for your edification, I have gone to great lengths to locate a photograph from countless envelopes stashed in dozens of dusty boxes stored on several shelves in our basement. By inserting this picture (see next page), it will undoubtedly allow me to shorten the text by nearly a thousand words.

The glamorous actress shown above is portraying the role of a seasoned Blister Ruster demonstrating the proper use of a pumper gun to spray the dreaded ribes plant. She is, as you might have surmised, the young lady who eventually became my bride. For those who may question the reality of this carefully posed scene, there are just a few minor adjustments required for true authenticity: she would be wearing boots instead of sneakers, her perfectly coiffed hairdo would be covered by a hard hat, a pair of work gloves would hide her soft hands, and, had she actually been attempting to eradicate a plant, both she and the spray nozzle would have been down at ground level. Other than that, it's fairly accurate. Well, at least the trees are real.

The third, and most frequently utilized method, was the dragline approach, in which each crew member would cover acreage less infested with our quarry. The dragline operator would lay out a length of cord along the edge of the "lot" to which he was assigned; he placed a second cord, parallel to the first, some 15-20 yards from the initial line.

He would then zig-zag between the two draglines, scouring the area for the enemy, using his "hodag" as a pointer. This tool (the hodag) resembled a small pick, but with a two-pronged fork on one end of the head and a three inch wide blade on the other end.

Once a plant was found, the two-pronged fork was used to dig it up, below the crown; if done above the crown, it would quickly sprout new growth and live to kill the white pine another day. A red chemical, identified by the non-specific name "goop," which was carried in a 16 ounce can by each worker, was then poured on any smaller root below the crown to insure that the plant had no chance of survival.

Regardless of the method used, each crew member kept a count of plants found and eliminated, by location. Such recording was made on a lot report, kept in a small metal clip board that fit in one's pocket, and which would later be combined with other lot reports by a crew chief and plotted on a map of the area.

This was but a small example (and as I was to learn in the years following, only the tip of the iceberg) of the government's typical need to generate countless paper documents in order to somehow justify the expenditure of vast sums of taxpayers' money.

OK, botanists, your seedy little segment is now over. Was it good for you?

****

Following a morning of lectures, charts, slides and the like, we went out into the field to seek our first live exposure to these hated gooseberries. Oh, did I happen to mention the elevation of Yellowstone National Park? The average for the park is 8,000 feet, but many of the areas in which we were to be working were often in the 9,250-10,250 foot range above sea level, such as Mount Washburn and vicinity.

Coming to these high elevations from the roughly 3,400 foot altitude of my Montana home was enough of a challenge; but for those appointees arriving from New York, Louisiana, Maryland etc., there simply was not enough oxygen to immediately sustain the body for the hiking activities required in this particular summer job.

Therefore, in addition to learning which types of plants to eradicate (ribes), those we should allow to live in peace (raspberries), or those to absolutely avoid (poison ivy); it was also essential for all of us to get in satisfactory hiking condition.

There were more than enough of these wild currant and gooseberry things near camp headquarters to test our visual skills; i.e. to differentiate between the bad guys, and the harmless, but sometimes similar looking ones. However, to also help us with our conditioning, we were taken by truck to an area requiring an elevation gain of some 1,000 feet while performing our initial search. During my first few days, I was amazed at the great condition of the various crew leaders, who either led, or pushed us, up these steep inclines.

I discovered in my second year, when I was a crew leader myself, that I had been invited to start work about a week to ten days prior to the arrival of the new appointees. The advance time was supposedly needed in order for this smaller band of brothers to scout out on foot, the areas to be worked during the upcoming summer; but it obviously provided a great head start on becoming acclimated to the elevation, and getting both legs and lungs in shape.

While the main thrust of our summer labors was to protect the white pine from blister rust, a secondary (but in reality, most likely the primary) purpose for our presence in Yellowstone was fire fighting.

Bear in mind that this time frame preceded by three decades, the massive forest fire which devastated the park in 1988. Nevertheless, the edict at the time was that whereas fires could be fought by men on foot, absolutely no bulldozers or heavy equipment of any kind were to be utilized, and certainly no smokejumpers would be called in to assist with battling fires in the park.

The philosophy centered on the idea that certain things, like fires, were to be allowed to follow nature's course, up to a point; apparently fire crews equipped with only axes, pulaskis, and shovels, with perhaps a small chain saw or two in the mix, fit within such an approach.

There was no doubt that we "Blister Rusters" were all but guaranteed to be in better shape than any other park employees, due to all our hiking, along with the carting around of the equipment utilized in our pumper units, high fog guns etc.

Another part of our preparation for the upcoming summer was to practice digging a fire-line. Despite the fact that, pushed by a strong wind, a fire can readily jump over a highway or a river with ease, the fire lines we built were basically a shovel's width. Any roots crossing our line had to be cut, to prevent a fire from sneaking across to all the fuel awaiting it just inches away. (I guess this follows the adage that "The fuel is always more flammable on the other side of the fire line.") Any readily burnable material adjacent to said line was to be removed, along with overhanging branches being cut back.

Now that you, the reader, are well versed in the events of our first few days of indoctrination, let's move along, for heaven's sake!

******

Sub Chapter 7.2: Welcome to Pack Camp

Following the week or two spent getting the hang of things in and around Canyon Village, our base headquarters, approximately three dozen of us were assigned to a pack camp. It was situated some ten miles northeast by highway and another four hiking miles north and west down into a valley located between Canyon Village and Tower Falls. Some early arrivals had previously set up the mess/cook tent and the living quarters (eight other smaller tents) by the time we "hit town."

There were five cots in each tent; except for the camp boss and his assistant, who shared a single tent which also housed a large map table to plot our upcoming summer's accomplishments.

Not that it had been prearranged; but five of the seven of us young men who had obtained positions thanks to the father of our fraternity brother, had been assigned to pack camp, and we logically chose to reside in the same tent.

As a lowly pledge for nearly half of my freshman year, and not yet living in the house even as an active, I obviously did not know much about the four brothers with whom I was to share such close living quarters that summer. Before returning for my sophomore year, I had learned a great deal about that quartet, and they about me.

For example, one of my tent mates (who was later to become a Rhodes Scholar candidate) had numerous books among his personal stuff; while another (the only certified high school athlete in the group) had a footlocker filled with cartons of cigarettes. Of course, I was without idiosyncrasies or oddities of any kind.

Our camp boss was, I think, from Louisiana or possibly Tennessee; based upon the typical vocabulary spewing from his mouth, it was the consensus of the entire mini-segment of our fraternity that he was some illiterate backwoodsman who had found his niche in what would be a lifetime vocation, at least until his knees gave out. Somewhat later, I discovered that he had a postgraduate degree from Memphis State, and was not at all what that initial three month impression had made him appear to be.

Pack camp was the perfect assignment for me. We normally worked Monday through Saturday; those chaps wishing to enjoy the pleasures of electricity, hot water showers, flush toilets, ice cream at the Hamilton Store, movies and (oh yes, I almost forgot) some connection with members of the opposite sex, could then hike out to the highway where a truck would be waiting to transport them back to the base camp in Canyon Village.

As my summer objective was to stash away as much cash as possible for the upcoming school year, and as there was nothing upon which to spend even a nickel in pack camp, this was where I spent most weekends.

Added enhancements included the opportunity to fish in any number of ideal deep cut banks of the stream running through the valley. "Red," our camp cook, was always more than willing to fry up such a catch, as long as I was willing to share some with him. We had horseshoe pits and volleyball equipment, as well as a multitude of paperback novels available for our pleasure to make for a leisurely Sunday prior to another six days of physical exertion and blister bursting while blister rusting.

True, we had to do our laundry and take showers by what can only be considered primitive methods; but it just made those once a month or so trips back to civilization all that much more special to those few of us who chose to stay in camp most of the summer.

Not having attended any type of camp as a preteen, as had a few of my boyhood friends, I was not at all sure what to expect from spending the summer in one, with a group of guys well beyond the Cub Scout stage of life. I did learn several new skills that probably did not come from the scout handbook, although some may have. For example, I had never considered the need to sweep our tent floor daily, despite the fact that said floor was itself, DIRT.

Then there was the relocation every ten days of our urinals (actually just a ditch dug behind the tent area). We were to pour lye or some other powdery substance into the abandoned site, prior to digging yet another similar ditch about twenty feet from the previous one. I could never figure that out, as unlike the "two-holer" located up the hill, which contained solid human waste, the ditch's contents quickly drained away each day.

You must all have certain songs which transport your thought processes back to some particular event in your past. One of that summer's more popular songs was "Volare." As we pack camp residents were hiking the final steep half mile to the awaiting big yellow truck on the highway, it became habitual for all thirty or so of us to begin singing that song at the top of what remained of our lungs. Why we had picked this song with which to serenade any surrounding wildlife or tourists, I do not know, as I doubt that any of us could have translated such words as "Nel Blu Dipinto Di Blu."

Nevertheless whenever Dean Martin or others belt out those lyrics on some "Old Person's Radio Station" all these decades later, I can still envision myself struggling to make it up the remaining real estate of the mountainside between me and the truck, and to make certain I finished within at least the first half of the group (that damn testosterone, you know).

If it happened to snow, which was not all that illogical at that altitude, we might be given a minimum four hours of work splitting firewood or accomplishing various camp tasks; as it would have been all but impossible to locate ribes under even a thin blanket of snow.

If the snowfall was forecast to continue for more than a single day, we were advised that no work (and no pay) would be available for X number of days. In those situations, employees would take off for some sight seeing; or in the case of those of us from Montana, perhaps travel back to our homes for a brief visit.

On just such an occasion, one of our tent mates invited any of us who might be interested, to come to his home during our weather-related furlough. Three of us accepted his offer. Once we had hiked to the awaiting truck and were driven to Canyon Village, we quickly showered, and hopped in his car for the drive to his home in Laurel, Montana (near Billings).

Doug was his given name, but that summer he came to be known, at least within his immediate circle, as the "Bleached Lobster," due to his ultra blond locks and his propensity to become red as a beet, from even limited exposure to the sun. He was the former star high school athlete described previously, and possessed excellent reflexes. Furthermore, it seemed that he had driven more miles than the rest of us put together.

These talents were never more desperately required than during this half-day drive. An icy overpass was anxiously awaiting our arrival, as was a potential newspaper headline such as "FATAL FLAMES FRY FOUR" or something not quite so flamboyant.

While deeply engrossed in discussing some aspect of the female gender, as you might imagine, we hit the patch of ice. The steering wheel was turned slightly towards a point between, say, 10:30 and 11:00 to allow Doug to maneuver a moderate curve on the highway. The momentum of the vehicle immediately caused us to be traveling sideways, with the right side of the vehicle leading the way.

Our earlier conversation was instantly replaced by something akin to gallows laughter, as each of us intuitively realized that if (when) the ice changed to dry pavement, the car would begin a series of flips, from which there was no hope of survival.

Fortunately (and that is definitely an understatement), Doug was somehow able to steer into the slide just enough to bring the wheels back to where those of us in the back seat could simultaneously view highway and the hood ornament, directly in front of us, at a point just below the rearview mirror; rather than looking in sheer terror out the side window as we had just been doing.

The only aspect of this near fatal flip more amazing than it not happening, had to be the incredible control exhibited by all of us in keeping our sphincter muscles performing their duty by keeping our shorts from turning brown.

A few years ago, my wife and I happened to watch again the Sean Connery/James Bond film *Goldfinger* which we had initially seen during my Navy days. In it there is a scene in which the villain runs an expensive automobile through a crusher, while a dissenting former associate remains inside the vehicle. When the compacted package of metal remaining from the car and its occupant appeared, I mentioned that my life could well have ended in a similar manner on that trip to Laurel early in my Yellowstone days.

****

Sub Chapter 7.3: Eight Hand Picked Studs, And Yours Truly

Our camp cook went by the nickname "Red," although such moniker must have been bestowed on him quite a few years earlier; what little hair he currently possessed was somewhere between light shades of gray and white.

Red had been the head chef at some swanky Miami resort for many winter seasons, but spent his summers as the presenter of fine meals for the Blister Rust Crews. Although he had a complete kitchen in which to operate at the base camp near Canyon Village, he had given it up to take care of us in the pack camp, much to the envy of those remaining topside.

One Sunday toward the end of August, I happened to be the lone camp member not to have made the trek up and out. Red and I were visiting outside the cook tent when we heard the whinny of horses; we looked down the trail and observed Fred, the packer, riding into camp. Fred was the camp's weekly source of food, mail and supplies; but he normally made trips during the week while all of us were out in the field. As he drew closer, we noted that he did not have the usual team of pack horses trailing behind him; although there was a two-legged individual following him at some distance. What was going on?

Red handed him a cup of coffee from the ever ready pot kept on one of the stoves, while asking the purpose of this unexpected visit to our humble quarters. Fred advised us that a fire had been spotted; everyone topside had been called out to fight it. The powers that be had requested that Fred be sent down to pack camp to bring Red back out to run the meal preparation for those fighting the fire. That had to mean it was a pretty sizeable fire, since they were going to such great lengths to relocate Red.

During a typical work week, we could accumulate up to a maximum of 48 hours in any given week, weather permitting. On a fire, however, one often worked 16 hours per day, which put crews into overtime mode by the middle of the week instead of just the eight hours on a Saturday.

Realizing I had missed being included in the firefighting, because I had remained in pack camp, I was temporarily bummed out, thinking of all that time-and-a-half pay I would be sacrificing. My disappointment was short-lived; Fred went on to explain that he was taking me along as well, to assist as needed to get Red to the fire site.

By now I recognized the fellow on foot. It was a co-worker named Stan, who had just been released from the infirmary where he was recovering from some ailment; while he was not yet up to joining the crews fighting the fire, he could remain in camp to both regain his strength and to safeguard the camp from anyone who might chance to be hiking in the area, and stumble into our otherwise abandoned camp.

Skipping ahead to the next day, I accompanied Fred and Red as we covered some 22-23 miles cross-country from the nearest highway to a point within a couple of miles from the fire. As I had never cared for horses; had never ridden one; didn't want to add that skill to my limited repertoire; and definitely considered myself to be in the best shape of my young life, I had walked the entire way.

Red, truth be known, probably had no prior equestrian training either; and certainly looked it, as he rode quite ungracefully over those 22 plus miles, as well as the four miles out of pack camp the afternoon prior. Our cook weighed in at around 260 pounds on his 5'6" frame (yes, he enjoyed his own cooking; sometimes to extremes). He would have had difficulty walking 25 blocks, let alone the 25 miles to the fire; so ride he did, ALMOST all the way, but not quite.

We approached a small brook, perhaps two feet wide at its widest point. Red, compassionate man that he was, felt his horse certainly deserved a few mouthfuls of cool water, after having carried him all those miles He allowed his steed to ease down the steep terrain adjacent to the brook.

Unfortunately, the horse lost its footing momentarily, and to right itself, quickly jumped to the other side; it then turned immediately back in the direction from which it had come. Even more unfortunately, Red had lost his balance when the horse made its initial jump; when the horse reversed course, Red continued in the original direction and became airborne until hitting a stump, head first, on the opposite bank.

I'll refrain from getting too graphic here; while specific details may spice up descriptions regarding matters of sex, they are far too bloody to my liking when describing injuries to someone.

Red's scalp had been peeled back from just above his right eye to a point about three inches into where his hairline would have been, had he had hair. Surprisingly, his bleeding was not as extensive as might have been anticipated from such a head wound.

Fred and I moved Red to a nearby flat and shady spot. We determined it made more sense for Fred to proceed on horseback to get help, so he continued on to the fire while I remained with what I truly expected was soon to become a corpse. I did my best to clean away dirt and blood, while using compression to keep the loosened skin in place.

After what seemed an eternity to me, but was in fact, just over two hours; Fred returned, leading an octet of firefighters to my location. One of them had a first aid kit; he applied tape and bandages to keep the injured area on Red's head from further bleeding, although far short of attempting any sort of stitches a la Rambo, in those Hollywood extravaganzas years later.

We had no means of communicating with anyone; but at the fire site, someone had radioed Park Headquarters for assistance. Meanwhile the Blister Rust Control Supervisor, who was coordinating the fire fighting, handpicked the eight members to be pulled from the fire and sent with Fred to help evacuate Red.

As a result of the radio contact, a plane soon appeared overhead; it had been sent from either Bozeman or West Yellowstone. Attempts were made to drop some items to us; the first consisted of a stretcher and some K-rations. However it was either dropped too soon, or the winds were stronger than they thought, as the items landed nearly as far away from our location as was the fire. A second drop contained a metal five gallon container of water. While it landed within a hundred yards of us, it basically exploded on contact with the ground. The only thing we salvaged from either attempt was the parachute carrying the too fragile vessel of water.

One member of our party had a small hatchet he had brought from the fire camp; he proceeded to cut and limb four small pine trees growing nearby. While the selection of trees in the immediate area was limited, it must be said that he couldn't have chosen four trees any greener (and therefore very heavy) had he been specifically assigned to do so.

With the parachute, its cords and the four trees, we built our own stretcher of sorts. It was assembled such that, in addition to two long sections extending beyond the "bed" both fore and aft (a couple of terms I learned later during my Navy days), there were cross-bars at both ends. Therefore, six people at a time could carry the stretcher (three at the front, three in the rear) with three more ready to slide into the rotation as needed.

I mentioned the rescue team pulled from the fire as having been hand picked; such selection had been made to result in a group of the biggest and strongest fire fighters available for the evacuation. While I was thankful to have all these "studs" on hand; it only served to point out my "less than studly stature."

The largest of the group was the assistant boss from pack camp, Bob, who reminded me of a Minnesota Viking. (No, this was still a couple of years before the current NFL Team came into existence; but he did look like a picture of a Viking I recalled from grade school geography class, and he had played football at a small college in Minnesota.)

A second member, Fritz, was within a few pounds of Bob, and was one of those guys who liked to show off by wearing just a fish-net material t-shirt to breakfast; while the rest of us had on long underwear tops and a wool shirt, and still found ourselves shivering until the sun arrived to make its impact on the day.

Still another was Don, a tight end (back then we just called them "an end" although, truth be known, he was often "tight" from imbibing heavily on Saturday nights) for the BYU football team. You might guess he was not a practicing Mormon.

The other members were only slightly less gargantuan, except me, at a strapping 5'9" (5'10" on a good day if I was really stretched out) and 150 pounds soaking wet.

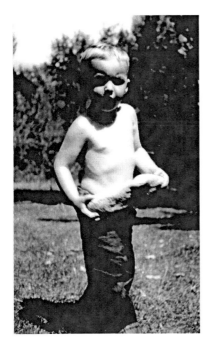

In anticipation of someday having the need to help carry 300 pounds of dead weight for great distances, I worked out with rocks as a child.

Each of us had a full canteen; the guys from the fire brought full ones with them and Fred had filled mine from his before he returned to the fire. We also had the aforementioned hatchet and two boxed K-rations also brought from the fire. Deciding it was unlikely we'd get any more attempted assistance from the now departed airplane, and that if we didn't get moving with Red, he'd never make it; we commenced our journey towards the highway, to what we hoped would be an ambulance rather than a hearse.

To compliment our limited supply of food and water, we also lacked a compass. What we did have was plenty of spirit. We carried our patient in six-man rotating shifts, starting at durations of fifteen minutes, subsequently reduced to ten, until dark, using the sun as our only means of direction determination. As our green pine stretcher weighed nearly fifty pounds by itself, the addition of our patient gave us a total weight to carry in excess of three hundred pounds.

Red drifted in and out of consciousness, and when he did awaken, we did our best to force small amounts of water and whatever segments of food from the K-rations (a piece of cookie or canned fruit) he might be able to swallow without choking.

Had we been at the fire, there would have been sleeping bags for nocturnal warmth, but as it was, we had to settle for sitting around a large campfire we had built. Yes, someone had thought to bring matches.

We covered Red with our outer shirts to keep him warm. They may not have smelled all that great, but he didn't seem to mind. It was all but impossible for the rest of us to sleep; the portion of the body facing the fire was uncomfortably hot, while the opposite side was freezing. That is not to say the temperature was below 32 degrees; but late in August at that altitude, after the sun has set, it can feel mighty brisk out. Mostly we spent the night shifting positions adjacent to the fire while telling jokes or stories, singing raunchy songs, checking on Red, and hoping that we were moving in the right general direction.

The morning sun finally peeked out from behind the mountains so we could continue our journey. Though a pot of coffee might have been a great way to kick-start the day, we had none; so a small sip of our diminishing water supply had to suffice. For me the sacrifice was not as great as it was for most others, as I had yet to acquire a taste for that caffeinated product. (I added it to my list of bad habits a year or two later, while studying for some final exams.)

The lack of some sort of breakfast, however, made for a lot of noisy growling of complaint from all our stomachs. My latest meal had been a hastily packed ham sandwich around noon the previous day, as we had anticipated arriving at the fire camp by early afternoon, where food would be plentiful. My co-rescuers were probably in much the same boat as I, as they had been pulled from the fire shortly after lunch as well. That said, I neither uttered, nor did I hear, a single complaint about starting the day sans food of any kind. The focus was entirely on getting Red to expert medical attention.

Our outbound route was nowhere close to being the shortest distance between two points, as might have been the case if we had we possessed a compass; still, about four o'clock that afternoon, we began hearing distant sounds of traffic and determined we must be within a mile of the highway. One of our nine-man crew jogged on ahead to try to locate the ambulance and advise the medical team to be prepared. He was successful, and they relocated to the site where we would most likely exit the mountainside.

Similar to one of those scenes from a heartwarming film in which miners are pulled from underground tunnels, or a space shuttle lands successfully after some tense moments in Houston Control; when we first appeared at the crest of a divide above the waiting emergency crews, a big cheer erupted.

While the six of us manning the stretcher at that point knew not the source of the energy it took to make each careful step of the remaining 150-200 yard descent, no one dared to attempt taking our package from us, until we reached the awaiting ambulance.

We had carried our 260 pound patient on the world's heaviest stretcher, over roughly twenty-five miles of unfamiliar terrain; with no compass, no food other than the K-rations reserved solely for Red, and only very limited hydration via tiny sips from four of the nine canteens we carried (the remainder being saved for Red).

There we sat: hungry, thirsty, filthy, exhausted and horny. Yes, despite whatever other conditions may exist for the vast majority of guys; that last one always seems to be present, regardless of circumstances.

With the precaution not to drink too much, too quickly, we were given some greatly appreciated water. We were then loaded into the back of a truck, taken to a nearby government mess hall, allowed a few minutes to clean up (superficial at best) and seated at tables to partake of a feast. The steak given each of us was larger than the plate on which it was served, requiring a second plate for the potatoes, corn, salad and rolls; a third plate was needed for pie and ice cream. I may have enjoyed better prepared cuisine in subsequent years, but I doubt that I ever appreciated a meal any more than I did that one.

Before continuing, let me assure you that Red not only survived, but following nearly two years of treatment and rehabilitation, he returned to Yellowstone as a cook for the Blister Rust Control Main Camp near Canyon Village. He never again ventured to any forest fires.

****

Sub Chapter 7.4: "Meanwhile, Back at the Ranch"

The morning following the successful evacuation, my eight companions returned to the fire to continue battling the blaze; much to my disappointment regarding the resulting hit to my financial situation, I was being sent back to pack camp.

The decision had been made that once the fire had been conquered; those fighting it would probably not choose to go back to such mundane work as ribes eradication for what few days of the summer remained. More likely, they would head back to their home towns or college campuses, to spend some of their hard earned fire fighting funds prior to starting classes.

I was dropped at the trail leading down to the camp, and told to join Stan, who had been guarding the camp. The two of us were start bringing in all of the equipment from its various locations; once that project was complete, we were to begin breaking camp. If you thought I was going to say "breaking wind," that would also have been true, due to the somewhat limited variety of dining options available to us, as will be described in greater detail further on.

Since the duration of the fire fighting somewhere above us was unknown, we were given no timetable for the completion of these assignments; so we made the executive decision to perform them meticulously. (I suppose some outsider might better have described it as "without a sense of urgency" to which I'd have to agree.)

Some days we would make both a morning and an afternoon trek to a pump site, hauling back to camp various

168

combinations of trash cans, chemical containers, gasoline, hoses, tool chests or the actual pump. If the site was quite a distance from camp, we might pack a lunch and limit our equipment removal to a single trip for that day.

Regarding the packing of a lunch, our menu selection for such a meal had now become somewhat less diversified than it had been during normal summer operations in the camp. As Stan and I were the sole occupants of the camp, there was little reason for the packer to make his weekly delivery of supplies. Surely we had sufficient items on hand to sustain us for the near term. Let's take a closer look.

Whereas a ham sandwich might have been a typical staple in one's lunch early on, the remaining ham currently hanging outside the cook tent, while ample in quantity for the two of us happened also to be filled with maggots. Our sandwich choices were therefore limited to either tuna fish, of the canned variety, or peanut butter.

The main course for dinner was also, of necessity, sandwiches. One exception might be a "surf and turf special" consisting of the aforementioned tuna, combined with some beef jerky Stan had purchased while topside a month or two prior. To supplement these entrees, we had ample canned fruit and vegetables; unfortunately these items were packaged in #10 tins, suitable for a dozen hungry individuals, but far too much for just a pair of diners. As there was not any refrigeration in camp, whatever was not eaten at a given sitting had to be tossed. The latest shipment of fresh oranges was still edible, while the containers of milk were just beginning to turn. A limited amount of bacon remained for frying, but the eggs to accompany it had already passed the point of no return.

To recap, while we may have grown tired of various combinations of tuna, baked beans, canned corn and peanut butter; we were never hungry. Had either of us been coffee drinkers, there was an ample quantity of it available, but as we were not, water was the beverage of choice for all our meals.

To provide some variety to our days, when Stan and I were not out hiking hither and yon to bring in more of the equipment; we would begin disassembling tents and breaking down cots, folding both types of items for storage within a still standing tent to keep them dry until they could ultimately be packed out. Eventually only the cook tent and one sleeping tent remained.

Around 9:30 one morning as Stan and I contemplated what more we could do to prepare for everything to be hauled out, we heard the approach of some Blister Rusters. Upon arrival, they advised that the fire was under control, with just a few mop-up crews still on the scene; therefore the six of them, along with the packer and several pack animals, had been sent down to complete the camp breakdown. Nick Reeves, the Blister Rust Control Superintendent (aka the top honcho) was to arrive that afternoon to oversee our progress.

As Stan and I had been able to accomplish so much of the preparatory work in advance, the eight of us had the packer's first load completed; and he was moving down the trail with it by high noon. When our new arrivals learned the limits of available menu items, one of the crew said, "I'm in the mood for some poultry, and I don't mean Chicken of the Sea! Let's go bag a grouse or two."

If you read the earlier chapter about my first hunting success with grouse, you'll recall that I mentioned these birds possess little of the self preservation skills of many other upland game birds. They do nearly everything but impersonate those "head in the sand" ostriches, when it comes to evasive action.

It was, therefore, not surprising to any of us, that once we had located some grouse; with our superior numbers, even while lacking weapons beyond rocks and big sticks, we were able to quickly dispatch two such fowl to enhance our noontime meal. When split amongst eight diners, two grouse did not provide an extensive portion of poultry per person; still it was a welcome delicacy in a sea of canned goods, especially for Stan and me.

Following our meal we continued preparing another load for the pack train. You'll recall my mentioning that our egg supply had reached the point where no sane individual would be tempted to boil, scramble, fry or otherwise prepare them for ultimate consumption. Despite them not being fit for human ingestion, there were "dozens of dozens" of them on hand in need of disposal.

A couple of us COULD have carried them out of the immediate camp area and buried them, or just left them for magpies or various four-legged critters to dispose of over time. However, the phrase "Boys will be boys" must have slipped into the thought process of one of our crew; he grabbed a handful of them, sneaked around behind a pile of tent canvas, and lobbed them at another member of the crew, just for laughs.

Naturally such a prank could not be allowed to take place without proper acknowledgement, so the injured party raced to the source of the ammunition; he picked up a cardboard layer of eggs (containing 36 units) with which to commence retaliation. Having no desire to be left out of such activity, the six remaining individuals soon joined in the festivities; in no time at all, a full fledged rotten-egg battle was brewing.

About the time our supply of foul smelling unborn chickens was dwindling to its final few missiles, a loud voice called out, "Just what in the hell is going on here?" Yes, the arrival of our esteemed supervisor, forgotten in the heat of battle, had come to pass.

As he looked at his eight egg-covered and stinky employees, he sternly commented, "If you men are not mature enough to perform the task you've been assigned, then maybe I'll just send you down the road and find someone else that can follow instructions."

In mere seconds, the guilty octet realized something that the boss, a heartbeat later, also saw with crystal clarity: there WERE NO OTHER EMPLOYEES to complete the task. Good, bad or indifferent, not to mention putrid, we were the ONLY Blister Rusters who had not departed Yellowstone for the summer.

Nick began to chuckle, saying "Oh, hell, at least you didn't get any of those eggs on me." We were relieved at his change in attitude, and began to laugh along with him; but suddenly it just didn't seem right for him not to get down and dirty with the rest of us.

So when he walked over to what was left of our egg supply and reached inside, several of us let him have it with what few "shells" we had in our hands. He fired back, quite accurately, I might add, with the few remaining pieces of ammo; then he said,

"Ok gentlemen, lets wrap this project up. The packer told me he would be just a half hour or so behind me leaving Canyon Village, so he'll be here pretty quick."

Thus was completed the first of my five summers as a Blister Ruster in Yellowstone National Park.

****

Sub Chapter 7.5: A Whole Lotta Shakin Goin On

I returned to Yellowstone the following summer as an experienced ribes picker, and had been elevated from just a lowly crew member to the position of Crew Leader. One of my new responsibilities was to whip into shape the new recruits coming aboard. However, my just completed second year of college had not included any mountain climbing or other physical exertion worthy of mention, so I was hardly in condition to "shape up" anybody else.

One of our returning veterans, a fellow named Ted, had been designated as an inspector (sort of an "auditor", if you don't mind me tossing around one of those cool accounting terms). As such, Ted did not lead a crew in eradicating ribes, but instead hiked from site to site, checking on the level of satisfaction with such eradication. If he found more than a single missed bush on a given lot, then that lot had to be reworked. His inspection involved only limited time per lot, but was adequate to determine acceptable or unacceptable work. His reports showed not only which lots had to be redone, but the name of the crew worker involved.

Multiple "gigs" naturally resulted in the offending employee being doused with syrup and tossed to the awaiting paws of the Grizzly Bear population. Well, perhaps that's a slight exaggeration; but he would be called in for an attitude adjustment, retraining, or some other disciplinary action.

I mention Ted here, as I looked up to him as the perfect example of what was required to hike up and down rugged terrain with seeming ease. I confided to him that I was more than apprehensive about trying to lead the latest arrivals, as I had yet to build up my own legs and lungs for the task.

Ted told me to simply "act the part" for openers, as these new guys wouldn't realize that I was not yet ready to "play the part." They would be far too concerned about barfing their guts up, or having a heart attack, to notice my physical condition. Next, he said that when we started hiking, I should go as fast as I could, for as long as I could; and when I felt I could go no further, to take just one more step, and then one more after that.

It may be true what is said about image being everything, because, strange as it may seem, I quickly discovered that I was looked upon by many of the newcomers as a "mountain goat" who delighted in pushing them beyond anything they felt their bodies were capable of performing. Hopefully it (the goat part) was no reflection on my choice of deodorant, or soap used to wash my clothing.

Once the basic training period had been completed, and the various regions of the park designated for work that summer had been assigned, I found myself (not that I was lost or anything) leading a crew working near Tower Falls and residing at the nearby Roosevelt Lodge, both of which are located in the northeastern portion of Yellowstone. Our camp consisted of four cabins: three for the crews and the fourth for the camp boss and three crew leaders, of which I was one.

Cabin living was quite a step up from the dirt floors of the prior summer. For one thing, we had electric lights rather than Coleman lanterns, and with said electricity, we also had the opportunity to utilize a phonograph player.

As I write this, technology has brought into common use i-pods, MP3 players and other advances, thereby making predecessors such as compact discs and audio tapes (let alone 8 tracks) seem antiquated. But we actually had "vinyl" way back when, and we thought those thirty-three-and-a-third rpm records were the "Real McCoy" to use another ancient phrase.

Bless our poor camp boss, who had an excellent selection of albums, along with a portable record player. As the summer progressed, another crew leader and I may have made our boss wish he had not brought along the music, as we played his records constantly; all too often, we also attempted to sing along with such groups as the Four Freshmen, trying to duplicate the harmony on the record while probably destroying the harmony within our cabin.

****

As our crews hiked our way from the highway into the work area each morning, reversing direction at day's end, we typically passed numerous chipmunks; they were particularly plentiful in a rock outcropping located not far from the highway.

One afternoon while heading back to the truck, one of the little critters was completely exposed in an open area, just as all these big creatures approached, clomping along in their boots. Being cutoff from a protective cavity amongst the rocks, he jumped up into the nearest white pine tree and quickly scampered toward the top. To his probable disappointment, the tree in question was all of eight feet tall, if that.

Jerry, my harmonizing cabin mate, expressed the thought that our abode would be enhanced by adding a pet of some sort, and since there were no moose nearby, that we ought to consider a chipmunk. When our camp boss shrugged his shoulders, Jerry took that as ascent, and stepped up to the tree as he might a puppy cage in a pet store. He began speaking to the little fellow, asking how he'd like to spend some time with us.

The quivering object of our conversation, having already climbed to the very top of his hiding place, was situated just inches beyond the immediate reach of our brave pet acquirer. Jerry simply extended his hand, palm up, while bending the top of the small tree to the level of his eye; the striped Disney-like character fell into Jerry's awaiting digits, placing its front paws over its eyes upon landing.

Jerry named him "Plop Albicaulis". The surname came from the Latin "pinus albicaulis" (not to be confused with "penis all but calloused") for the white-barked pine tree which we were so valiantly attempting to protect from the deadly Blister Rust fungus; the first name resulting from the way it had "plopped" into his hand.

Plop quickly adapted to his new home in our cabin. We made a cage of sorts from some wood scraps and a little piece of wire screen; he generally resided in there during the work day. I say "generally," as there were a few occasions when we had failed to properly secure the screen, and he thus had free roaming opportunities within the cabin.

Surprisingly he never attempted to escape, although numerous routes to the outside world were readily available to him. He would climb from floor-to-cot-to-map table with ease, and would entertain us by shelling and eating peanuts we had acquired from the store at Roosevelt Lodge.

One of the times when he was missing from his cage upon our return from work, he was discovered burrowed down inside the foot of one of our sleeping bags. All in all, Plop was a very welcome addition to our summer home.

****

In addition to the four cabins of Blister Rusters, along with the sizeable number available for rent by tourists, there was one cabin housing four or five college age female employees. I suppose today, with coed dorms on college campuses being the norm, those gals would have lived in the dorm area housing all the male employees of the lodge, but this was back in the late 50s, and a young lady's reputation definitely required such segregation of living quarters.

Other than an occasional basketball game on the outdoor court with some of the Roosevelt Lodge guys, I don't recall having much association with them. The same was not necessarily true of the handful of ladies. It was not unusual for a foursome or two of bridge to come together from the inhabitants of our five non-tourist cabins, and over the course of the summer we all became well acquainted.

One of the gals, Elaine, happened to be attending the same college as was I, although we had not met prior to that summer. As fate would have it, Bob, our camp boss, also transferred from his college in Minnesota to ours the following fall quarter. To carry this little rabbit trail just a tad further, once back on campus that autumn, Elaine introduced camp boss, Bob, to Karen, one of her sorority sisters. Bob and Karen later married, moved to California, had four children and have continued to enjoy sharing the same quarters for some five decades thus far.

But this is not supposed to be an excerpt from the society section of a newspaper, so I'll hop off that rabbit trail, as this segment relates, not to a rabbit, but to a chipmunk.

Having built a friendly relationship with our neighbors of the female persuasion, and more recently having added the tiny new resident to our cabin, it seemed only fair that we should allow these lovely ladies the opportunity to meet Plop, at some point.

Therefore, one evening following work and dinner, we invited any of them not otherwise occupied, to stop by our cabin for formal introductions. Plop was an immediate hit! ("Oh, isn't he darling!" "Is it alright to pick him up?" "May I pet him?")

Plop, although young, even in chipmunk years, proved to be your typical male in short order. As he was climbing up the arm of one of the girls, he spotted the opening at the neck of her sweatshirt, and adeptly crawled inside.

I'm not sure that I need try describing what followed for the ensuing thirty to forty-five seconds, but I'll give it a shot: (a) Shrieking by the invaded female; (b) "Oh, my God!" or howling laughter by the others of the fair sex; (c) Male hosts standing around trying to decide how we could help out the victim, without getting slapped.

Amazingly, the poor girl experiencing the lustful advances by Plop did not pee her pants during this adventure; she must have had incredible bladder control. Having had his way with our nearly hysterical guest, Plop ultimately poked his head back out and exited the premises, without assistance from any of the males.

I somewhat regretfully admit that my failure to volunteer as a "personal search and rescue hero" to this helpless soul, by trying to locate Plop during his inner attire wanderings, would have to be considered, in retrospect, an obvious missed opportunity on my part. To this day, no one has yet to accuse me of being a "fast mover" with the ladies.

****

176

The majority of the summer was relatively uneventful..............

I kept track of the phenomenal baseball season of Roy Face, of the Pittsburgh Pirates, who won eighteen games against just a single loss that year as a Relief Pitcher.......

Once during work, as I was hurriedly returning to the pump site from some outlying dragline lots I had been inspecting, I rounded a bend and came practically face-to-face with a startled moose. Talk about a big sucker! I carefully backed away and avoided what could well have been a quite serious, if not fatal, confrontation..........

On a warm Sunday afternoon, a couple of us hiked up behind Roosevelt Lodge to a place called Lost Lake or Hidden Lake or something similar, and went skinny dipping. That was some mighty C-O-L-D water! As we were about to exit the lake, we heard voices, and noticed tourists hiking the trail just above us, necessitating our remaining near some protective lily pads for another couple of minutes until they had passed.

Same lake, same lily pads,
but on a different visit

177

As you can imagine, these tourists would have been unable to observe anything worthy of note, as the icy water had caused more than sufficient "shrinkage" of body parts normally covered for the sake of modesty. Decades later I could not stop laughing at a "Seinfeld" episode, in which the Jason Alexander character was observed, sans swimming suit, by a couple of females; he responded to their laughing and finger pointing by exclaiming, "It's Shrinkage!"..........

But to reiterate, nothing had happened to differentiate this summer from another until one evening in the latter half of August, ... when everything changed dramatically!

****

It was late, just after 11:30 p.m., and by all rights we should have been sleeping soundly, but we were not. All of our map work, plotting results from the day's accomplishments, had long since been completed; but our lights remained on as we were individually "doing our thing" of writing letters, reading books or sketching a drawing (one of the crew leaders was an artist of sorts). Suddenly the map table started bouncing around; then the cots, and finally the whole cabin began to shake.

As lamps, pencils and other paraphernalia crashed on the floor from the table and/or shelving in the cabin, Bob (who had spent time in Japan during some previous military service) walked to the door and opened it, while saying, "My friends, we're having an earthquake, and it's no piker!"

We followed him out the doorway and watched in amazement. Viewed with the aid of light from the moon, the ground seemed to be rolling, as if someone had been shaking out a long rubber mat to straighten it out, while cabins similar to ours looked like bouncing boats on a choppy lake. No trees were uprooted, at least from our viewpoint, but we kept our eyes toward the sky, in the event something happened to come crashing down toward us.

As for our good friends in the cabin of female savages, we later learned that when the earthquake hit, they assumed it was a bunch of us trying to scare them by rocking their cabin, and they had kept calling out, "C'mon you guys. Cut it out." until they finally realized it had to be something other than a juvenile male prank on our part.

The quake had a magnitude of 7.5; it was centered near Hebgen Lake (close to the town of Ennis, Montana) and covered an area from British Columbia down through Wyoming. More than two dozen deaths were reported, most of which occurred from a landslide above a campground.

For quite some time afterward, the loss of life in that campground was only estimated, as there was no way to remove the massive boulders to search for bodies. It was necessary to rely upon information from outsiders, who reported that so and so had supposedly been camping in Yellowstone, and had not been heard from after the earthquake.

****

The morning following the initial quake, I was reassigned from the Blister Rust Camp to assist Park Rangers, working out of the Old Faithful area. The function, for lack of a better name, was labeled as "tourist control." I spent the remainder of the summer in that capacity.

Most of the time I had but two assignments; one of which was v-e-r-y b-o-r-i-n-g, with the other only slightly less so. Neither one was even remotely close to the days of rigorous physical activity to which I had become accustomed.

The road beyond Madison Junction (from Old Faithful) was not open to the public, due to numerous rock slides, but tourists could still visit various sites along the way before having to turn back. Although there was a "Road Closed Ahead" sign about half a mile prior to the closure, more than a few park visitors had to see for themselves every last inch of accessible road; they would drive right up to the barricade, and the lonely but ever so friendly human who manned it. I was that lonely, but friendly, human.

I would be driven to my sentry position in the morning before the roads were made available to the general public, and be picked up in the evening after things were shut down for the day. While I had no journal with me to share my solitude, it might have come in handy to jot down some of the comments of occupants in vehicles having to turn around at my outpost in the wilderness.

Some examples (with my unspoken responses following them): "Is it unsafe for us to be out this far?" (No, if it was, the government, in its infinite wisdom, would have placed the blockade back a mile or so where it WOULD be safe.) "Do you get lonely out here all by yourself?" (You must be kidding. I have this very sexy life-size blowup doll hidden behind that pile of rocks to keep me company, but folks like you keep driving up to interrupt us.) "What happens if another earthquake hits while you are out here without any transportation?" (What would happen if I DID have transportation and another quake hit and swallowed up my vehicle, or me, for that matter?)

The hours (as I recall, I had a ten hour shift from 8:00 a.m. until 6:00 p.m.) dragged on endlessly. I actually looked forward to the arrival of one of these tourists, who, like a person overwhelmed by an irresistible urge to touch a bench to see if the "wet paint" had dried yet, just had to confirm that the road was actually closed.

I played a variety of mental games to pass the time, such as guessing whether or not the next vehicle would contain children; or how many different state license plates I would observe during my shift; or the make or color of the cars seen most frequently. I politely turned away every driver but one, during my time on that secluded outpost.

The exception was a rather gruff sounding, no nonsense man; he pulled up to the barricade late one afternoon and advised that, despite my well rehearsed spiel, I would simply have to let him through. I had been given numerous excuses by folks who "absolutely have to meet our parents in Mammoth" or "I'm a contractor and have worked in far more dangerous situations than this" and that sort of thing.

As I politely persisted with my denial of his request for me to drop the barricade, he said, "My reason is in the back, if you have to know. It's a dead body." Then he smiled, and provided me with a pass he had been given by a ranger back at Old Faithful, to allow him through, admitting he had just wanted to give me a hard time.

When not involved in manning that remote outpost, my alternate assignment was to patrol, on foot, the area around the Fountain Paint Pots (a popular tourist stop a few miles north of

Old Faithful). Once officials had determined that the parking lot and most of the boardwalks in the area were stable enough to allow viewing by the public, ropes had been placed across the few areas considered unsafe, with signs hanging from the ropes every few feet, reading "Do Not Enter" or "Keep Out."

Despite the fact that many brilliant individuals visit our national parks every year, it would seem that such individuals deposit their common sense at the park entrances and do not reclaim it until exiting the park at the end of a vacation.

I was amazed at how many people would try to cross over or under the ropes between the "Keep Out" signs; when confronted, they would say they had not seen the sign just a few feet away. These same individuals would undoubtedly have tried to sue the government for damages, had they fallen through an area of thin crust and been severely burned.

This temporary assignment ended my second summer in the park.

****

Sub Chapter 7.6:

When Fred Astaire Met Ginger Rogers

I cannot read a single note of music, but I thoroughly enjoy listening to many varieties of it; and numbers performed by a good dance band rank high amongst my favorites.

At the time I was working there, the Yellowstone Park Company hired maids, waiters/waitresses, clerks, cooks, and dishwashers (aka "pearl divers" to the other savages), some of whom had included on their applications the fact that they played musical instruments. The YP Company would then assemble a group of roughly half a dozen such musicians to form a dance band; by day these employees performed duties similar to others hired for the summer, but at night, for an additional bump in pay, they would play for dances at various locations throughout the park.

Normally consisting of piano, bass, drums, sax, trumpet and trombone; the band would perform for guests in the Yellowstone Lake area three nights each week, while both Old Faithful and Mammoth received a single night each.

In those good old days, poor college students (such as me) without personal means of transportation experienced no problems hitchhiking to Yellowstone Lake from the Canyon Village area. I had successfully hitched my way to such dances during my previous two summers.

I recalled spending many a fruitless Friday or Saturday evening during high school dances following ballgames, at which all the girls typically gathered together in one area while the boys kept to themselves, with "never the twain meeting," unless some couple happened to be going steady. However, having advanced to college and joining a fraternity, I had now acquired at least enough moxie to comfortably approach a member of the opposite sex for the purpose of suggesting a spin around the old dance floor; I also knew how to gracefully back off if I was rejected, with or without accompanying laughter.

One evening, early in my third summer in the park, I had managed to obtain a ride from Canyon Village to Lake Lodge where a dance was scheduled. That same day, a young college coed had arrived from her small town in Indiana to begin duties as a cabin maid at Yellowstone Lake (over the strong disapproval of her father).

Always an outgoing gal, she had rapidly made friends with her counterparts; when one of them suggested she ought to initiate her summer by attending the dance with them, she figured, "Why not?"

She was wearing a white Kappa Kappa Gamma sweatshirt when I spotted her across the dance floor; as we also had the same sorority at our college, I had a logical opening. It was something along the lines of "Might I invite a lovely Kappa to share a dance with me?" Much to my delight, she gave me a very pleasant smile and offered me her hand.

As this beautiful, blue-eyed blonde eventually (just over two years later) became my blushing bride, I would like to say that I can recall precisely the name of the song of that first dance we shared; but I'd be lying.

This is my one and only lifetime dance partner

To Exchange Vows

The band normally opened and closed each evening's dance with an up-tempo version of the jazzy "Gone with the Wind." Don't scratch your head wondering why they picked that "Tara's Theme" number from the exceedingly long *GWTW* film. No, the song played by the band was composed by Herb Magidsen and Allie Wrubel. While they had several successful songs written together or with others, somehow their names don't roll off the tongue like Rogers and Hammerstein, or Simon and Garfunkel. As for the song, you'd definitely recognize it if you heard it.

However, I know it was not that particular number to which we first danced, as the band had already played two or three numbers before I had stepped out in faith to ask for the dance.

Furthermore, this initial contact was far from "love at first sight" for either of us, so there would truly be no reason to have recalled our inaugural dance melody. Nonetheless, it proved to be just one of several numbers to which we danced that evening; not to mention countless spins, twirls and "cheek to cheeks" set to music over more than five decades subsequent to that fateful meeting.

Our night of dancing both slow and fast selections was devoid of any stepping on toes, stumbles or other mishaps; which was not always the case when asking a perfect stranger from another part of the country to trip the light fantastic.

By evening's end, having learned each other's names, colleges, home towns, work locations and a few mutual topics of interest; we agreed that future dances ought to be on our common agendas. Despite my usual shyness, I did pull her in close for a very pleasant goodnight kiss before she had a chance to turn away. I then made my way back to the highway to commence exercising my thumb in order to obtain a ride back to Canyon.

That summer (with the obvious exception of meeting the fabulous female who later became my wife) was uneventful, when compared to my first two summers. That is to say there were no earthquakes, major fires or injured cooks to pull us away from our assigned duties. I was designated the camp boss for an outfit working out of Mammoth Hot Springs for a portion of the summer, but still managed to make it down to Yellowstone Lake with some frequency.

Our "relationship" (back in the days before that word took on the meaning it has today) was casual to say the least. We were not "dating" in the true sense of the word, but did enjoy each other's company, and did have a few actual dates in addition to meeting at dances. We caught a couple of movies in West Yellowstone with two other couples; took hikes into some areas not generally accessible to the vacationing public, as I had a master key to government locks; and went swimming on more than one occasion in the Firehole River.

Montana guy and Indiana gal
on one of our "non-dates"
in Yellowstone Park

Several things have changed in the many years since I worked in Yellowstone, starting with the road system. Today a visitor could easily miss a substantial portion of viewing opportunities simply by staying on the main highway and not taking any of the turnoffs or side drives. During my days there, these sites WERE the main road. A perfect example is the Firehole swimming area.

The terrible forest fire in 1988 may have taken away some of the desirability of this popular spot. Without question, when my wife and I stopped to revisit it a few years ago, it certainly did not come close to what we had experienced many decades earlier.

Allow me to partially describe that old swimming hole. Imagine deep, slow moving water, warmed by numerous upstream geysers flowing into the otherwise icy river, forming a pool-like floating opportunity some fifteen to twenty yards in length; the river then opens into a wider, more shallow and faster moving area, adjacent to a sunbathing (or picnicking or drinking) segment of land.

Tall cliffs border the deep waters, and many visitors (but never yours truly) would jump or dive from them, into the river. Years later when viewing the scene in *Butch Cassidy and the Sundance Kid* in which the anti-hero types jump from a cliff into the river to escape the posse, I thought back to those Firehole jumpers/divers. In reality, the cliff in the film was substantially higher than those adjacent to the Firehole; but then again, Newman and Redford actually jumped only a few feet onto a platform, covered with padding before letting special effects take over.

****

One evening, following a more physically taxing day than normal, I had decided not to attempt hitchhiking down to Yellowstone Lake. However Jack, a co-worker, offered me the use of his Volkswagen at the last minute, so I accepted his offer and decided to surprise my young Kappa friend.

When I appeared, unannounced, at her dormitory, she not only displayed less enthusiasm than I had anticipated, but actually seemed quite displeased to see me. "Why didn't you call me? Did you just think I'd be sitting around waiting to see if you happened to show up? I'll have you know that I already have a date for tonight."

Not wishing to give up quite yet, I asked when her official date was to begin, and she advised he would be picking her up at 9:00. I then suggested that, since I had wheels (albeit borrowed ones) for the first time in our acquaintance, we had plenty of time to drive down to the lake and visit, prior to the time her scheduled date was to commence. After all, it was a beautiful summer evening, she looked ever so lovely, and there was the promise of a gorgeous Yellowstone Park sunset to be shared. She somewhat begrudgingly acquiesced.

Somewhere around 8:15, she said I needed to take her back to the dorm so she could get ready for her "real date" of the evening; much as I'd have enjoyed extending my time with her, I started the car without argument.

We had parked on the beach at the end of a fairly narrow draw coming down from a camping/picnic area, with the front tires sitting right at the edge of the lake. I had determined that it would be relatively simple to put the car in reverse, and retrace my route back up to the campground.

Perhaps this is the time for me to mention that I had never before driven a Volkswagen, and among other things, had never tried to put one in reverse. When Jack loaned me his car, he had instructed me in the shifting of gears for smooth forward progress; but as the vehicle had been positioned for departure without the need to "back up" first, that particular portion of indoctrination in the successful operation of his "Bug" was somehow overlooked.

Needless to say, the shifting mechanism on this loaner car did not function with any comparable similarity to that of my old grey Plymouth, which was currently sitting back in Montana.

We slowly inched our way deeper into the water's edge, as I continuously guessed (incorrectly) at the proper positioning of the gear shift; during this time, she provided ongoing verbal abuse ("Can't we just turn around? What do you mean you can't find reverse? Are you intentionally trying to make me be late?"). All of her comments did nothing to aid me in this embarrassing situation.

Following the adage that even a blind squirrel finds a nut from time to time, I eventually (probably no more than a frustrating minute or two) found reverse, backed the VW up the draw to the campground, and drove my companion back to the dorm in ample time for her bona fide date that evening.

Now, dozens of years later, when she tries to get me moving a bit more quickly to turn off a ballgame and come to the dinner table; or to hustle it up to get ready for church; or to finish reading a particular section of the newspaper; or to otherwise expedite the pace of my movements, I will typically reply, "What's the hurry, sweetheart? Do you have another date tonight?"

****

Sub Chapter 7.7:

Jellystone Adventures with Yogi Bear

I mentioned that one of the perks of a camp boss was being the recipient of a master key to all government locks on any gate in the park. Such a key allowed entrance into fueling areas to gas up the big yellow truck in which we transported the crews. Furthermore it allowed us to drive beyond locked gates to otherwise inaccessible (to the public) areas to set up our pumps, trash cans and hoses for a work site (or to at least substantially reduce the distance such equipment had to be carried). It also provided access to all garbage dumps throughout the park.

Since my job description was in no way to be confused with those sanitation engineers who picked up trash and delivered it to the various landfill depositories, there was no work-related reason for me to require access to such sites. On the other hand, a late night visit to one of these areas in one's auto could almost guarantee the sighting of one or more Grizzly Bears.

Whether trying to impress two sweet young things on a typical double date, or just as an afterthought for a car full of co-workers coming back from a movie in West Yellowstone; it was nothing short of awesome to pull up to the edge of the trash pit, park, and shine the headlights on these hump shouldered grizzlies, especially when they would rear up on their hind legs.

In thinking back to the indoctrination sessions given to all of us at the commencement of each summer, I do not recall ever being specifically restricted from visiting the garbage pits, and more or less taunting the grizzlies; so I was not technically violating any rules. Yah, right!

Regardless of the properness or lack thereof, it was definitely a foolish thing to be doing; as a grizzly can move very rapidly, and could easily rip the door from a car before its occupants would even realize that they were in jeopardy.

While it may sound absurd to someone reading these words, I have the distinct feeling that the chief grizzly (aka "Big Bad Bear") convened several of his brethren for an executive bitching session during one such visit by me. He probably expressed his displeasure with such comments as "I've had it up to my hump with clowns like these!" and recommended that they seek at least a small modicum of revenge on the two-legged critters that had been disrupting their dining; he then distributed a paw-drawn sketch of me as the enemy poster boy.

Whether or not such a meeting by these grizzlies actually took place, it is a fact that during my fourth summer in the park, one of them decided it was payback time, if for no other reason than to see how I liked MY meal being interrupted.

****

Before detailing this little adventure, I need to provide just a tad of background, such that you may have the best possible understanding of what transpired on the day in question.

Let us begin with my tree-climbing skills. As a child living in the mountains just outside Missoula, Montana, I had a favorite tree on the hillside across the stream from our home. This bit of foliage might best be described as something found in *Tree Climbing for Dummies*. The branches all but formed a ladder; should the climber desire to relax while either ascending or descending, there were numerous branches forming a comfortable "V" where the butt could be parked with ease. Although I had climbed one or two other trees in my youth, I certainly never became proficient at such activity; furthermore, my most recent attempt at such climbing had probably occurred no later than at the tender age of twelve.

The next bit of background relates to the unwise mixture of sunshine, sun lotion and beer. A sensible combination of those three items can make for a great afternoon. Unfortunately for me on one particular Sunday, I was far from sensible; the proportions of sunshine, suds and protective cream as I spent the day swimming and sun bathing near the Firehole River, was heavily skewed in favor of both sun and beer over sun lotion.

As a result, I began the workweek the following morning with not only a bad hangover (yes, I know most folks can drink beer all day and not suffer any consequences, but I was not one of those folks), but my legs were as red as a ripe pie cherry. They were so raw and sore that it took great fortitude to simply pull on, ever so slowly, my blue jeans.

The final item of background involves bears and their relationship to trees. Black bears, the type that could often be seen mooching from tourists for handouts along the roads in Yellowstone, are extremely agile tree climbing creatures. Grizzly bears are not known for such climbing skills.

****

The photo appearing on the next page may be of interest to those of you who have never beheld a bear begging for breakfast.

Very old picture of Black Bear family panhandling from my parents, years before I worked in the park. Note the "Folgers®" nameplate above the license. This was my dad's company car during his many years with that coffee company.

Ok; by now you should have a vivid picture of my physical condition on the day in question, so let's proceed. I had been assigned to spend the week assisting Ted, as he inspected lots in an area recently completed by one of the crews. We exited the truck and divided the lot sheets, after which he smoothly strode off; whereas I took a moment to advise my tender, raw thighs that if they survived the day with me, I'd be more than generous in the application of volumes of soothing lotion or first aid cream at day's end. I somehow survived a morning of lot inspection, arriving at my lunchtime destination on schedule.

I grimaced as I watched Ted sauntering toward me across the steep terrain of Mount Washburn, part of one of the higher mountain ranges in Yellowstone National Park.

"About time you showed up" I commented sarcastically. "If I could entice these painfully sunburned legs up this motherlovin mountain, with my blue jeans impersonating P120 grit sandpaper rubbing against them each step of the way, the least you could do was to get here on time. You'd think we were out in the boonies or something."

"Hey, I didn't force you to spend the whole afternoon yesterday down at the Firehole River with nothing but a swim suit on your miserable body, and a few too many cold beers in your cooler. So don't go bitchin to me about your damn sunburn."

"Remind me of this conversation the next time YOU have a lapse of good judgment, which, knowing you as I do, will not be too far off."

"It's a deal. Let's dig into our lunchtime's enticing entrée and see whether our stomachs will be appreciative or not." Ted replied.

Briefly thereafter, we had settled our scrawny butts on the ground in such a manner that we could individually lean back against our own huge White Pine Tree, of which there happened to be two in this immediate locale. We had been separated all morning, but had planned to meet for lunch at this prearranged spot in order to compare the results of our morning inspections.

As I was untying the rag knot of the cloth bag containing yet another soggy sandwich (an all-too-typical result of having unintentionally crushed the little cardboard half-pint container of milk packed with said sandwich), I glanced over my right shoulder, and rather imagined that I was observing a slowly approaching animal of substantial size.

I then looked back at Ted, noting that his eyes had suddenly grown to the diameter of middle sized Frisbees®. I quickly realized what it was that I had just seen, but not fully comprehended. Yes indeed, it was a massive GRIZZLY BEAR! (In a different setting, I would probably add the adjective "magnificent" as well, but from where we were sitting, it was not that setting.)

You can imagine the feelings experienced by Ted and me at that moment: an adrenalin jolt causes hair on the neck, arms and assorted body parts to stand at attention; while droplets of perspiration begin trickling down the body like a battalion of snails commencing a marathon. (If you haven't recently been in a situation where you were up close and personal with a live Grizzly, think of a scary movie in which the sweet young thing steps into a darkened room where the monster, the killer, or a startled cat suddenly makes his presence known.)

Almost simultaneously, we muttered "Holy shit!" or some other highly intelligent expression of concern, and immediately jumped to our feet.

Ted grabbed the convenient, low hanging limb of one of the pair of pine trees and quickly pulled himself further up to one of those convenient "V" branch combinations, where he could sit with some degree of comfort.

Although a few seconds slower, I, too, stepped up to my tree, looking for a handy limb to commence my climb. Sure enough, there was a nice sturdy limb; unfortunately for me, it happened to be nearly ten feet above the ground.

Brief commentary on my situation: Had there been no bear, but rather a wealthy individual standing there offering me a cool million dollars if I could successfully climb that tree, he would have retained his money with ease. Although my legs were in great shape from all the hiking, my upper body strength was sadly lacking. In high school I probably ranked at the bottom when it came to rope climbing, chin-ups and the like. My sunburned and badly chaffed thighs would have eliminated the prospect of shinnying up to a point where I could grab the closest limb. Finally, my jumping ability epitomizes the "White Men Can't Jump" theory to the "n'th degree."

Nevertheless, while no amount of money could have motivated me in this all but impossible task, "Yogi Bear" (for lack of a better name) must have provided me with some secret source of adrenalin, muscle power, pain killer or whatever; and miraculously I was up in the tree.

Unlike the situation in Ted's tree, my selection of branches was quite limited. In fact, I had a solitary limb on which I was able to stand. It was about five feet above the initial branch, or about fifteen feet above ground. There was another one, some seven feet higher, which I grasped with both hands. Thus, whereas Ted was relaxing in his "Made by Mother Nature" recliner, I was stretching out my limbs between the tree's limbs. I felt like what I imagined someone on a medieval "rack" might have been feeling just before someone began turning the wheel.

Meanwhile, our four-legged visitor circled beneath the two trees, looking up at us with interest, while a pink tongue occasionally licked what, on a human, would be its lips. Ted still wore his hard hat (mine had not survived my ascent into the tree); after thirty minutes or so, he tried throwing it at the bear to drive it away. The critter simply pawed at the lining inside, then knocked it aside. Similar diversions were attempted with our canteens and metal lot report holders with similar results; the bear simply sat down.

Ted had a new insight: "I've got an idea. How about if you start spouting a bunch of that accounting mumbo-jumbo from your college courses to our visitor? If nothing else, it'll leave out of sheer boredom."

"Right, Ted. I'm afraid it's gonna take a lot more than me spewing descriptions of debits and credits to dispatch that damn Grizzly."

Just past 3:00 in the afternoon, almost as if checking a wristwatch and deciding it was time to punch out for the day, our uninvited guest slowly stood on all fours, looked up at us one final time, and proceeded to meander down the mountain. We waited at least another fifteen to twenty minutes after it was out of sight before leaving our position of safety.

Taking a circuitous route above the departure path of the bear, we made our way back to where the truck was parked. We sat in the cab awaiting the arrival of various crews as we reflected on our eventful, if unproductive, afternoon.

I then and there made the conscious decision to refrain from interrupting future dining hours of those park residents for the duration of that or any future summer.

****

Sub Chapter 7.8:

Choosing the Right Time and the Right Place

Before abandoning recollections of those wonderful summers in Yellowstone, I would be remiss should I fail to mention the aroma that permeated the numerous geysers and hot pools. The descriptive "rotten eggs" would certainly fit, if you will; or more scientifically, you could substitute hydrogen sulfide gas.

Any logically thinking individual would quickly express a preference for the enchanting fragrance of a rose, or perhaps the summer smell of an outdoor barbeque, among other options, rather than choosing to attack one's nasal cavity with the foul odor of those geysers. However, there was an upside to them.

To put this seemingly illogical possibility into proper perspective, bear in mind that, as a male, it had somehow never entered my thought process that a member of the fair sex would EVER experience flatulence. When God removed that rib from Adam back in the garden to form Eve, I figured He must have laughingly replaced it with another device, the sole purpose of which was to provide man with the ability to "break wind" for his own personal entertainment.

Conversely, despite being the delicate creatures they are, women's powers of femininity are so far superior to men's powers of masculinity. Even if having just digested a large bowl of chili, or a side of baked beans with ham and potato salad; a young lady would not only never find it necessary to "let a fart," she would not even "think about" doing such a boorish thing.

Boys, on the other hand, and that could be expanded to all males, I suppose, consider farting to be just something that guys do. They may laugh after (or during) the activity; they may experience trying to "light one" with a match (possibly causing personal injury on occasion); they may have contests for the loudest, longest, smelliest or quietest such fart; they may attempt to play a tune or at least provide a background rhythm section with them; and, of course they will come up with endless jokes about farts.

Jack, the guy who had loaned me his Volkswagen several pages back, had once kept a bunch of us in stitches as he described the seven categories into which all farts existed, with names for each, including the "Fizz," the "Fuzz," the "Fizz-Fuzz" and the "Rattler" among others. Eventually there comes a point when such frivolity, at least in mixed company, is determined to be best left in juvenile film comedies.

With maturity, males actually make a conscious effort to avoid passing gas, in an attempt to make a better impression on a female in whom they have even a mild interest. Despite the desire to "hold it in" while in the company of one or more of the gentle sex, men's eating habits tend to work against them. All too frequently, such bad dining options result in males needing relief from a serious buildup of gas at some point, so as to avoid suffering internal pain beyond comprehension (that is, if one does not compare it to something like, say, CHILDBIRTH).

This brings me back to the upside of those noxious fumes in the vicinity of geysers.

Say you are a guy riding in a vehicle with a charming young lady, en route from Yellowstone Lake to Canyon Village. You have carefully shaved, showered, brushed your pearly whites, all that pre-date sort of thing; you opened the car door for your lady friend and even allowed her to select the radio station for the drive. Suddenly you begin to sense the onset of gas buildup in your stomach. Now is NOT the time to blow it! (You can take that literally or figuratively.)

Your escape hatch from this untenable situation is just a mile or so down the road, so tighten up those glutes and hang on. Once you reach the site of one of these geysers, slow the car a bit, and look admiringly at the steaming scene. Then, as you ever so quietly allow the gas to slide from your backside, comment about the magnificence of these natural wonders of science, if only they didn't have that terrible odor.

I can't confirm whether this process will work every time, or if instead, that the highly intelligent female riding beside you is simply giving you some leeway for your originality, as opposed to simply shifting your buttocks on the car seat and blasting away with a total lack of chivalrous intent.

Chapter 8

Up Close and Personal with Celebrities

Having a front row seat for a performance by one's favorite symphony, singer, comedian, rock star, musician, magician or even politician, is something to be desired by nearly anyone. We all seem to relish the idea of getting up close and personal with those considered to be famous.

That said, I have difficulty comprehending what is so fantastic about simply possessing the autograph of some celebrity. Only you (and perhaps some hotshot handwriting analyst) can be certain that the signature scrawled on a program, tennis ball, napkin, T-shirt or other object is really that of the person, rather than a total fake.

Being in possession of such an autograph somehow tells the outside world that for one brief, shining moment; you were actually close enough to a certain individual to obtain his/her signature as proof of such closeness. Of course, even if it is nothing more than a forgery; if you possess a great bit of salesmanship, you may still convince others of what you know, in your heart of hearts, to be an outright lie.

But what the hey? If an autograph is something you've always wanted, then go for it. As for me, I just cherish the memory of having heard any number of fine musicians, watched a noted actor perform in live theatre, or marveled at the seemingly unbelievable skills of a top notch athlete; while leaving the autograph chasing to others.

As with any broad statement like that, there is bound to be at least one exception to the rule, and mine is spelled out a few pages further along in this section.

****

My first contact with someone who might have been considered somewhat famous happened when I was but a young lad of around five years. I was in a Kansas City railroad station with my parents, awaiting a train to somewhere or other, at the same time Harry James and his band were present.

My mother pointed toward the popular band leader and suggested that I walk over and ask for his autograph. Being an extremely obedient child, I did as she requested, wandered over to the band members standing around, and began visiting with them.

What follows is a sort of loose regurgitation of what I told my mother following my visit, and which she much later related back to me. (There is no way I'd be able to have recalled such detail on my own from such a tender age, especially now that I am well into my senior years.) To assist you in keeping track of who is speaking, here is what could be categorized as a helpful key: "HJ" represents Harry James; "Me" represents me.

(HJ) "Hello there, young man." (Me) "Hi."

(HJ) "Do you like music?" (Me) "Yes."

(HJ) "How about big band music?" (Me) "Uh, huh."

(HJ) "Who is your favorite band?" (Me) "Artie Shaw, I think." (Uproarious laughter from other band members.)

(HJ) "Do you like trumpet players?" (Me) "Uh, huh." (Notice my extensive vocabulary?)

(HJ) "Who is your favorite one?" (Me) "Oh, I guess Louis Armstrong." (More laughter.)

(HJ) "How about movies?" (Me) "Sure."

(HJ) "Who is your favorite movie star?" (Me) "That's easy. Betty Grable." (Even greater laughter from the band. While I seemed to have no idea who this Harry James guy was, I certainly knew the name of the world's top "pinup," who just happened to have been the wife of James at the time.)

After a few more questions and more laughter, at the expense of the band's leader, their train arrived and I returned to my parents. In addition to inquiring as to what all the conversation and laughing was about, my mother asked if I had gotten an autograph. I replied, "I guess not. All he did was write his name down on this piece of paper."

****

I had the good fortune to be introduced to live theatre early on in my life. While my dad was traveling around the country, providing for us by selling coffee, candy or rice products, as I've related elsewhere; my mother and I would take in a movie at least twice a month. Better still, whenever the Montana Masquers, a theatrical group within the local university, scheduled a performance; my mother and I would nearly always be in attendance.

One of my earliest recollections of such live theatre was the play *Winterset* by Maxwell Anderson. I couldn't tell you today what the plot was, or whether or not it had a happy ending. However there was a "bad guy" character named "Trock," whose role was performed by an actor named Carroll O'Connor.

Yes, this was the same Carroll O'Connor who was later to become famous as Archie Bunker on the television hit show *All in the Family*. It would be an understatement to say that I was completely mesmerized by O'Connor's performance that night.

The following spring, the City of Missoula, the university and various members of the citizenry had decided to co-sponsor an extravagant outdoor pageant entitled *As Long As the Grass Grows*.

The title related to one of the many bogus treaties forced upon the Indians by our leaders in government, in which they were promised certain (less desirable) portions of the land through which they had freely moved for decades, prior to the arrival of the white man. They were promised such territory for "as long as the grass grows and the water flows." I guess you could say it was a sad precursor to the oxymoronic, "Hello, I'm from the government and I'm here to help you."

Ok, the unfairness of the sad situation is not the point of this segment; so let me return to the topic at hand, namely some sort of hero worship on my part.

The pageant was to be performed at Dornblaser Stadium on the campus of the university; this was also the site of generally disastrous football games for the college eleven. Various members of the community were given the on-field roles of soldiers, Indians and pioneer families; meanwhile the entire event was being narrated over the public address system by Mister O'Connor, Irish brogue and all.

Included in the "Cast of Dozens" were roles for three pioneer women and three or four children. Without attempting to determine how any of those roles was filled (there were certainly no auditions), I wound up as one of the children, while my mother was one of the three pioneer ladies.

My mother and me in costume

None of us had speaking roles, but we were all required to attend numerous rehearsals to learn where we were to be at various stages of the production, and the actions we were to take in those places. We had very elaborate costumes, considering that I figured we'd just look like a bunch of ants to people up in the stadium watching the pageant.

Without question, the fun part for me was to sit in rehearsals listening to and observing O'Connor, shirt sleeves rolled up, explaining things to the "actors" of whom I was one, thereby receiving specific direction from this idol of my youth. (Yes, I'll admit such adulation dated back no more than a year or two, but when one is still in single digits, age wise, such perspective may be distorted just a tad.)

****

Several years later, the University staged a production of Rogers and Hammerstein's *Carousel*. Professor John Lester was assigned as the Music Director. (Yes, he was the husband of the patient lady who had pounded away on the piano while teaching us juveniles the elements of ballroom dancing years earlier.)

My mother, who had been a promising dancer in New York in her younger years, was currently the Director of the Ballet Theatre for the University, and had been selected to do all the choreography for the musical, while Carroll O'Connor (who had returned to Missoula for a brief stay to take a class, teach a class or something along those lines) was the Stage Director for the show.

O'Connor was quite personable, treating me like a long time friend as I frequently sat beside him during rehearsals; when he discovered that my father was quite adept with a camera, he asked him if he would be willing to shoot photos of various scenes for use in pointing out things to the performers.

The "in-charge triumvirate" for Carousel:
Marnie Cooper, John Lester and Carroll O'Connor

Although I was no longer mesmerized simply by being in O'Connor's presence, as had been the case at the time of the pageant, it was fun watching him put the various actors through their paces.

One more small point of interest (at least to yours truly) was a comment I had made to my mother, with whom I frequently discussed numerous actors, actresses and films, regarding O'Connor, after he began appearing in supporting roles in movies. No longer considering him to be bigger than life, even while he was sharing the silver screen with the heavyweights of Hollywood; I had described him as "sort of a poor man's Rod Steiger."

Little did I ever anticipate that, years later, following O'Connor's breakout role as Archie Bunker on television, he would, in fact, assume the role in the television series *In the Heat of the Night* for which Steiger had won an Oscar as best actor in the Hollywood film of the same name.

****

During a pleasant afternoon in the early 1950s, I happened to be standing on a street corner by the Florence Hotel during the campaign stop in Missoula of the young running mate of presidential candidate Dwight D. Eisenhower.

A small platform had been erected in front of the hotel to accommodate the political speech by the Vice Presidential hopeful, as well as seating for various dignitaries. Also accompanying Richard Nixon was his far more charming wife, Pat.

Following the brief campaign speech, I had some time to waste before I was to meet my mother at some prearranged location elsewhere in town. I entered the hotel and got on the elevator to ride up to the mezzanine, from which I would be able to look down at people walking around in the lobby. Just as the door was about to close, a man asked the elevator operator to please wait for a couple more people to get on. One of those people was none other than Pat Nixon.

Such an occurrence would be impossible today, even in an out of the way whistle stop spot like Missoula, Montana. I would never have been allowed within forty feet of anyone in the campaign party, let alone the wife of the candidate, even had Mrs. Nixon said something like, "Oh, surely he can ride up in the elevator with us. Besides, he was in here first." No, I'd instead probably have been spread-eagled against the wall of the elevator and frisked for weapons, and then some.

However this was still the age of innocence, so none of that occurred. Instead, Pat Nixon looked down at me, smiled, and asked if I had heard the speech by her husband. I nodded in the affirmative. (I was still not big on verbal responses, as you can see.) She then asked if I had received one of the campaign pins, and when I shook my head no, she reached in her purse and handed me an "I LIKE IKE" pin.

I did manage a polite, "Thank you" prior to exiting the elevator; such response at least proved to this pleasant lady that she had not been addressing some mute. Although I was never wildly enamored of her husband in the years following, I always carried a soft spot for Pat Nixon throughout her life. Again, I did not get an autograph. Big deal!

****

In 1949, the Mann Gulch Fire took the lives of thirteen men, including Eldon Diettert, the brother of one of my classmates, Doris Diettert. It was the first such tragedy of fatal proportions experienced by the Smokejumpers, headquartered in Missoula. Many years later the event was the subject of a book published posthumously by Norman Maclean (who also had written the more well known *A River Runs Through It*).

Within a year of the fatal fire, Hollywood decided to capitalize on the general idea of a firefighting disaster; however they chose not to follow actual events other than to place the setting in Montana.

They brought both Victor Mature and John Lund to Missoula to star in the movie, but in the early stages of production, had to scrap what little film had been shot and start from scratch. First, Mature (the super-strong star of *Samson and Delilah* who had that ill-fated free haircut from his co-star) broke his leg riding a motorcycle during a lapse in filming. At roughly the same time, Lund (perhaps best known as the voice of radio's *Yours Truly, Johnny Dollar*) was attacked by a swarm of bees and wound up in the hospital (along with Mature), being treated for life threatening swelling from multiple bee stings.

The movie *Red Skies of Montana* was finally completed in 1952, with former "bad guy" Richard Widmark replacing Mature, and young hunk, Jeffrey Hunter, filling in for Lund. I did not obtain autographs of either the original stars or their replacements, but did have the pleasure of watching some scenes that were filmed locally.

A prominent doctor from Missoula was given a role in the movie as, you might well imagine, a doctor. He had a single three-word line to recite, and it was rumored that it required some two dozen takes before this man of science had satisfactorily completed his brief screen career. The scene in question involved a doctor treating an injured firefighter; his line was, "He needs plasma." All things considered, I'm sure his numerous "real patients" were pleased to have a medical practitioner with less than Academy Award quality acting skills, as opposed to someone who wouldn't know a cancer cell from a catheter, but had "played many a doctor on TV."

****

Way back in the segment about our local minor league baseball team, I said I'd be following up later with the origin of the team's name, "Timberjacks." "Later" has now arrived, so here is that bit of background with probably needless additional detail tossed in, just because that's what I tend to do.

A couple of years after the release of "Red Skies," Hollywood revisited the Missoula area to film an outdoor action movie entitled *Timberjack*. Right off the bat, a bunch of us (uneducated) kids began badmouthing the project by saying "Where did they get such a goofy title? Nobody calls someone who takes down big trees a Timberjack. Everybody knows the proper word is Lumberjack." There was even a local ballclub from nearby Bonner, Montana, named the Bonner Lumberjacks. We rested our case, to use one of those flowery legal phrases.

Many, many years later, I happened to discover that the movie's title came from a novel of the same name by Dan Cushman. Is it too late to apologize to the moguls of movie town about my inappropriate put downs?

While the top billing went to Sterling Hayden, numerous supporting roles were given to actors who, at various stages in their careers, attained some level of stardom. Included in this category was Elisha Cook (shot by Jack Palance in *Shane*); Chill Wills (of *Giant* and the *Francis, the Talking Mule* films); Jim Davis (television's Jock Ewing on the hit show *Dallas*); and Hoagy Carmichael (better known for numerous songs he wrote, including "Stardust").

It seemed only logical that with all these movie stars staying in our little town, we common folk might bump into one or more of them in such popular locations as Penney's, Wards, or any number of restaurants. Sadly, from my perspective, I did not see a single one of these actors during the filming, although I was in the audience for the World Premier of the film, when most of them made an appearance.

The only incident involving any of those celebrities related to good old boy, Chill Wills, who apparently enjoyed the spirits to a slight excess; he was definitely not in full control of his faculties for the premier, practically falling down twice as he attempted to ascend the stage.

I did have an older friend who confided to me that he had been sitting in one of Missoula's less crowded bars, nursing a beer; when Hoagy Carmichael wandered in alone, walked to the piano, sat down and played for over an hour. It made me wish I had been on the scene. What a treat!

****

At the beginning of this chapter, I mentioned a personal exception to my general opinion about autographed paraphernalia. Here it is.

Most Saturday afternoon B-movie fans of my vintage placed Roy Rogers in his proper position as "King of the Cowboys." In descending order, Roy would have been followed by the likes of Gene Autry, Hopalong Cassidy, Rex Allen and various others. Having always marched to a slightly different drumbeat, my favorite was Tim Holt.

Unlike many of the other stars of kids' western flicks of the day, Holt had also appeared as a supporting actor in major film releases opposite such luminaries as Humphrey Bogart (*The Treasure of the Sierra Madre*), Joseph Cotton and Anne Baxter (*The Magnificent Ambersons*) and Henry Fonda (*My Darling Clementine*) to mention just a few. Perhaps that gave him a bit more prestige or something in my estimation. For whatever reason, he was my cowboy hero of choice.

During the period when I was immobilized with polio, my parents contacted RKO Studios, or whoever handled Tim Holt's public relations, telling them of my illness. I knew nothing about such contact, but one day in the mail, I received three 5X7 photographs of Tim Holt in various cowboy poses. Two of them contained only the autograph of the actor, but the third actually had written across its top, "Get well, Ken. Best wishes. Tim Holt."

Those photos may well have been autographed by some secretary, but I never considered them to be anything short of authentic and deeply personal.

Do I still possess these glossy Hollywood promo shots today? No, along with my (unquestionably priceless) collection of baseball cards, half a dozen favorite books that I read and reread repeatedly, and a few other treasures of my youth; these pictures wound up being tossed by my mother somewhere along the way. (Isn't that something that mothers are hard-wired to do, just to give their offspring an excuse for not starting life with a fortune from such collectibles?) As luck would have it, the only item not tossed, but instead carefully included in a "memories scrapbook" made especially for me by my parents, was that Harry James autograph. Go figure.

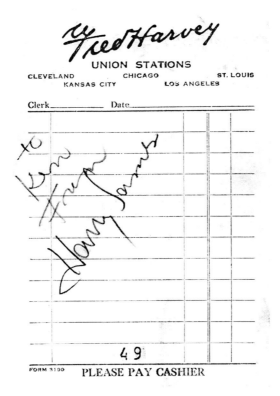

Chapter 9

Departing Downtown; Bound for the Boonies

In contrast to my close proximity in Missoula to elementary school for the 1st Grade (our house was on the corner, directly across the street); by the 2nd Grade, I was practically in a different time zone. Our home in Pattee Canyon was now all but completed, and it became my place of residence until I began college. This was a bit of an adjustment for me, but the plusses far outweighed the minuses.

****

Sub Chapter 9.1: "Hey, It Beats Walking!"

One obvious change was the method by which I was transported to the doors of our school. In the beginning (1st Grade) I simply walked down the sidewalk from our porch, crossed the street (first looking both ways, as all young children have long been taught) and entered the halls of knowledge. As the distance between those halls and our new home had now expanded to somewhere in the 4-5 mile range, transportation was provided by the school system.

There were too few children living in Pattee Canyon to justify the use of a school bus, so the local cab company was contracted to provide rides for us. Although a bus may have been too large, a normal taxi lacked sufficient room for those of us who did reside in the area, so the cab company's HEARSE was the vehicle of choice.

Now if you are of the opinion that seven consecutive years of starting and ending each school day enclosed within a hearse would make an otherwise stable young man consider taking up the segregation of debits from credits as his life's work; I really have no valid opposing theory to present to you, so think what you will.

The back seats, in this somewhat unique unit of transportation, could be folded down completely to allow a casket to be loaded within; but it also contained jump seats for mourners. As youngsters generally more interested in playing than in attending school, we probably felt we qualified to belong in this "mourning" category.

****

Sub Chapter 9.2:
"OK, George. We'll Keep It Just Between Us."

When we first moved into Pattee Canyon, the roads were unpaved; but that had changed within our first year of residency, when wonderful, dust-free blacktop was installed all the way from town to just twenty yards further up the road beyond the end of our property. With the passage of a second year, the paving had been extended all the way up to the picnic grounds, which were situated another couple of miles further up the canyon.

These picnic grounds were a popular summer meeting place for families, complete with horseshoe pits, massive picnic tables, a softball diamond, fire pits with grills, and plenty of firewood. Not infrequently, my family would attend such gatherings, and I even requested to have a couple of my birthday parties there.

The area was also a popular late evening "make out" location for college students, both before and after the road leading to it had been paved. Ours was the last residence one passed prior to reaching the picnic grounds, and thus was also the closest possible location with a telephone. Yes, this was obviously "BC" (Before Cell phones).

It was not unusual to have one or more such students knocking on our door to use our phone in order to call the young lady's dorm or sorority to provide any number of lame excuses for being out beyond the curfew. Rules were both strict and discriminatory, as related to the time for students to be safely enclosed within their housing facility.

As to strictness, dormitory and sorority doors were locked after a certain hour, with tardy students placed on some sort of disciplinary log. Discrimination was exceedingly evident; rules were applied differently for females (must be inside by 10:00 p.m. except for Friday or Saturday when an extra hour was added) versus males (no restrictions whatsoever).

The head custodian of the picnic grounds happened to also be the principal of my elementary school. He was a friend to all, regardless of age, and was often invited to share the table with those having picnics; he was also frequently asked to fill in for a game of horseshoes.

His name was George Blakesley, but was known as everyone as simply "George." By this time I may have been in the 4th grade, and despite having had just the one school principal on which to base any judgment, determined that I had drawn the world's best, directly out of the chute.

Our school was built similar to a bi-level house, such that upon entering the front doors, one could walk down to classrooms whose windows looked up to the ground outside, or walk up to the so called main floor. Here were situated additional classrooms, a combination nurse's office/break room for staff, an area overlooking the gymnasium, and finally, the principal's office. My classroom that year was on that main floor. Unlike a true bi-level, there was yet another floor containing an auditorium and still more classrooms for upper grade students. That last sentence is not relevant to anything, but provided simply for full disclosure.

On any given day, when arriving for classes, or going to and from recess, or during the lunch hour; it was all but inevitable that a student would cross paths with our school's beloved principal. He was amazingly quick at learning the names of new pupils in his school, while still retaining those of returning students. Considering that there were two classes for each of the eight grades, with each class consisting of around twenty five students; we are talking some four hundred individuals. Of course, all four hundred of us knew HIS name from the get go.

Because of the frequent and friendly summer evening contact I had experienced with our principal, it seemed only natural that I should refer to such a close acquaintance by the name I had used at the picnic grounds. That is to say, I figured "we were tight."

I think he may not have heard me when I initially greeted him with a "Good morning, George" and simply overlooked it the first time or two that I said "Hi George" when we passed one another in the crowded hallways. However, about the fourth or fifth time I acknowledged him in such a familiar manner, he called me into his office to relate the facts of life, at least as they pertained to proper decorum within the walls of the school.

He explained that while he was "George" at the picnic grounds, that he would really appreciate it if I would use the more formal "Mister Blakesley" during school. Being the close personal friends that we were, I naturally complied; keeping to myself the knowledge that were it not for the sake of "appearances," we would always be on a first name basis with one another.

****

Sub Chapter 9.3:
"What Was It You Said the Easter Bunny Left Me?"

I realize that the famous, long-eared, pink-nosed carrier of colored eggs was in no way involved; but you'd have to admit that I had a pretty doggone interesting surprise awaiting me in our front yard on my first Easter morning in Pattee Canyon. Allow me to provide you with just a few more details, by setting the scene.

My parents tended to stay up rather late at night; would unfortunately have to be considered "light polluters" by today's standards; and often had music playing a bit more loudly than they might have, had there been neighbors living nearby. All these tendencies were in full operational mode on the eve of my first Easter in our new home.

On one wall of our living room was a built-in gun rack which contained three shotguns, three or four high caliber rifles, two smaller (.22 caliber) rifles (one of which was mine), a couple of antique weapons and assorted shells and bullets. My father was forever advising me that I should ALWAYS CONSIDER A GUN

TO BE LOADED as part of my training related to firearms and the shooting thereof.

Another family member involved in the night's event, but not previously mentioned, was our little dog, "Stuffy." His name carried over from a description my dad had given him the day he joined our household, "Small Stuff." The courage of this combination Cocker Spaniel-Water Spaniel could never be questioned; however his ability to learn from mishaps was dubious at best, as was painfully exemplified by repeated sessions of removing porcupine quills from his nose.

This is me with "Stuffy" some four years and a dozen porcupine incidents before the lion visited.

Oh, yes, we also had a couple of housecats.

All descriptions of what transpired, while I was engrossed in getting my beauty sleep, were provided to me after the fact by my parents.

213

Although it was the night before Easter, it was really no different from any other night, as our family neither attended church nor promoted the "rabbit thing." I had gone to bed, while my parents sat on the couch adjacent to our large fireplace, catching up on some unread magazines, popular at the time. The phonograph was playing a stack of records at a moderate volume. Nearly every light, other than the one in my walk-out basement bedroom, was illuminating at maximum radiance; and as the fireplace had somewhat overheated the living room, our front door was open, leaving only the screen closed. Stuffy, our brave watchdog, sat outside on the front step.

In a manner similar to that described in Clement C. Moore's popular Christmas story, "Out on the lawn there arose such a clatter; my mother sprang from the couch to see what was the matter." My dad was right behind her, well aware that Stuffy was barking in a manner neither of them had heard him do previously.

The scene on the front lawn (well, no grass had yet been planted, so it was just a flat area of dirt between the driveway and our house, if you want to get technical about it) was as follows: a tiny (fifteen pounds soaking wet) dog was advising a mountain lion (somewhat larger and far heavier than the aforementioned canine) that he had not been invited onto the premises. The big cat was on his hind legs, which made him seem even taller than he already was; and he was about to swat away the barking dog at his feet (paws?).

My dad immediately headed for the gun case. However, my mother, who figured she could not possibly be observing what her eyes were trying to convey to her brain was actually taking place (in today's jargon, she must have considered it "surreal"), simply shook her head and returned to the couch.

As my dad was taking down one of his high powered rifles, he noticed my mother's actions and hollered, "Close the damn door!" She promptly arose from the couch and did so. He then asked her to help him find the appropriate bullets for his weapon of choice. (Despite his warnings to me about always considering a gun to be loaded, none of those in our gun case happened to be so at the time.)

She handed him three different cartridge containers before finally selecting the correct ammunition; he quickly loaded some bullets into his 30-06, returned to the doorway, opened both it and the screen, and stepped outside.

By now the cougar had reduced the distance by at least a third from the previous viewing; yet somehow, had been unable to cuff away our brave little watchdog. My dad took aim and brought down the too rapidly approaching lion with a single shot. Meanwhile, I slept soundly, obviously being used to assorted loud noises during a given night's repose.

When I awakened my parents Easter morning, they told me there was a surprise awaiting me just outside the front door. After I had cautiously observed the inert body of the big cat resting near our front door; my dad had me don my cowboy hat, cap pistol and holster, and had me cradle my real .22 caliber rifle, while standing next to the prone figure. He then took several photos for posterity. While not typical of my daily pre-breakfast routine, I didn't really consider the event to be all that big of a deal, until vehicles began arriving with radio and newspaper personnel to report on it.

A local veterinarian advised my parents and the media on the scene, that the lion had apparently been attracted to our house cats. Further, the cougar must have been somewhat deranged to have thrown caution to the winds by approaching such a fully illuminated and noisy structure, plus a barking dog, (and ultimately high caliber fire power) just to get to those much smaller felines. The mountain lion story made not only the local papers, but those all over the country, plus a couple of magazines.

I guess the facts, as presented to local reporters, were not sufficiently sensational for some national publications; when the story went out over the wires, it was somewhat embellished by inserting comments such as "the wife kept handing unloaded rifles to her husband as the dangerous intruder approached their front door." A typical example is shown on the following page.

Third Rifle Is Loaded And Gets Mountain Lion

MISSOULA, Mont. (U.P.)—After sweating it out with two unloaded rifles, Ken Cooper finally managed to shoot a mountain lion just 20 feet from his front door.

Looking out the door to see what his dog was barking about. Cooper saw the lion sauntering up the front walk. He sent Mrs. Cooper for a rifle.

It was unloaded. She went for a second rifle—also unloaded.

The third rifle she brought was loaded and Cooper shot the beast "within 20 feet of the door and still coming."

A local restaurant contacted my parents, to see if they had taken any photographs of the big cat. When my dad gave them an 8 X 10 of me holding my .22 rifle, standing next to the ill-fated intruder; they posted it prominently above the front door. All those exiting their establishment saw a picture of a seven year old boy with the caption, "Mountain Lion Shot by Ken Cooper in Pattee Canyon, April 5, 1947." Although I was not "Ken junior," since my dad was Kenneth whereas I was simply Ken, the implication was definitely misleading.

This is a copy of the misleading photo
which could be viewed over the door
when departing the local restaurant.

Another photo from the same morning:

*"Look, I'm truly sorry it had to come down to this; but I
warned you time and time again not to use my mother's
vegetable garden as your own personal litter box."*

That first picture remained over the door of the restaurant
until the building was demolished many years later as part of some
renovation project. I did occasionally have some classmate new to
Missoula, who happened to see the photo, ask me, "Did you really
shoot that mountain lion?"

After the skin had been tanned, it became a fixture next to my bed; it was the first thing my bare feet hit upon arising from slumber. During the period when I was in college, and subsequently the Navy, some mice chewed off the tail and two of the paws. The remainder of the pelt currently hangs diagonally on the wall of our family room, with a copy of the 1940s vintage black and white photo hanging next to it.

To show how fleeting (or, more accurately, "non-existent") was my fame, not a single one of our four grandchildren has ever so much as commented about the origin of the pelt, or why some little kid's picture rests next to it.

****

From time to time, one of my young friends spent the night with me. Even though we were not all that far from town, it was in many ways quite removed from what "city" kids were used to experiencing. We would frequently have deer grazing on the open hillside across the stream from our house. Coyotes could be seen, and definitely heard yipping, on many evenings. Even a bear now and then wandered into view; but no more mountain lions.

The mere presence of the small stream, which contained fish in ample quantity, if not great size, provided a form of entertainment not generally available in town. If we chose not to go fishing, we could always build dams, chase frogs, or have contests splashing each other as one of us attempted to cross the creek on a log while the other lobbed large rocks from the bank.

In the winter, we might toss some loose snow into the water; then we'd light a two-inch firecracker (long since categorized as illegal), planting it in the snow/slush, and try to guess how far the slush would fly when the explosion took place. In the summer, my little guests and I could sleep on that hillside in our sleeping bags, under the stars, while listening to any number of sounds of creatures spending the night nearby.

For one of my birthdays, just a few years following the mountain lion's visit, I invited several friends up for a birthday party. Unbeknownst to me, my dad had slipped out of the house following dinner and birthday cake, and ventured up the hill. Having selected an appropriate location, he then set up a can with two holes punched in one side; he placed a candle inside, faced the two holes towards the house, lit the candle and returned to the party.

I do not know how he had arranged it, as I was never able to duplicate the idea, but his contraption looked like an animal with glowing eyes when viewed from our driveway. He really had the kids going for a while, agreeing with them that, yes; it very well could be another mountain lion, or at least a bear.

****

A resident of our town apparently decided one evening that his trash company's monthly fee was just too doggone expensive and/or that a trip to the city dump was too far to drive. His (or her) Plan B was to transport and deposit some half a dozen sacks of garbage in the ditch directly across the road from our home.

Naturally, my parents were furious at such an act of thoughtless littering, and were further concerned that our dog would start digging into the sacks and get sick from their contents; or worse still, find a chicken bone that could get stuck in his throat.

Therefore, our family, excluding the dog, began picking up all the messy stuff, depositing it in one of our own trash cans and a couple of empty boxes we had. Upon completion of our cleanup, rather than placing the repacked containers where we normally kept our garbage cans, my dad put them in our car, which I though was rather unusual.

Much later that night, Dad drove into town. Among the bottles, cans and other garbage, he had found some magazines and mail which provided the address of our earlier visitor. He located the home of the offending party and methodically spread the contents of the trash on his front lawn. I would love to have seen the look on that person's face when he exited his house to go to work the next morning.

****

Chapter 10
Things Better Left Unsaid or Undone
(With 20-20 Hindsight)

My foot really isn't all that tasty, although such lack of flavor apparently does not register with my brain cells, considering the number of times I seem eager to continually insert it into my own mouth.

It is part of my nature that I would always prefer to make another individual feel loved, proud, glorified, appreciated or other such descriptions, as opposed to their opposites; however, all too often, my mouth is operating just a few miles per hour faster than is my brain. Sometimes my inherent ignorance is to blame for causing me to say something regrettable. Here is one such example:

There was a large park not far from our elementary school in which were planted what seemed to me to be an unlimited number of rose bushes. The various beds of these plants were scattered throughout the park, such that there were no completely open grassy areas in which one could play softball, without having to avoid stepping into yet another bed of the thorny things.

In my more mature years, I have grown to appreciate the power of a rose, a dozen roses, a rose bouquet and all that good stuff. As a young lad, however, I saw far more value in a game of softball between two competitive teams, or even an entertaining game of "workup" if the number of players was limited; I naturally assumed that my opinion was shared by the majority of society.

Around lunchtime one day, I happened to be at the home of my friend, Conrad, whose mother was hosting a group of ladies in her living room for some sort of meeting. Conrad and I were about to depart for an afternoon at the swimming pool, but he had misplaced his swimming goggles. While he hurriedly scanned various parts of the house in search of the goggles, his mother asked me to come in and meet the other ladies before we left.

I somewhat grudgingly stood amongst them, trying to act polite, while Conrad's mother advised everyone that I lived in Pattee Canyon. One of the ladies asked me whether I liked being out in the country better than living in town; and what the advantage of one location might be over the other.

I responded that, in my opinion, the only real plus of living in town would be the numerous city parks where one could play ball, as no such spaces existed in Pattee Canyon. Had I left my comment there, and we zipped off to the pool, all would have been just fine.

But no, yours truly had to amplify the comment just a little bit; adding how one of the best possible locations in town to play ball had been made all but useless by the stupid rose gardens that someone had decided to place all over said park.

The room became incredibly quiet; thinking they had serious business to conduct, I excused myself and joined Conrad, who had, by now, found his missing goggles and was finally ready to go.

What I later discovered, was that Conrad's mother was the President of the Rose Society of Missoula (or some similarly named group) and had been the recipient of several awards for the rose gardens in the aforementioned park.

To her great credit, she possessed far more open-mindedness towards the thoughtless comments of a young lad, than I had the common sense to judge the viewpoint of an audience to whom I was making such ill advised comments. Incredibly, I was still allowed to be friends with her son, and was even invited to spend the night at their house on occasion.

****

My vocabulary, by the time I was in high school and driving a car, fell into two categories; these extremes could be identified as polar opposites.

I had always considered the use of correct grammar to be important, and furthermore, when in mixed company, took great care to eliminate anything offensive from conversations in which I was involved.

There were no "She don't" or "I ain't" or "Him and me are going" types of phrases, nor did my discourse include any risqué words or insinuations. I had even been told at one time by a young lady in one of my high school classes how much she admired me for my reputation of being such a gentleman, both in word and deed. (Perhaps that could be translated to mean that I was definitely a dull dud for a date, but I had generally considered it a reputation worth nourishing.)

Of course, when I was in the exclusive company of guys only, I seemingly felt the need to balance such lofty language by including an ample supply of expletives in my "manly conversations."

Unfortunately, in the heat of battle, one's brain often does not have the time to properly sort out what races toward the tongue for verbal expression.

Excessive nervousness on the part of a young man taking a girl friend home from college during the holidays, for example, could cause the guy to twist "I need to purchase two tickets to Pittsburgh" into purchasing "two pickets to Titsburgh." (I know that is an old joke, but it does make the point.)

The pain resulting from having hit one's thumb with a hammer can bring out any number of expletives before the brain can slam the door on such vocal explosions. Excitement, or panic, may also bring forth words not generally planned. In my case, it was some combination of the latter two that caused my lapse.

I was on one of my frequent double-dates with Doug, and two young ladies whom we had somehow convinced to spend the evening with us. Following a movie, we all hopped into my '49 Plymouth sedan to go get a milk shake, hot chocolate or other treat. I was about to exit the parking lot into the street; when out of nowhere came the sound of screeching tires, a blaring horn and the accompanying vehicle, going the wrong way on a one way street, and stopping (barely) within a foot of my door.

There was no screaming; it happened so quickly that we'd never have known what hit us, had it hit us. Ever so quietly, although still quite audibly, I uttered "fuck," as the offending vehicle backed up, pulled around us and sped away.

No one said a word. Nobody laughed. Not a single "Nice mouth!" comment came from anyone in our car. Nor did I apologize. We all just sat there for perhaps 30 or 40 seconds, at which time I finally broke the silence with, "Well, who'd like to go get a milk shake?"

Today, "f-bombs" are used as verbs, nouns, and adjectives; they are prevalent in movies, books, cable television, and, unfortunately, even in elementary school conversations. That said, they now carry about the same shock value as a weather forecaster advising of "partly cloudy conditions."

Such was definitely not the case back in the 50's. Had someone at the time decided to establish a pyramid of naughty words, it would probably have run the gamut from the messy, but harmless "snot" at the bottom, elevating on up through "butthead" and "son-of-a-bitch" plus a lengthy listing of far more crude ones; but only at the very pinnacle would be found the ultimate expletive "fuck." One might argue it is more than a little bit sad that no words remain in our vocabulary which would cause even the raising of an eyebrow.

To further drive the point home, most of you are familiar with the songwriting team of Jerry Leiber and Mike Stoller. They created numerous hits back in the 60s including "Love Potion #9" and "Charlie Brown" along with Elvis favorites such as "Jailhouse Rock" and "Hound Dog." The duo also wrote a completely different type of song which was recorded by several artists, with Peggy Lee's rendition becoming by far the most successful. In it, she reflects her disappointment after some initial excitement involving a major house fire, with similar feelings after attending a circus and still later experiencing a failed love affair. Just as she laments in the song, were Peggy to have been handed the now truly emasculated listing of powerful venting words, she would have had no choice but to say, "Is That All There Is?"

Perhaps we should go back to "shucky darn" or some other totally innocent exclamation to show that we are REALLY upset or excited.)

****

Enough about my mouth; let's move to my head. While I have not always used it, I have always had the desire to retain it.

There's an old joke I first heard while standing in the cafeteria lunch line in high school (although it may have originated back in early Rome, with the wheels of racing chariots having been replaced in the version I heard by a railroad train). Here it is: "A cat was racing across a railroad track, but before he could reach safety, a wheel cut off the end of his tail. He turned around to look at the damage, only to have another wheel cut off his head. The moral to the story: Don't lose your head over a piece of tail."

Whether or not one finds any humor in that joke, decapitation, while prevalent in history, literature and film, is no laughing matter. Like most high school students, we studied *A Tale of Two Cities* in which Sidney Carton gallantly took Charles Darney's place at the guillotine. At the movies I watched the evil Lana Turner face her beheading appointment with the executioner in the 1948 Technicolor version of "The Three Musketeers." Public television presented Anne Boleyn, who lost her head, and the position of wife, to Henry VIII. *Alice in Wonderland* brought us the Queen of Hearts constantly shouting "Off with their heads." Ichabod Crane and the Headless Horseman come to mind. All sorts of stories and jokes bring up "chickens running around with their heads cut off." The list is endless.

One weekend, my high school friends, Conrad and either Doug or Wayne (you know how it is with twins, it's just difficult to remember which is which, but I think it was Doug) and I were contemplating the topic of sledding, which was brought to mind by the recent arrival of some excessive, powdery snowfall. I mentioned that I had a toboggan my family had acquired somewhere, and how, on the right type of mountain, it could provide an exhilarating ride. Because the hill behind our home was neither steep enough, nor long enough, to provide for many thrills on that flat-bottomed sled, it had seldom been used.

Currently, at the base of Pattee Canyon, lies a full-fledged residential neighborhood. But when I was in high school, only a few homes had been built in the area; most of those sat on the north side of the main road going up the canyon. Across the street were no more than a handful of homes along the edge of a fairly long and steep hillside.

A short time later, having considered various options available, the three of us were standing at the top of the aforementioned incline, attired in assorted snow gear. We were ready to initiate the toboggan on a slope worthy of its full potential.

There is no steering mechanism on a toboggan, as one would find on a sled with moveable front handles; riders instead control the direction of their course, to at least some extent, by leaning to the left or right. Admittedly, we had not studied this steering methodology in advance. As our initial run towards the bottom built up speed, we were far too busy laughing to be concerned with leaning in either direction for any purpose other than to feel the added gravitational pull from such twisting and turning.

The powder flying in our faces prevented even limited visual acuity, but our bodies did seem to excel at leaning in unison; in no time we reached the base of the hill, covered in snow and feeling exhilarated from our rapid ride.

Then we looked around to see where we were in relation to where we had started out our initial climb; discovering in the process that we were significantly south of our point of origin. As we began our ascent for a second run, we observed the pathway of our inaugural ride, and nearly stopped dead in our tracks.

Less than three feet from the imprint of the sled, at a point roughly a third of the distance from the foot of the hill, sat a large trailer; the metal base of it would easily have decapitated all of us, save those thirty some inches of life-saving space. It wasn't that we hadn't seen the trailer from our take-off spot; it was just so far to our right that its presence was not even considered before we pushed off. Suddenly the "rush" of moments before was replaced by the realism of our "near miss." Interest in continuing this activity quickly waned.

Chapter 11

I Doubt That I'll Ever Forget THIS Class!

I experienced all sorts of memorable classes during my college years. I was blessed with some outstanding professors, along with some others who had no business whatsoever being in the teaching profession. Unlike too many of today's students, I never suffered from the frustration of being taught by a "TA" while the regular professor was off doing research, or writing a book; for that I am ever so thankful. Naturally, I did have some "interesting characters" amongst the individuals conducting classes during those years.

There was the Economics instructor who would continually pop lifesavers into his mouth throughout class. Too often, students (including me) spent more time counting the number of candy insertions he would make during a given session, rather than the topic being covered that day.

A short-term member of the Business School faculty set the bar rather low for us, by stating on the first day of instruction that he "allowed one cut per week" without impacting our grade. As we met three times per week, with a two-hour class on Monday and a single hour on both Wednesday and Friday, it seemed only logical to cut his Monday class, if one was inclined to cut any of them at all. I was not particularly interested in the subject being taught, but was required to take it as a part of my Business School curriculum. The presentation was extremely boring and it was scheduled in the afternoons; so I must admit that I took advantage of more than one such cut, over the course of the quarter.

On the other hand, the top guy in the Accounting Department, Jack Kempner, gave us a markedly opposite introduction on our first day of class, setting guidelines for his course, a CPA Review, which was a preparation for taking the twice yearly CPA Exam.

His spiel was somewhat as follows: If, when called upon, we could not give a reasonably adequate answer to any question he might pose; sufficient to indicate that we had, at the very least, spent enough time on that day's assignment to be familiar with the topic being discussed, then we might as well not come to class that day. He continued by saying that if we chose not to attend a class for that, or any other reason, then we probably ought to drop the class. He further suggested that if we dropped the class, we should strongly consider changing our major; we should definitely save the time and money involved in registering for the upcoming CPA Exam.

No, I never missed a single one of his classes; I did pass the CPA Exam, as did a remarkably significant number of his students. He had high demands of our time, with comparable expectations for our success, and we tended to meet them.

Among the rigorous, ridiculous, resplendent and regrettable hours expended in these and other varied experiences in my college coursework, one that stands out above all others was a night class having something to do with Speech.

It was taught by a very theatrical (overly dramatic?) red head; a lady not quite ready to admit that more years had passed than she would have desired. I'll not dwell on any of her idiosyncrasies, though she exhibited more than a few such antics during the ten or eleven weeks she held us in captivity, so to speak.

Among various readings in which we participated, was Dickens' *A Christmas Carol*, in which I was assigned to read any lines belonging to "Tiny Tim," for the simple reason that I was the only class member who, at the time, could generate a presentable falsetto.

Another dramatization dealt with young people trying to stand up to Russian tanks with nothing other than sticks and stones; we were divided into two groups chanting: "Dead yet?" "He will be." "Dead yet?" "He will be." These vocal outbursts were made in much the same manner as fans sitting on opposite sides of a football stadium shouting: "Go" and "Broncos" (or some other team name) back and forth during a ballgame.

Near the conclusion of the course and for a large portion of our overall grade, we were to speak for roughly seven minutes on a topic of our choosing to the rest of the class, without the benefit of notes.

My friend, Wayne, with whom I had signed up for the class, selected the topic of "memory" for his presentation. He practiced giving his speech to me, as I did mine to him; based on that before class preview, I'd have given him high marks for both content and speaking skills.

To this day, I have utilized some of the points in his speech to assist me in my ability to recall numbers, or other things one seeks to pull from the recesses of the mind. For example, when trying to memorize a long series of digits; group the numerals such that you need remember only two or three large numbers, instead of eight or nine individual ones. By that, he meant you should break down "975346280" into "975" (i.e. nine seventy five), "346" and "280."

Wayne had breezed through his introduction, and had everyone's full attention in this interesting and helpful subject; but about three or four minutes into his presentation, he suddenly stopped.

Wayne stood, looking around the room, saying nothing. After a moment or two, our instructor interrupted the silence to determine the reason for his failure to continue. Wayne calmly replied that he was terribly sorry, but it seemed that he had forgotten the balance of his speech.

As Wayne had a reputation for being somewhat of a goofball, his fellow students thought it was just part of his typical humorous approach to things, to claim to have forgotten a speech on the topic of "memory;" and they were all but rolling on the floor in laughter. Wayne, however, was dead serious on this occasion, and he simply returned to his seat.

While he may have had a lapse of memory on the topic of the same name, the event is etched in MY memory bank forever.

****

Chapter 12
Memorable Dining Experiences,
For Better or Worse

"Oh, I forgot. I don't bake regular pies.
My repertoire is limited to those mud
filled specialties I showed you before.

****

When someone has gone without the essential intake of any form of liquid for an extended period, an otherwise taken-for-granted sip of water may taste like the most heavenly elixir imaginable. For someone similarly lacking the tiniest morsel of solid food over a lengthy time frame, a portion of a saltine cracker would equate to the finest of hors d'oeuvres.

Because my wife has become an excellent chef, baker and cook, our mealtimes rank amongst the best available anywhere. She jokes nowadays that her favorite meal is "leftovers" (due to the reduction of preparation time), but her "leftovers" are nothing short of a feast revisited.

My bride developed her culinary skills over time. When we were first married, even boiling water could prove a challenge, and we experienced more than a few discards ("Hamburgers Hawaiian" anyone?) along the journey towards future dining delights. During our half century of wedded bliss, we have also enjoyed dining out now and then.

As I look back over the years, there are more than a few recollections of questionable items that have found their way into my mouth (without even counting my foot on far too many occasions). That I survived ptomaine poisoning or worse, speaks more about God's hand of protection than it does the (underutilized) use of common sense He bestowed upon me.

In no particular sequence, here are a few of those experiences. Some of them involved some pretty good stuff; others, maybe not so great.

****

I've mentioned that with the presence of numerous college students in our town, the list of money making opportunities was not at all lengthy. One of the few existing, although admittedly infrequent, such happenings, was that of selling refreshments at our college football games.

At the time I write these words, my alma mater, the University of Montana, has an excellent football reputation, albeit at the next level below that of the Oklahoma, LSU, Southern Cal, Texas or Alabama teams. However, at the time being described, our teams lacked such elements as sound coaching, tackling, blocking and…..well, to put it succinctly, we sucked. Nevertheless, the wooden stands at the base of Mount Sentinel tended to fill with a reasonable mix of students and townspeople, as long as the weather was anything close to being decent.

For each game, some six to eight people were hired to sell hot dogs and cupped beverages to those in attendance. Beer was surreptitiously consumed by many of the fans, but was not available for sale by the sanctioned vendors. Becoming chosen as one of these lucky few vendors was difficult; although if a person obtained such a slot and performed to expectations, the likelihood of being chosen on a subsequent Saturday's game increased significantly. My friends, Doug and Wayne, had managed to be selected for the initial game of the season, and because they vouched for me afterwards, I too, was accepted for such a role for the remaining games.

The pay scale varied, but was slightly higher for those persons actually carrying product around the stands. As I recall, such "carriers" purchased full baskets of pop and hot dogs for a few cents less per item that the sale price; when they had sold everything, they would retain their profit as their pay. On a good day, selling multiple containers of product could result in $15-$20 of clear profit for some four hours of effort; especially if good service and a smile brought a "Keep the change" response from even a few customers.

One member of the concessionaire team, which on my initial day of such work happened to be me, was given a flat rate of $10 to work beneath the stands; filling paper cups with soda from tanks, spreading mustard on buns, adding the hot dogs kept in a heated steamer, and wrapping them for the carriers.

The guaranteed income was a positive, and $10 was a sizeable piece of change at the time; however, missing out on the chance for even greater riches selling product in the stands, along with the fact that we did not get to see any of the ballgame (and some cynical individual might say "And the problem with that would be?") provided the downside. I apparently passed muster, along with spreading mustard, in my entry level assignment; much to my delight, I was promoted to the loftier position of seller for subsequent games.

We vendors wore an apron containing pockets, in which we carried all our money; this allowed us to make change with only minimal delay. Certainly the last thing we wanted to hear was "Hey, down in front!" while breaking a large ($5 or $10) bill.

It had been quite some time since the "Grizzlies" had proved victorious on the gridiron; but on one abnormal Saturday, our boys were holding their own against the then first place University of New Mexico Lobos (in the old Skyline Conference). Late in the game, one of our local heroes intercepted a pass and ran it back for a go-ahead score; this play had the entire audience on its feet cheering loudly, including yours truly.

What made the momentary excitement a bit more costly for me than for those surrounding me was that, while jumping for joy and all that sort of thing, a not inconsequential number of the coins in my apron pockets remained elevated as I was descending from my jump. That may not initially seem like a problem, since what goes up must come down; but when said coins reversed their flight pattern, they failed to return to the apron pockets. Instead, they landed on the stands and slid down the subsurface, lost to me forever. A few thoughtful fans recovered dimes or quarters that had landed on seats nearby and gave them back to me, but my day's profits (and even a portion of my starting capital) were significantly reduced.

Back now to the dining example. At the end of each game, after financial transactions were completed and the supplies had been loaded up; rather than toss leftover hot dogs into the trash, where they probably should have gone, our employer kindly distributed such items to any of us who might want them. Such benevolence also kept the trash receptacles from overflowing. For one of the games late in the season, the crowd had not been as large as anticipated; naturally there were more of the uneaten "franks" than usual. As a result, Doug, Wayne and I took in excess of three dozen of those delectable dogs home as a bonus.

Having worked up an appetite during the game, we each wolfed down about four bun covered wienies, immediately upon entering the home of the twins. We then walked over to the field across from their house and tossed around a football for another half hour or so, returning to down another three or four now rather chilly (not chili) hot dogs (how's that for an oxymoron?) for our definition of dinner.

No, we had not refrigerated them; they were still sitting on the table in the shoe boxes in which they had been carried home. Lacking a more exciting activity, the three of us decided to see a movie, and (finally) put the remaining 12-14 soggy dogs in the refrigerator. When we arrived back at their house after the movie and the short mile or so walk from the theatre, we were moderately hungry, so we extracted the shoe box and its contents from the refrigerator and placed it in the oven, heating up a delectable late evening snack.

Yes, I can hear you saying to yourselves, "Where were the responsible parents while we three put our young lives in danger?"

As best I can recall, their dad was at a conference; their mom, who was a nurse, was probably working a late shift at the hospital, little knowing that she could well have had the three of us admitted to the stomach pumping section of the hospital for treatment during her shift. I have no doubt she would have overridden our food foolishness, had she been home at the time.

****

I first discovered pizza as a young lad, when my parents hosted a cast party at our home following one of my mother's annual "Evening of Ballet" weekends at the University of Montana Fine Arts Theatre. It was sort of a BYOF (bring your own favorites), although my folks provided the basics. A couple of the dancers brought pizza, which was not even in my obviously limited vocabulary at the time.

My initial thought process was as follows: "Cherry pie, peach pie, banana cream pie----delicious! Pie crust, tomato sauce and cheese----disgusting!" Or so I thought, until being all but forced to "Try just one bite." Naturally, it has been a favorite staple of my diet ever since.

Our fraternity house employed a Scandinavian lady, Mamie Yonce, as its cook during two of my years living there. She had some wonderful recipes, and succeeded in keeping all of us quite well fed; but as in my case many years earlier, she had no knowledge of pizza.

One of the brothers working in the kitchen mentioned pizza to her one day, and she said she'd certainly be willing to try it out for us. Somewhere in translation, some of the details about ingredients and preparation must have gotten confused. What resulted, while far different from any pizza I'd eaten before (or since), was so amazingly good that no one wanted to tell her what she prepared wasn't actually pizza.

She had rolled out some regular pie crusts and placed them in pie pans. Then were added some tiny Swedish meat balls she had prepared, a little tomato paste, some canned tomatoes (with most of the juice drained off), a few finely diced onions, assorted spices of her own choosing, and topping it all off with a liberal sprinkling of cheese.

She baked it topless (the pie, not the cook) in the oven. It may not have appeared on the menu at Shakey's (the first popular American pizza chain), but it was definitely a frat favorite during her stay with us.

****

Testosterone-filled teens might argue that in matters of sexual intimacy, there is no such thing as too much of anything; over time, however, they learn that variety (time of day, location, position, attire or background music) can certainly provide a lot of positives.

In the matter of dining, it takes far less insight to realize that even the finest meal, if repeated for more than a day or two, quickly exemplifies the law of diminishing returns. In other words, repeated repetition results in redundancy.

Take Thanksgiving dinner, for example. While most of us overindulge on that particular Thursday, to our temporary regret, we savor the aroma emanating from the kitchen in advance of the meal, slowly taste that first bite on our plate of goodies, and have nothing but compliments for the preparer throughout the meal. The same basic elements repeat as "pretty good" on day two, and have slipped to "not bad" by day three; but thereafter, for whatever days the leftovers remain to be eaten, they generally produce a "This again?" groan.

While stationed in Newfoundland for some two plus years of my Navy obligation, I saw many fellow officers come and go. To honor such arrivals and departures, the Officers' Club had what was called a "Hail and Farewell Dinner."

A Lieutenant (Junior Grade) named Don was the Officer-in-Charge of the club, and had an extensive education in Hotel and Restaurant Management, which probably provided him an exciting and economically enhancing profession following his brief Navy stint. His years in Newfoundland partially aligned with mine, as he had arrived only six to eight months in advance of me. We were on a committee that selected entertainment groups to bring to the base from stateside, and thus I got to know Don fairly well. He added many improvements to both the menu and the overall operation of the club during his assignment.

My first dinner took place prior to the arrival of my wife; afterward, in a letter to said bride, I went on and on about this fantastic meal, describing some of the delights to which she had to look forward.

I suppose it would be fair to remind the reader that whereas we began our married life without excessive debts from college, like those that burdened many of our counterparts, we had absolutely no savings, no cash reserves, nada, zip, nothing. Therefore what may have seemed like an outstanding dining experience to a couple of near paupers like us may have been considered far more pedestrian, to those of greater means. Still, it was worth writing home about, so to speak.

The meal commenced with a shrimp scampi appetizer, and I mean those shellfish were some really big hummers. Next followed Chicken Kiev (similar to what I would now call chicken cordon bleu), enhanced by tiny, seasoned, new red potatoes and French style green beans with slivered almonds, all followed by a dessert of grasshopper pie.

This latter item, lest you think it is something one might have seen on a television reality show like "Survivor," is instead a chilled, minty (as in crème de menthe liqueur) green pie on an Oreo cookie crust; with the contents also including white crème de cacao, marshmallows and whipping cream, for the ultimate in smoothness.

Add in the finest coffee to top things off (and bear in mind that there had been a few cocktails preceding the meal) and it was downright fascinating to this young Ensign.

Although intending to impress any new arrival, or to allow each departing officer a dining memory to take to the next assignment; due to an "If it ain't broke, don't fix it!" mentality on the part of Don and his chefs, or for some other reason unbeknownst to me, I must go on to report that we experienced that IDENTICAL MEAL at practically every such Hail/Farewell event, until it became all but tasteless to us.

****

In a similar vein, but something for which my wife and I were entirely to blame (OK, maybe it was just a little bit more my fault, like say 90 percent), relates to lobster, beef and a very large freezer.

Beginning with the freezer, it had belonged to my wife's parents and had been in storage since shortly after the death of her father. Her mother had moved to smaller quarters until she ultimately remarried, at no time having need for said freezer. As we newlyweds had no furniture of any kind, and as her mother and stepfather still had no interest in it, my wife became the recipient of this large appliance. About the only items of note which the government had to ship to Newfoundland for us were our 1956 Chevy Station Wagon and that freezer chest, both of which probably weighed nearly the same.

Moving on to the lobster; it was available for purchase directly from traps at a couple different locations just off the base for the even then ridiculous bargain price of 50 cents per pound. As the Enlisted Men's Club was included in my area of responsibility on the base, it was a simple matter of taking any quantity of these crustaceans to the club's kitchen; there to be dropped into boiling water to prepare them for our subsequent dining pleasure.

During our first full year, we enjoyed this luxury on only a limited basis, but in our second year, we expanded these seafood purchases markedly, and placed them in our big freezer. As for the beef, we opted to purchase a "side" through the commissary, and had it packaged for storage, adjacent to the lobster.

238

Having only recently reached the point at which we no longer had too little income to allow such extravagant purchases, we could now schedule either "a surf" or "a turf" meal, whenever the mood happened to strike. Still, our pattern of poverty had become so habitual during our initial year or two of wedded bliss, that we tended to ration out the finer cuts of cow or choice lobster tail options rather carefully, making each such occasion a memorable one.

Possibly as a result of experiencing one of those taste tantalizing plates, accompanied by a pre-meal alcoholic beverage or two, and/or a glass of wine during said feast, we chose to enjoy each other's bodies for dessert one night. As fate would have it, all the pieces fell into place that evening for the creation of a baby.

As you might imagine, in no time at all during the weeks following, my better half began experiencing something she called "morning sickness," although it seemed to last far beyond just the morning hours. The idea of lobster was entirely out of the question, and big steaks or roasts seemed not all that desirable either.

Suddenly it was January. My tour of duty was to end in March, the baby was due the latter part of April, and the doctors advised that my wife should probably schedule her departure flight no later than early February for the safety of both mother and child.

The morning sickness was no longer present, but many portions of steak and lobster remained. We took an inventory of our freezer and decided we might need to increase the frequency of preparing our cache of "yummies."

Departing from our former schedule of an occasional special treat of lobster tail or steak, we suddenly found ourselves having steak sandwiches for lunch and lobster tail for dinner; a lobster salad for lunch and a big roast for dinner; kabobs for lunch and.......well, you get the point.

In retrospect, while I would certainly not recommend that someone drink his entire canteen of precious water during the first half hour of a six hour hike, nor spend $2,995 of an allotted $3,000 budget on the first day of a week long vacation; there is no question that by hoarding these food items as we did, it wound up diminishing the pleasure we might otherwise have experienced.

I should add, as much as we have always loved lobster, it may have been another three or four years before we felt the inclination to order it in a restaurant or to prepare it in our home.

How strange it was at the time to have had cravings for such mundane fare as macaroni and cheese, chicken, or even peanut butter on any given day, only to find ourselves forced to feed on those former favorites from our freezer.

****

I believe I have left no doubt in your mind that we were not exactly in the chips during the formative years of our married life.

My wife had been working two jobs during her final year of college, following the death of her father, a small town attorney, at age 49. Had he lived, he may well have become, if not wealthy, certainly what one would consider "well off" financially. Unfortunately, he had several businesses in addition to his law practice; all of them were highly leveraged (included were a furniture store, a funeral home, and a building and loan company). His death brought about a disastrous domino effect on his businesses, leaving his wife and daughter with nothing (other than the huge freezer mentioned elsewhere in these writings).

My parents, while not destitute, had no savings to assist me with college. However, my Yellowstone Park job during the summers, along with furniture delivery and snow removal jobs during the academic year, had allowed me to complete school with neither assets nor liabilities to my name.

Still, having no college debt hanging over our heads placed us in a far better position than what faces many young couples today. Nevertheless, we began our lives together lacking an urn into which to urinate (or in today's vernacular, "we didn't have a .pot to pee in").

****

I had owned a 1949 Plymouth sedan since high school which used approximately equal quantities of gasoline and oil at each fill up. My wife had a 1956 Chevy Station Wagon in need of more than a simple tune up, and it was beginning to rust. We traded my vehicle to a guy in Indiana (my wife's home state) to cover the cost of adding a few thousand more miles to her wagon.

I had been accepted to attend Navy OCS (in Newport, Rhode Island), which commenced about a month following our wedding. As an officer candidate, I received the same pay as a seaman recruit, plus a very small housing allowance. We considered ourselves quite fortunate to be able to rent a two-room apartment in the home of the Navy Chaplain for OCS, who probably charged us far less than he might have been able to obtain on the open market.

My wife picked up a minuscule amount of babysitting revenue during my months at OCS; once I obtained my commission as an Ensign in the U.S. Navy, we took what was referred to as a "dead horse" loan, which was basically an advance of six months pay. It gave us some cash to put in the bank to provide for first and last month's rent, plus a damage deposit, for housing during Supply Corps School in Georgia; but with no monthly pay coming in, those cash reserves were quickly depleted.

****

Just to put things in perspective, in reference to monetary value, and to place something in this segment related to "dining experiences," there was a hamburger chain named Burger Chef (long before Burger King). I think it originated in Indianapolis, Indiana, back in the 50's, and was probably second only to McDonalds at the time we were in Georgia. I believe it was later taken over by Hardees and is no longer in existence in its original form.

Whether by pure chance, or because my wife was a Hoosier, we favored Burger Chef over the Home of the Big Mac. They had a radio commercial set to music that still remains in my head, (which is not necessarily good, as the same can be said about the tune played over and over by the ice cream truck that frequents our current neighborhood between May and September. I'll not give you that tune's title, lest the mere mention might drive you to near insanity, as hearing it does to me.)

Anyhow, without attempting to describe the melody, the words to this musical jingle went something like this:

"For fifteen cents, a nickel and a dime,

At Burger Chef, you eat better every time.

Just a nickel and a dime will get:

French fried potatoes, big thick shakes,

Or the greatest, fifteen cent, hamburger yet."

(Yes, those were obviously the "good old days.")

****

After Georgia, I was sent to Brooklyn for a six week Navy Exchange Management Class. Upon seeing a large mouse (or small rat) in the first apartment we considered renting in Brooklyn, my wife let out a scream heard all the way to Yankee Stadium up in the Bronx; so we kept looking until we were able to find more suitable quarters, albeit a tad more pricey.

To help make ends meet, and to retain some personal sanity while I was in school, my youthful bride found employment with "Miss Rae's Services." I must admit, the whole thing sounded more than a little bit suggestive, but she convinced me it was similar to a Kelly Girl temporary agency. (Oh, REALLY, sweetheart??) She actually was assigned to some interesting companies, including Time Magazine, during the six weeks we spent in Brooklyn.

Although we had, by now, paid off the "dead horse" and I was getting my military compensation on a regular basis, we still tried to be frugal and not spend everything that was coming in; therefore, we always sought out inexpensive ways to spend our non-working hours in New York.

Sightseeing was naturally at the top of our list, and the low cost subway fares allowed us to see a wide variety of tourist attractions, from Coney Island to Central Park; from Yankee Stadium to Yonkers and much more.

*No caption required,
other than that my wife
far more closely resembled
her cutout than I did mine.*

16th ST. near BOARDWALK
CONEY ISLAND

One crazy night, while we had yet to master the subway system, we kept crossing the East River via trains: back and forth, to and fro, hither and yon; feeling as if we were residing in déjà vu-ville, just trying to get back to our apartment following one such touristy visit.

****

The USO provided us with one of the best possible deals, in the form of free tickets to Broadway shows and other events.

Two stipulations: I had to wear a suit, rather than my Navy uniform, as the tickets provided were given out to "paper the house" as it were. In other words, they wanted us to appear to be fully paying customers. Often the tickets provided to us were for prime seats which would not look good being empty.

The second thing was that we never knew what show we would get to see, until about 30 minutes before curtain time; so we never knew if we were in for an evening of comedy, drama, a musical, or some combination thereof, until our place in line hit the front and we were told what was still available.

Included amongst the titles of various shows we had the privilege to take in, none of which we would ever have been able to attend, were it not for the wonderful USO, were the following: *A Funny Thing Happened on the Way to the Forum* with Zero Mostel; *Tovarich* with Vivien Leigh (Hollywood's Scarlett in *GWTW* and Blanche in *A Streetcar Named Desire*) and *Jennie* with Mary Martin of *Peter Pan* and *South Pacific* fame. (*Jennie* opened the night before we were in the audience and closed the night after we were there, but it was NOT our fault!)

****

As for the dining comment about New York during our stay, if we had considered a meal eaten out in the form of Burger Chef's fifteen cent specialties to be an "event" for us in Georgia, then Tad's Steaks would classify as its successor in the Big Apple, prior to attending a Broadway show. While we've never darkened the door of a Tad's, subsequent to our six weeks' stay in New York in the early 1960s, and might well find it not to our liking today, it was one heck of a bargain at the time.

For (as nearly as I can recall) only $1.19, one could consume a steak, baked potato, salad and a slice of Texas Toast. The steaks were placed on a flaming series of grills producing, I am certain, the maximum quantity of carcinogens possible.

But we were young and foolish. (If you don't believe me, just ask me about going without a shirt, a hat or sun lotion in Yellowstone and the Tetons.) Cancer was not on our current list of things that would EVER happen to US. From our perspective, it was a great meal for the price, and for that stage of our young married lives.

****

Having exposed the reader to the three big "N's" (Navy, New York, Newfoundland), it is time to regress to the age of innocence (which, for me, covered roughly the first twenty plus years of my existence.)

There was a small café in Missoula, situated next to the Wilma Theatre; it was owned and operated by a hard working Greek gentleman named Syrros. His son, Bill, was a classmate of mine in both elementary and high school. The establishment was known as the Palace Candy Shoppe, in that they did sell boxed candy as well as an assortment of menu selections; but its claim to fame was the Coney Island.

I realize that a wiener, frank, hot dog or other name for this food item is held in very low esteem by dining critics (and anyone involved in the processing of them); however, in the hands of Mr. Syrros, the Coney Island was considered to be nothing short of a superb dining experience. My limited resources and frugal nature limited the frequency of my purchases of these Coney Islands, but when I really wanted to treat my tummy, that was the place to go.

The franks sat on a device in the front window for passersby to observe, revolving on heated bars, which rotated them counterclockwise, and seemed to say, "Come on in and check me out."

The buns were always warm, with just a hint of moistness, and freshly chopped onions were the favorite item of garnishment. However, the secret ingredient had to be in the meat sauce that was very lightly ladled onto the frank, after it had been placed in the bun. That sauce contained some very finely ground beef in a brown juice, seasoned with just the right combination of spices. I can almost taste one of them now.

One fall, I was invited to a birthday party for Bill at his home. I naturally assumed that the highlight of such a gathering would be: not cake, not ice cream, not games that would be played, nor gifts being opened; but rather, an unlimited supply of those mouth watering delicacies, the Coney Islands.

One of the greatest disappointments in my young life hit me directly in the chops that day, when Bill's mother produced a huge turkey and various side dishes for our meal. I kept looking around for the Coney's, but it was not to be. An otherwise fine meal left me wanting for what, sadly, would not be served.

So ends this thrill-packed segment of menu scanning, aka, my dining misadventures.

****

Chapter 13

Colder than a Witch's Chest

(And Other Weather Related Events)

****

Sub Chapter 13.1:

"Anyone for Christmas in Iowa?"

Johnny Brodsack, an Iowa friend of my dad, had also moved his family to the wilds of Montana, more specifically to the Billings area. These two transplants maintained contact with some degree of frequency, and Dad would always stop by to see John and his family when salesman trips happened to place him in Billings; while John and his wife, Lois, came to Missoula to visit on a couple of occasions.

During one such get together, the topic of packing up their respective families and heading back to spend an upcoming Christmas in Fort Dodge, with Iowa friends and relatives, was agreed upon. In late December, after first driving the 300 plus miles to the Brodsack home in Billings, six of us from the two families squeezed into our car and headed east.

Our journey placed us somewhere in Nebraska at the same time a heavy winter storm was passing through. While I was totally without concern about the accumulating snow, as was the (slightly older) female youngster in the car, the adults were checking maps for the nearest town and considering options available; all the while trying to keep the wheels moving forward, and on what they hoped was the highway.

As fate would have it, a small bar in a rather ramshackle two-story structure, slowly became visible. To no one's surprise, there were no patrons parked out front, and only a snow-covered pickup truck at the side of the building gave any indication that someone might be around.

John and my dad made their way to the door, which was not locked (in those days of innocence, few people bothered to lock anything). The proprietor and his wife were sitting by a wood stove reading, and expressed mild surprise to have someone at the door.

Although they were not anticipating serving customers during such inclement weather, they immediately invited all of us inside to share both the warmth of the stove and shelter from the storm. Their bar was not a combination café/bar, and thus they had no food items available for sale, other than some bags of chips and peanuts displayed at either end of the bar. They also had a couple of boxes of chocolate candy which were potential prizes for a punchboard.

As I recall those punchboards, they were sort of a precursor to today's lottery tickets. For something like 50 cents per plug, a customer "punched out" a circle of his choosing on the front of the board with a device about the size of those "keys" on a can of coffee used to twist off the metal binding when opening the container. Then the tightly compressed paper that had been poked out was unfolded to identify the prize won, if any. Prizes could be cash ($5 or $10) or a box of candy.

These sugar, salt, and grease-enhanced products, our hosts generously offered to share with us; and, nutrition be damned, we equally willingly accepted, as the contents of our vehicle lacked meaningful types of edible items of any kind.

The owners had their own small bedroom at the back of the building, but advised us that there was a room upstairs, containing a double bed (along with some cases of bar glasses, toilet paper and napkins, some filing cabinets, etc.) where we could spend the night. They even had a couple of large blankets we would undoubtedly want to utilize, as there was no heat in the room.

While distant by a couple of decades from the communal living that was later to become prevalent amongst hippies, our two families did our best to get cozy under the pair of blankets, while lying sideways on the sole bed.

Despite a lack of anything resembling a decent night of sleep, we were extremely thankful to have avoided spending what could have been our "last night ever" in a stalled vehicle, buried in drifts of snow, in "Nowhere, Nebraska."

248

About 9:30 the following morning, we were greeted by not only sunshine and blue skies, but the welcome sound of a snowplow approaching. We quickly packed up what little we had brought in from the car, thanked our "Good Samaritans" for their kindness and headed our car towards the rear of the plow (which, fortunately, was clearing the road in the direction we needed to take).

****

Our Christmas in Fort Dodge was memorable, not only because we lived to tell about it, but for a couple of other observations.

I had the opportunity at my grandparents' house Christmas morning to witness first hand, one set of cousins (offspring of my father's brother, a radiologist) who ripped the wrapping from a seemingly endless array of gifts, as if in a race to the finish.

Upon completion of this package opening ceremony, the eldest of the three children commented, "Is this all I get?" while I just sat there bug-eyed. (Although I had never had to settle for a "lump of coal" and typically counted multiple gifts with my name on them under our tree; we had always taken turns unwrapping gifts and pausing to thank each other for the thoughtfulness of the giver. Witnessing the attitude of my apparently badly spoiled cousins made an indelible impression on me at my relatively young age.)

Later that day we relocated to the home of my mother's older brother. My Christmas gift from his branch of the family was a ping-pong ball gun, along with a half-dozen perfectly harmless units of ammunition. To operate this "toy," the shooter would insert a ping-pong ball in the end of the barrel, take aim, and quickly pull back on the handle affixed to the front of the gun, with the resulting air pressure projecting the ball toward the target.

My uncle declared that something as light as a ping-pong ball, possessing such a smooth, round surface, could not hurt anyone or anything, as might be the case with something that was both heavy and rough-edged.

I naturally tested his theory by shooting at the posterior of my aunt, while she was reaching for something under the tree; for my action, I received a frown, but no verbal chastisement. I also made several attempts at hitting my uncle's hand which he held up as a practice target (with nary a wince by him on the few instances when I happened to hit it).

Having convinced myself that no object in the household need fear my sharpshooting, I began seeking other targets, while the adults were engaged in conversation in the kitchen. I found an ideal one in the form of a decoration on the mantle of their fireplace. It was a tiny tree on which about five glass balls (the fragile kind one would hang on a regular Christmas tree) were placed.

Wouldn't you know it, I suddenly evolved from a rank amateur into an Annie Oakley sharpshooter; on my first attempt I shattered three of the five colored balls, and totally disrupted the post-meal conversation of my elders.

My uncle quickly accepted all blame for the incident, as he had given me a false sense of safety as related to this weapon of moderate destruction (or WMD for you military-minded folks). I learned that a seemingly harmless device (gun, sling-shot, bow and arrow, dart et al), even while using allegedly safe rubber, cloth, soft plastic or plain water as ammunition, could cause the loss of an eye or worse, a lesson which has served me well over my lifetime.

Our return trip to Montana provided no inclement weather, and thus no memorable recollections.

****

Sub Chapter 13.2:
"So Just How Cold WAS It?"

Several localities in our wonderful United States have attempted to utilize the "Turn lemons into lemonade" philosophy, in reference to their less than balmy winter weather. International Falls, Minnesota; Fraser, Colorado; and Cut Bank, Montana, are three such towns, whose claim to fame is that of being considered the coldest in the nation.

Now Missoula, to my knowledge, never made, nor even considered making, such a claim. That is not to say it did not get more than a tad chilly now and then, during its winter months.

One morning in the Student Union of our university campus, during a break between classes, I was playing a hand of bridge with a fraternity brother, his girl friend and one of her sorority sisters. At some point during our game, it must have become evident that I was not the wealthiest member of our foursome.

It couldn't have been the cardboard covering the hole in the sole of one of my shoes, as I kept both feet planted firmly on the floor; perhaps it was that I was drinking water instead of coffee or hot chocolate, as were my table mates.

In any event, Sally (the girl friend, and ultimately wife, of my fraternity brother) seemed sensitive to my frugality, and commented that she'd heard her dad mention he might be hiring another pair of hands in the stock room at his furniture store, if any of us knew of someone in need of extra income.

Without expanding further on needless details, other than to emphasize the "It's not what you know, but who you know" approach to job interviews; I was shortly thereafter the newest employee of Lucy's Furniture, working for Sally's father, Oscar Shiner.

Although a good word from his daughter undoubtedly got me in the door, so to speak, something about "my outstanding work ethic, politeness and overall reliability" (not to mention Oscar's concern about potential financial liability) soon brought about a slight modification to my job description.

Oscar called me to his office during my second week and asked if I had ever driven a truck. I replied that my position in Yellowstone, as a Camp Boss, had included transporting my crews from site to site in a truck about the size of that used by his company to deliver furniture.

He then explained to me that his regular driver was a nearly ideal employee during the mornings, but he had recently developed the bad habit of stopping for a drink or two in the afternoons, making unsafe his p.m. deliveries.

The other person working in the stock room was a part-time college student who, while a hard worker, had some "emotional problems" (which Oscar chose not to disclose, but in retrospect, might have been something akin to someone displaying a manic/depressive condition).

OK, I'll admit it. Disregard those lofty descriptions a few paragraphs earlier. As you can plainly see, I was about to get a promotion by default.

Oscar told me he would give me AN EXTRA QUARTER, increasing my hourly wage from $1.00 to $1.25 (at the time a substantial difference) to take over the afternoon driving, provided I did not mention the rate change to either of my two co-workers.

(For those of you familiar with the musical *Oklahoma*, you may recall Jud Fry's bidding war with Curly for Laurey's picnic basket of goodies, repeatedly focusing on the phrase "And two bits." And so it was with me.)

I told Oscar my lips were sealed, and eagerly maneuvered into my new position and pay level.

****

Most deliveries required two men, but once in a while the items purchased could be handled by a single person. One such instance involved a small kitchen table, four chairs, a hanging lamp fixture and some bar stools; bought by a family in Seeley Lake, a favorite summertime recreation site some 50-60 miles north and east of Missoula.

However, this particular Saturday morning was about six months removed from anything resembling summertime. The temperature that day may have been balmy compared to that in Cut Bank, International Falls, et al; but at 36 degrees south of zero, I wasn't about to surrender them any bragging rights.

I have driven trucks with bad springs and shocks, others with brakes that were all but non-existent, and some that were all but impossible to shift from gear to gear without awakening folks in the next county, but I don't recall any in which the cab so closely resembled a colander. The heater did function, but it definitely was overmatched by the porousness surrounding the seating area.

I arrived at my destination without incident, although I did have to stop a few times to scrape the windows, as the so-called defroster was unable to keep up with Mother Nature, Jack Frost and all that gang. The residents were delighted to see me, as they thought the delivery might be called off due to the weather conditions, and they invited me to come inside to warm up prior to unloading their purchases.

My return trip to Missoula seemed to last forever. Despite the few minutes I had stood in the customer's kitchen warming up, and the limited exercise from moving their acquisitions from the truck to said kitchen immediately thereafter, I was still quite chilled from the Missoula-to-Seeley Lake trip.

Before I had logged even ten miles back towards town, I was shivering. To make matters worse, the wind picked up. There is a song from the musical *Paint Your Wagon* entitled "They Call the Wind Maria" which, today, would easily make my list of top 100 favorites, but what I was calling the wind on that particular morning was nothing you would find in a family newspaper.

I made it back to the store with my nose both red and runny, and my hands so cold that I could not move my fingers. (Even when my arthritis acts up from time to time in the present, it does not come even remotely close to what I felt on that day.) I gingerly placed the fingers of my glove-covered hands into the indentions on the wrought iron radiator next to Oscar's office, and allowed the warmth to permeate the gloves until my hands began to again feel some life.

No frostbite, no amputations required, and my nose eventually stopped dripping; but decades later, I have never again experienced such prolonged coldness.

****

Chapter 13.3:

"Let It Snow, Let It Snow, Let It Snow"

OK, what's the big deal? Everyone has experienced vivid examples of extreme heat or cold. There are other elements of weather that make an impact on people during their multiple years on this fair planet.

Take rain, for example. Noah and his assorted duos of passengers could stake a valid claim for the all-time record for frowning at inclement weather forecasts over nearly a six-week period.

In a similar vein, though on a far lesser scale than that of Noah's passengers, while serving a winter internship with a Seattle CPA firm, I made it a morning ritual to check my extremities to see if I had begun developing web feet and hands.

No, it did not rain continually all day, every day, during the 90 days of my stay in the "City by the Sound," but not a single day passed without at least a brief period of having the wet stuff fall.

****

Snow is merely a variation of rain, albeit one generally limited to cooler climes. I love snow! I wouldn't want to live where it NEVER snows!

Snowballs tossed at girls I wished to somehow impress(?); hard packed missiles thrown with a bit more gusto at boys during down and out battles; creation of snow angels (not all that "manly" I suppose, but who cared about that sort of thing in elementary school?); forts built to withstand attackers; snowmen and snowwomen built as a child, then as a parent, and still later as a grandparent (and if I live long enough, maybe as a great-grandparent); the perfect surface over which to glide while on sled, toboggan, skis or snowboard..... Snow has just so much going for it, what's not to love?

I've shoveled countless compacted flakes of the stuff over the years. One winter in college, I was fortunate enough to find a 12 unit motel owner, who hired me to remove snow from his sidewalks and small parking lot "by hand" for ten dollars per snowstorm.

He had no motorized equipment, and could not afford to hire someone with a plow to clear the area for the few guest rooms he had. It was terrific exercise, and it provided me with much needed "fun money" for the occasional movie, alcoholic beverage or (wonder of wonders) going on a date.

Of course, snow is not always given a warm reception, and if it were, it would probably just revert to rain anyway. (Sorry about that. What I meant to express is that snow is not restricted to pleasant things such as "White Christmas" or "Frosty the Snowman" happiness, or the beautiful "Currier and Ives" winter scenes, or even the title of children's story time favorite, "Snow White." Unfortunately, snow can often equate to collapsed roofs, missed events, back injuries, heart attacks, frostbite and death.)

When I was no more than a year or two into elementary school, a college student who had been hiking in the mountains, not more than a couple miles from our canyon home, was caught in a surprise snowstorm. He apparently panicked, became disoriented, and froze to death, before he was found the following day.

Aerial photos of the immediate area, near where his body was located, indicated that he had walked in circles along the side of the terrain, always reversing direction just before nearly reaching the stream running at the base of the mountain, only to return to the high ground.

My father, following this tragic event, counseled me that it made sense to utilize such high positions on a mountain to seek visual contact with civilization in the form of buildings, roads or power lines; however, once descending from such heights, to continue in my descent, as such valleys and streams located therein would almost always, if followed, allow me to reach safety.

****

Sub Chapter 13.4:

"Snow: Tolerable; Wind: Terrible"

Although I have not broken out a specific chapter concerning my time in the Navy, there will be or have been references to that period of my life, as it relates to other bits of subject matter. As the topic at hand is focused on weather related recollections, and there were a few during said Navy life, sing a few bars of "Anchors Aweigh" and follow me to the Province of Newfoundland, where I was stationed for nearly two and a half years, during which I experienced some interesting weather, among other things.

One of the first sights observable when approaching the landing strip on the Naval Station in Argentia, Newfoundland, is what appears to be a large pair of breasts protruding from the water; as if some gargantuan bathing beauty was floating on her back in the bay, awaiting the arrival of yet another testosterone-filled junior officer. This rock formation, which generated a similar appearance from land as it did from the air, had been given the unofficial name "Mae West" by all those stationed in or around the Naval Base.

In thinking back to having spent well over two years at Argentia, where the most famous landmark was a pair of boobs sticking out of some water; and coupling that experience with having previously spent five summers in Yellowstone and Grand Teton National Parks (with the mountain range in the latter allegedly named by a French trapper, who considered them reminiscent of the female anatomy, what with "Teton" being French for "nipple"), it is no wonder that I may have become somewhat fixated on the chest area of approaching females from time to time.

While the view from the air, when making the landing approach, may be more alluring, this one from ground level still makes the point(s).

The most significant meteorological aspect of the area was the wind. Oh, sure, we had snow there, to which I'll relate shortly, but nothing stands out in my memory (or could stand up to most anything) as those winds. I got so used to leaning into the wind, or leaning back against it, depending on which way I was trying to walk, that upon my return to the continental United States, I practically fell down attempting to rely on something that was no longer present.

The most severe wind in the entire area was on the base itself, which was made quite evident when a moderately light snowfall of an inch or two could close down all ground transportation, simply due to drifting. The streets adjacent to the landing area for planes were cut deep into the ground, such that even a truck's height would not extend above the level of said runways. These roads would literally fill to the level of the surrounding land from the drifting snow.

On one (and only one) occasion, my young bride and I decided to visit the lone tennis court on the base to hit a few ground strokes back and forth. I should have guessed as I approached, that it was not an oft-used facility. Whereas the baseline on a standard tennis court consists of a painted line perhaps three inches wide, the baseline on this one was the end of the concrete, behind which was a drop-off to a cinder like bit of ground cover. In other words, one could trip on the baseline when moving forward following a serve, or might stumble off (spraining or breaking a limb) while moving backward to reach a topspin lob.

However the real concern was the strength of the wind. Even standing near the net to warm up by hitting half-volleys to each other, it was all but impossible to get the ball over the net if facing the wind, whereas barely touching the ball with the wind at one's back, would carry it well beyond the drop off point, otherwise known as the baseline. In other words, if choosing an outdoor sport to play on that Naval Station, horseshoes would beat badminton hands down.

****

New arrivals of married officers and enlisted personnel were placed on a waiting list for "On-Base Housing." The wait could range from as few as three months to as many as eight, prior to which, families had to find housing in one of the surrounding small towns.

I had initially lived in the Bachelor Officer Quarters (sort of a large dorm), but as I was anxious to have my sweetie with me sooner, rather than later, had managed to find an apartment vacancy in the nearby town of Placentia (not to be confused with placenta, which, as all you mothers and obstetricians know, is associated with providing nourishment to the embryo during pregnancy). She joined me very soon thereafter.

Our second floor apartment was one of eight in the two-story structure, with the other seven occupied by enlisted personnel, who were either awaiting housing on base or had chosen to live off base and take the cash-in-lieu of such housing. Although the outside walls of our building were of sufficient construction to keep out wind, snow and cold, the interior walls were on the opposite end of the spectrum.

You can visualize how thrilled was my young bride when I welcomed her to the illustrious Orcan Apartments, our off-base living quarters for several chilly months.

One evening, as we sat watching the Beatles appear with Ed Sullivan (or some other exciting program on our tiny eleven inch, black and white television set), we kept hearing a strange "swishing" sound coming from the wall to the adjoining apartment, even over the noise of the television.

When we passed our neighbors in the hallway the next morning, I inquired about the unusual sound, and they replied that they had been painting. That may give you some idea as to the degree of audio privacy enjoyed by one and all. You might imagine, without any further elaboration on my part, some of the vivid love-making sounds flowing from one living area to another, even with absolutely no intent, nor desire, to be eavesdropping by any of the residents.

My young bride had been on the scene barely long enough to become partially acclimated to the wind, when Mother Nature decided to add some serious snow to the picture as well. The storm hit Placentia at about 1600 hours (to use the popular "military time" utilized by everyone, including civilians working on the base). Driving home that afternoon, I had more than a skosh bit of difficulty maneuvering our somewhat dilapidated 1956 Chevy Station Wagon from the base, stretching a typical twenty-minute drive into over an hour-long struggle.

The snow continued without letup all night, as well as the following day and night, accompanied by the ever present wind. The base had been closed to all traffic, so there was no problem with our inability to report to duty.

The next morning, or some 38-40 hours after it had begun, the storm stopped and the sunshine returned. Dressed in jeans, sweater, jacket, gloves and boots, I merrily descended the stairs to join my neighbors in digging out our vehicles. Approaching the entryway double doors, I came upon two other men standing there laughing. As I attempted to look through the glass portion of the double doors, I saw the source of their amusement.

The snow levels completely covered the doors, continuing how much higher, it was impossible to determine. The three of us headed up the stairs and began scraping the frost from the window leading to the fire escape. The snow reached halfway between the base of that window and the grate portion of said fire escape.

Deciding there was no time like the present; we opened the window and began removing snow from the stairs of the fire escape, which wasn't a slam dunk, as shovels had to be lifted to the level of the window before they could be tossed outward.

In short order, we had been joined by remaining residents, including even one of the gals who was in the advanced stages of pregnancy. She told us she figured she ought to be contributing to our efforts, just in case her "time" arrived earlier than anticipated.

In reality, it didn't take us all that long to reach the parking lot, even considering the methodology we utilized, which was similar to a sort of "water from the well" (pull it up and pour it out) procedure.

The snow had drifted heavily against the building and was packed in solidly due to the ever present winds. Rather than attempting to remove all of it, we instead dug a tunnel from the parking area to the doors. Upon completion, some of us took pictures to commemorate the event for disbelieving friends and relatives. I had conveniently left my camera in my desk at work, so was unable to take advantage of the photo opportunities until I could reclaim it.

Thanks to snow plows and a lack of additional snow, things returned to near normal within two more days, while yet another weather-related memory found itself firmly imbedded in my head.

I finally retrieved my camera to take
this shot two days following the storm.

****

Amongst the acquaintances my wife and I made early in our stay in Newfoundland, once we had obtained on-base housing, was a Navy pilot and his wife, who were always suggesting various activities we could do as a foursome, or perhaps as part of a larger group.

Bill and Jean had invited us to go bowling with them one evening, and in the course of events, suggested we form a team to compete in the Officers' Mixed Bowling League, which shortly thereafter we did (and won a few trophies in the process).

Another time they proposed renting a house for a weekend somewhere off the base with some other couples. While there, we could partake of some boating, fishing and hiking, plus a variety of great food and beverages. Their recommendation resulted in a very enjoyable gathering of eight or ten of us the following summer.

However, another of their ideas nearly turned into our permanent undoing, so to speak.

Bill had never observed a terrain that wasn't worth crossing. When our foursome was fishing together, he might recommend that we "try that little lake over there. It can't be more than a hundred yards from here." The presence of what was referred to locally as "buck brush" could modify a simple few minutes' jaunt to the water's edge into an obstacle-like journey requiring upwards to a half hour, and that was going downhill. The return trip (against the grain) might grow by another 20-25 minutes, minimum.

Given that premise (and certainly in retrospect), we should probably have given it a bit more thought when Bill called us one late winter evening to promote the idea of hiking into "this incredibly beautiful lake" that one of his fly-boy buddies had described to him. Instead, we readily agreed to his suggestion. Big mistake!

After filling a back-pack with sandwiches, fruit, canteens of water and a couple of treats for our dog, Tiffy, we met our friends at the prearranged parking spot around 9:00 a.m. (aka 0900 hours) on a sunny Saturday morning, ready to commence another adventure. There was existing snow on the ground, but it registered no more than four-five inches in depth.

I mentioned Tiffy, but did not describe her. She was our first dog as a married couple, though both of us had had various canines in our homes growing up. She was a black lab who probably could have been one of the best trained dogs on earth, had she been adopted by someone else; but unfortunately she was stuck with us, and we had left anything resembling a training manual back in the US of A.

Her name was short for Tiffany, from the film title about the coffee and Danish breakfast enjoyed by Audrey Hepburn outside the window of the famous jewelry store. Due to the aforementioned lack of decent training, Tiffy displayed little interest in coming to us when called; but as she loved going for rides in our car, she would always fall for the cheery "Let's go for a ride!" ploy and jump into our car once it was started. Although she deserved far better parents than we were, she was a wonderful family dog, including allowing our two boys to crawl on her, ride on her, etc. in later years.

Now back to "Fun with Bill and Jean." Within less than ninety minutes of walking we had located the lake in question. Completely frozen over and covered by drifted snow, we had to admit that it offered several outstanding scenes for an artist with a brush, as well as providing such a variety of shots by either an amateur or a professional shutter bug as to nearly bring him/her to orgasm.

We had decided to cross to the far side of the lake to eat our lunch near an out-cropping of large trees and rocks, before starting the return home. As you may rightly guess, the weather which had started off filled with sunshine and blue skies performed a complete "180" as we started across; before we even reached our dining destination, the sky was filled with snowflakes, and the ever present wind began to accelerate by a few knots.

Although you cannot tell from this poor excuse
for a photo, it was an extremely scenic area, at
least until the arrival of yet another snowstorm.

We rather quickly wolfed down our respective lunches,
realizing that our return trip could be slightly more difficult and
time consuming than had been the inbound trek.

As Bill jumped up to lead our caravan back to our point of
origin, he suggested that since we weren't staying out as long as
we'd planned; once we got back, showered and changed clothes, we
should all go out for an early dinner and top off the evening by
taking in a movie (the latter of which was FREE, just one of the
perks of our generally positive military experiences in Argentia).

Looking up, visibility had diminished; looking down, snow levels were accumulating rapidly, making it especially difficult for our canine family member to walk. She was forced to leap, rather than taking normal steps, while her nose and whiskers were entirely covered with flakes.

Traveling back across the lake, our earlier footprints long since covered by the blowing snow, I sensed that we were veering more to the right than we ought to be, though not to a significant degree. On the inward portion of our hike, we had followed a trail of sorts that took us between a couple of ridges for nearly two miles, followed by crossing a flat distance of nearly a quarter-mile, before reaching the lake.

On our return, as we moved from the lake to the flat area surrounding it, I mentioned my concern about the mild direction change; but Bill convinced me I was in error when he said, "Look over there. I think that's the draw we came through, just a little to the right." Embarrassed about my inability to sense the direction in which we had been traveling (and thinking I'd perhaps been too focused on the struggles of our by now exhausted retriever), I said no more….. For a while, that is.

After another thirty minutes, I noticed beside the trail a very large snow-covered evergreen tree that had apparently started to fall, but had become caught in another standing tree, leaving it at a sixty-degree angle. I didn't recall seeing it on our way in, and questioned Bill and the ladies about it. None of us, it turned out, recalled that scene.

OK, cut to the climax. We retraced our steps to the open area, traveled to our left some 250-300 yards, discovered another opening between two different ridges, continued through that mini-valley (carrying our poor black dog for nearly half of the way), and eventually arrived at the parking lot and our snow-covered vehicles.

We exhibited some nervous gallows type laughter about our close call with that guy in the robe carrying a sickle (or is it a scythe?), lifted Tiffy into the station wagon, and all but fell into the car ourselves.

We mutually agreed to call off the evening's plans until some later date and headed to our respective quarters for hot showers, whatever leftovers might be in the fridge, and an early visit to our warm, cozy and safe bed.

Oh yes, I am no longer averse to questioning others when my senses tell me we are going the wrong direction, even if I am still stubborn, as are most males, about stopping to ask directions.

Chapter 14

Juvenile (No Age Requirement) Attempts at "Talking Dirty"

****

"Rickety, rickety ree;

Kick 'em in the knee.

Rickety, rickety rass;

Kick 'em in the other knee."

****

At some point in the maturation process of little boys moving toward becoming young men; they may replace earlier career choices such as that of a fireman, a policeman or an astronaut, with an intense desire to become a GYNECOLOGIST. Whether or not such (misguided?) curiosity ultimately leads to the years of medical school required, an interest in things of a sexual nature tend to remain firmly ingrained in their makeup.

As mentioned earlier, I never heard language in our household that in any way related to sexual or bodily functions. For that matter, I do not recall overhearing much, if any, language of that sort in the homes of my friends' parents. Of course such absence was not the case out in the "real world."

Whether during sleepovers (indoors or in sleeping bags outside), or with groups of boys wandering around on the playground or in school hallways; there was ample discussion of things sexual or jokes regarding same, complete with excessive giggling. Those present, who might not understand the topic under discussion or the point of the joke would, in all likelihood, laugh even harder than others, simply to disguise their ignorance.

For example, one of these young lads might say, in his best impression of an Elmer Fudd voice, "She couldn't wun vewy fast, but you should have seen her twat." Those of us within hearing would practically fall on the floor in laughter, whether or not we had the slightest clue as to what this play on words was all about.

Next, one of the more astute members of our raucous bunch would follow with the joke about the airline stewardess (yes, before political correctness changed the title to Flight Attendant) who was making her way down the aisle of a TWA flight, asking if anyone would care for some TWA Coffee, to which one of her male customers replied, "No, but how about some of your TWA-T?"

Oh, we were such hilariously brilliant youngsters, were we not? Little did we stop to think that these profound pieces of humor had probably been around for some time; if not during the demise of the dinosaurs, at least since the day following the first TWA passenger flights in 1930 or the initial appearance of Elmer Fudd as a cartoon character near the end of the 1930s.

****

While no different from my contemporaries, albeit probably far less knowledgeable, I tried to concoct ways to give the impression that I was not only well-versed in matters sexual, but hopefully, exhibited erudition in describing same.

For example, with the help of the library's dictionary and encyclopedias, I might create a quiz, asking questions such as: "What is the name of the little bird about which a song was created by Gilbert and Sullivan for the light opera *The Mikado*?" Answer: "Tit Willow." "What is another tiny bird whose name sounds more like that of a small rodent?" Answer: "Titmouse." "What is an adjective describing someone who is the leader of a group in name only, while performing no actual leadership?" Answer: "Titular." "What does a cow have four of that a woman has two of?" Answer: "Legs." Then I'd ask why they were laughing, and inquire as to what they were thinking about anyway.

As years passed and I matured slightly (although I was now in college, that would obviously still be up for debate), I left behind such adolescent "boob" humor and became slightly racier by using questions such as "What is the name of the shrub (technically a tree) with soft grayish fur-like buds on long straight stems?" Answer: "Pussy Willow." "What is a word used to describe the behavior of a person who acts overly cautious or timid?" Answer: "Pussyfooting." "What was the name of the central female character in the book *Goldfinger* who provided assistance, among other things, to James Bond?" Answer: "Pussy Galore." Then the final question, "What might you anticipate finding in the well in the nursery rhyme "Ding Dong Bell?" The obvious answer would, of course, be "water." I truly thought I was God's gift to racy humor.

****

Another goofy pastime in this category was to take a popular song and substitute modified (as in: suggestive) lyrics, something I certainly do not consider to be unique. Although I'll provide a couple personal examples shortly, there's something I must do beforehand. As the first one relates to my wife, I need to describe a particular trait of hers which has necessitated my keeping this initial example to myself, rather than sharing it with her. Naturally, until and unless she reads this memoir, she would have no knowledge of it.

Despite being solidly grounded in her Christian faith, my charming wife is somewhat superstitious. For starters, any event falling on "Friday the Thirteenth" is a definite concern for her, especially if it involves driving. In addition, she will not "pass me on the stairs" in our home. She also shies away from things like black cats crossing her path, walking under ladders, breaking mirrors and so on. But she is absolutely adamant about the following: "Never sing before breakfast!" That even includes avoiding "Happy Birthday to you" every 52 weeks or so, until at least a few bites of the morning's repast have been taken.

To continue, although we've never made love to "Bolero" ala Bo Derek in the movie "10" of a few decades ago, we often have some sort of romantic music playing to enhance the mood for such activities. I have even sung to her afterward (admittedly not at a level with, say, Engelbert Humperdinck doing "After the Lovin'") as we've relaxed in the afterglow. But to reiterate her "Never sing before breakfast" edict: any morning sex, while typically involving melodious rhythm, an upbeat tempo and even thoughts of heavenly trumpets for accompaniment, would necessarily be totally "song-less."

Having now made you fully aware of these early-morning musical-rendering restrictions she's placed on me, I'll proceed to my first example of lyrical modifications.

On numerous occasions when I'd awaken a few moments earlier than she, the song "Carolina in the Morning" would pop into my head. The number, as you'll recall, begins with the line, "Nothin could be fina than to be in Carolina in the mo-o-o-or-nin." However, in the version playing on my mind's turntable and speaker system, I replaced a single word from that line, substituting "your vagina" for (and rhyming with) the geographic location in the original song. Obviously, as I was forbidden to sing it to her, I've had to keep it to myself for the first half century of our marriage.

****

Backtracking now to high school, during a rainy and gloomy late autumn Saturday afternoon, three of us had decided to goof around with a tape recorder. We began by creating sound effects to simulate a massive car crash (kicking around a metal waste basket on a linoleum covered floor), threw in some "Dragnet/Joe Friday" type dialog, and finally added some bogus commercials we had made up. It was an entertaining way to pass the time, with more than a few laughs occurring in the process.

One member of our trio was John Tebbe, a recent transfer to our school from back east. He measured in at well over 6'3", with gangly arms and legs, ears that made him look like an elongated version of Alfred E. Neuman (of Mad Comics and "What, Me Worry?" fame) and a dry sense of humor.

John said he had a great idea for a song for us to add to our previously recorded antics. He said he knew we must be familiar with the tune "Brazil" to which he had thought of some minor modifications. (Of course, he may have been plagiarizing something he had heard earlier, but it was new to us, way out there in Montana.)

He reminded us that the song included an instrumental segment that sounded like "bum bum bum; bum bum bum-de-bum" repeated several times before the melody kicked back in again, and he hummed it for us to be certain we understood.

He then told Wayne (the third member of our threesome) and me to sing words to the rhythmic ("bum bum bum" etc.) part of the song as follows: "Stroke that nipple, squeeze that titty; stroke that nipple, squeeze that titty" over and over, while he sang the (somewhat altered words of the) melody: "Brassiere, you hold the things I love so dear." There was a bit more, but you get the idea.

While I was not the one initiating such song modifications on that occasion, I certainly subscribed to them. It doesn't take much imagination to picture what I later did with the Rogers and Hart melody "Lady Is a Tramp." While I may have eventually matured in many other ways, I'll admit there has remained an awful lot of juvenile thought process imbedded in the area between my ears.

****

One of my favorite songs as a child was "The Old Master Painter," sung by Phil Harris. As puberty arrived and I discovered masturbation (an activity in which I was willing to spend as much time as necessary to master), I happened to reflect on that song from my youth, and re-titled it "The Old Masturbator." Then I set about thinking of similar plays on words in the same vein. I came up with a couple of examples: a person who debated subjects with the masses would be identified as a "Mass Debater;" or someone who works at a resort instructing fishing contestants in the proper method for baiting hooks, as a "Master Baiter."

****

While reading newspaper ads, I might be drawn to one for ladies' intimates or undergarments, and wonder what would happen if, for a "Half-Off Sale," they would show a bra covering only one breast.

Or I might visualize how a voluptuous blonde, strictly in the interest of improving mental acuity, could jump-start the thought processes of any males present, simply by "getting something off her chest."

Of course, more recently, when Victoria's Secret began advertising on television along with various print media, it was obvious that I had not been the only person who must have thought of such ideas, as their ads left nothing to the imagination;

in fact, any such ad made the "Playboy Magazine" foldouts of my youth seem tame by comparison.

Even later in life, I could be watching Reese Witherspoon in some film, and think to myself that if, rather than having become a successful actress, she had instead chosen to operate a house of ill-repute, she could have called it "Reese's Pieces."

At times I might modify a movie title or television show by making a very minor modification to one of the words in that title, or adding a word or phrase to it, thereby entirely changing the original subject matter into something sexual in nature.

For example, was I to do so with the Roma Downey/Della Reese television show, "Touched by an Angel," I might replace the initial "T" with a "D." While such modification might technically keep it within the classification of being "clean," it would definitely no longer be recommended for young family viewing, in spite of such categorization.

Still another modification to television might be exemplified by adding a prefix to a word in the title of a popular show, such as "Little Whorehouse on the Prairie." I might rewrite an ad for a popular wine such as Inglenook, by adding an "ie" at the end, thus modifying the text regarding the pleasure of such product. Or I might take an existing movie title such as *The Incredible Shrinking Man* and add "After Swimming or Sex."

****

If the addition of a letter or word suited my purposes, fine; but another way of doing so could be simply ending abruptly. In my typically long-winded manner, allow me to explain what I mean utilizing the following example:

In the latter part of the 1950s, the Kingston Trio recorded their updated version of a 1948 song called "Charlie on the MTA." While catchy, the song lacks any degree of realism; but it made them a gazillion bucks, so who am I to judge?

To give you a quick synopsis, if your recollection is a bit fuzzy, it tells the tale of a guy who takes the train every day to work somewhere in Boston. For openers, he apparently forgets his billfold, and to make matters worse, doesn't have quite enough change in his pockets to pay the full fare for his subway ride, which included one transfer. Being a real stickler for financial rules, the conductor (perhaps another of those darn accountants in disguise) won't let him depart the train, so the poor passenger is doomed to ride around in circles throughout eternity. Our hero's wife, while thoughtful and loving, must be something of a ditz herself. I say that because, in spite of the fact that she somehow (via an early version of GPS or perhaps just dumb luck) manages to locate her husband's fast moving railcar each afternoon; rather than giving him the money needed to allow him to exit the train, she tosses him a sandwich. (Little known fact: the origin of the popular SUBWAY ® Sandwich Restaurant chain may well have had its beginning from this subway sandwich tossing incident.) Of course, had she thought things through and given him the funds demanded by the conductor, there'd have been no updated version of the MTA number, and the Kingston Trio would have had to find a different song to follow "Tom Dooley" in their concerts.

Now (finally) I'll get back to my point of ending a song abruptly. Having what was probably an innate interest in oral sex, long before that esteemed United States President William Jefferson Clinton popularized it for the masses; at the place in the song wherein the wife makes her way down to the subway station to bring him some food, I simply ended the song at "Charlie's wife goes down."

****

What with my residence being situated well outside of town, it was more likely than not that I would spend a fair amount of time in the homes of friends after school or on weekends. Whether the parents were present or not, or even if my friend wasn't around at the time, was not relevant, as people seldom locked their houses.

A given afternoon might logically place a couple members of our "group" in the basement of John Wertz's house (another great place to hang out) playing ping-pong, even though John was not around to be participate in the game. Another afternoon I might be up in Conrad Colby's den watching television while waiting for him to return from a late class.

Sylvia Baldwin was the wonderful mother of twins Doug and Wayne, of whom I've written earlier, plus their kid sister, Kay.

Many years after the fact, when I had the quite pleasurable opportunity to reunite with Sylvia, her three offspring, and Conrad, she laughingly related to all of us an incident dating back to our high school days, shortly after their move to Missoula.

Sylvia had arrived home from her long day of nursing duties and observed a couple of feet protruding from the end of her living room couch. She called out, "Doug?" (No answer); then "Wayne?" (Still no answer); and next, trying to recall some of the names of the twins' new friends, "Ken?" (Third time not a charm either, resulting in no response). Tiring of this guessing game, she set down her armload of parcels and entered the living room to see who was attached to the long legs, smiling broadly as she then said, "Oh, it's just you, Conrad." to the soundly sleeping intruder.

Conrad (as an old married guy now, better known simply as Con) played the trombone in the high school band, which qualified him as the individual having the closest resemblance to being a musician in our frequently assembled foursome (although that really isn't saying much).

Rather than catching a few winks on the Baldwin couch, he would more typically enter their home, sit down at their piano (they did not have a trombone available), play the first dozen and a half bars of "Mister Sandman" and promptly stop. It was sort of a "calling card" for him. If any member of the Baldwin family happened to arrive home as Con was performing his abbreviated version of that 1950's hit by "The Chordettes," he or she would respond to such playing with a "Hi, Conrad."

****

Although most of the parents of my friends were what one might call pretty straight-laced, none fit that category more so than Don and Sylvia Baldwin. Prayers were always said prior to meals. Swearing was non-existent. I was actually somewhat surprised to observe that they had allowed their daughter, Kay, to place a sticker on the back of the toilet which boldly stated "IF YOU PROMISE TO KEEP ME CLEAN, I WON'T TELL OF THE THINGS I'VE SEEN."

Thus you can imagine my response one afternoon when I was hanging out in the twins' upstairs bedroom with Wayne; he looked me right in the eye and said, "Do you know that I can say

'FUCK' right in front of my mom or dad, and they won't blink an eye?" After I replied that if he did so, he'd never live to tell about it; he then said, "I'll go one step further. I'll even spell out the word, just to prove to you they didn't misunderstand, or failed to hear me."

We didn't place a wager on his assertion, but it just so happened later in the day, that I was invited to share dinner with the Baldwins. Neither Doug nor Kay was going to be home for the evening meal, so Sylvia insisted that I stick around to help them finish up the leftovers she was serving.

Just before we sat down at the table, Wayne walked into the dining room and addressed his mother with "Mom, if you see Kay," and paused for just a second, before adding, "Oh, never mind."

We then shared a typically scrumptious, Sylvia-made meal, after which Wayne and I decided to go shoot some hoops at the nearby elementary school. As we took turns displaying our skills with the big round ball, he said, "Ok, do you believe me now?"

Giving him a confused look, I asked him what he was talking about.

"I told you this afternoon that I could spell out 'FUCK' in from of my mother and she wouldn't blink an eye."

I gave him another blank stare, and said he had done no such thing, and to "just shoot the damn ball."

"Remember when we walked into the dining room? Mom was bringing in the potatoes, and I said to her quite specifically, 'Mom, F-U-C-K.'. Then I said 'Oh, never mind.'"

I thought back to the interchange with his mom, and suddenly realized what I had missed. His "If you see Kay" equates to "F-U-C-K," but I had heard only the former. Wayne had played yet another prank from his seemingly never ending repertoire.

****

As a general rule, conversations in a boy's locker room (or a girl's for all I knew) tended to include certain expressions that would typically be excluded from those carried on at "High Tea," a charitable fundraiser, or in a church. The phraseology in these sites was modified, such that while it was less offensive to sensitive ears, the overall meaning still came through to the listener.

For example, "Are you out of your fucking mind?" would be replaced with "Are you kidding me?" "Who gives a rat's ass?" would become "Who cares?" "Tough titty!" would convert to "Too bad." And so on.

In this vein, the term "Scared Shitless" was a rather vivid description, expressed by any number of people to portray a fear so intense as to have totally cleared out the colon.

As my small contribution to society at the time, I attempted to provide a couple of viable substitutes for relating such a feeling of fear, without resorting to coarse potty mouth language, while still providing the necessary specifics of the situation. While they were not guaranteed, even then, to be original, I proposed: "Petrified Poopless" or "It frightened the feces out of me." Oh well, a rose by any other name..............

****

One final episode in using a play on words took place during my years of employment with Peat Marwick Mitchell and Co, CPA's (at the time, one of the "Big Eight" CPA firms). I had been assigned by one of the partners to give a 20-25 minute presentation to the rest of my counterparts on some accounting topic for our monthly staff educational gathering.

I admit to having found such meetings to be sleep-inducing the vast majority of the time, other than when watching whichever poor staff member had been chosen for that month's dissertation: 1) sweat bullets; 2) lose his place in his notes; 3) stammer; or 4) set a new record for the number of "um" or "a" inclusions in his speech.

Somehow (divine intervention? annual bonuses? magic? lots of practice?), once these hopeless staff members attained even the entry level of management, their speaking skills immediately became equivalent to those of the finest orator around.

I have no doubt that, included amongst those attending such meetings, there were a select few who were attentive to every word spoken; those individuals were undoubtedly more likely to wind up as managers or partners of the firm. This scenario may or may not have been in the cards for me, although it's a moot point, as I left public accounting for a position with a supermarket chain before I had the opportunity to find out.

As mentioned, these topical meetings were, to my way of thinking, nowhere close to the exhilaration of a Knute Rockne halftime pep talk; but then I had always found the Journal of Accountancy (the Accountant's Bible?) to be the prefect solution to insomnia, and that perhaps slanted my viewpoint.

It was now my turn to be faced with the challenge of enlightening my associates, while not wishing to embarrass anyone who happened to drop off during my oration. After all, the Partner-in-Charge would be joining us in the room as well.

I had prepared a handout covering the topic of my speech in great detail, for those who really had a desire to accumulate a few more ounces of paper; but I gave only a brief overview from that prepared text during the actual speaking portion of the program.

Switching gears from those prepared notes, I posed a question to the audience: "If you were to arrive late for a meeting, and by so doing, missed out on the subject matter, could you quickly determine what was being discussed, and be confident in volunteering useful input in that meeting?"

The general consensus of the group was that, as highly educated certified public accountants, they could certainly zero in on the business at hand, simply by listening to a few key words or phrases; even without having been given an agenda of what was to be discussed.

I then asked them to envision two meeting rooms side by side; with the first being an assemblage of accountants, much like ours today, while the other one consisted of owners or operators of multiple houses of prostitution.

Along comes a bright-eyed, bushy-tailed accountant, newly promoted to his firm's management team; he had been held up in traffic, arriving just after the respective meetings had commenced. Because signs describing the groups in each room had been attached to the inside of the meeting room doors, once those doors had been closed, it was not readily evident which group was which.

Of the two rooms, our hero selected the latter. He quietly slipped into a vacant chair on which rested a handout of sorts, basically just a couple of sheets of paper with the heading "Possible Topics of Concern for Today's Discussion."

Despite the lopsided ratio of females (most of whom looked like they'd seen more than just a few tax seasons) to males, he felt confident that he must have chosen the proper room. He understood that firms were actively recruiting more women into the profession, so the number of these ladies in attendance was certainly understandable. Also, based on the topics listed on the discussion pages, any fool could see that they were common accounting terms.

Following is a partial listing of what appeared on those pages:

Average Cost Method….. Continuing Operations….. Horizontal Analysis….. Fixed Price….. Engagement Completion….. Deposit Method….. Bid and Asked….. First-In, First-Out….. Variance….. Lump Sum Distribution….. Goodwill….

Performance Measurement….. Dry Hole Expenses….. High-Low Method….. Double Entry….. Extent of Test of Control….. Returns and Allowances….. Face Value….. Discontinued Operations….. Full Absorption Costs….. Depletion of Assets…

Goods Available for Sale….. Appreciation….. Involuntary Conversions….. Business Combinations….. Certificate of Deposit….. Qualitative Analysis….. Foreign Exchange….. In Arrears….. Internal Control….. Standard Costing….. Swaps….

Detection Risk….. Value Added Activity….. Straddles….. Accumulation….. Non-Routine Transactions….. Closing Entry….. Passive Income…… Claim for Refund….. Installment Method….. Extraordinary Items….. Backup Withholding….. Private Placement….. Piece Work…. Cost of Goods Sold….. Period….. Inflation…. Claim for Refund….. Public Offering….. Control Deficiency….. Rate of Return….. Indirect Method….. Just-in-Time….. Co-Mingling….. Closed End….. Direct Labor….. Audit Sampling….. Dual Dating….. Variable Cost….. Clean Opinion…. Finished Goods….. Wash Sale….. Credit for Elderly and Disabled….. Tenancy in Common….. Instrument….. Yield….. Casualty Losses….. Deflation….. Negotiable….. Wrap Around….. Subsequent Event…..Turnover… Trust… .Last-In, First-Out…..

Merger….. Lay Off….. Output….. Extension….. Going Private…..
Leverage….. Options…..

Yes, he was a pretty smug young bean counter, until the moderator stepped to the microphone and began speaking………

The presentation to my fellow CPA's then ended, as did, in all likelihood, any hope of my advancement into management. On the plus side, no one dozed off that afternoon.

****

Chapter 15

This and That, In Order of Interest

(Or Lack Thereof)

****

Sub Chapter 15.1:

Not "Butt," as in Slut; But "Butte," as in Cute

Butte, Montana was once the home of "The Richest Hill on Earth" from which countless tons of copper have been mined. Driving through Montana today on Highway I-90, one would no longer be able to observe a hill, but rather a very, very large hole, exemplifying the landscape of Butte. The town has a fantastic history, replete with a wide assortment of diversified characters.

Growing up in Missoula, some 120 miles northwest of Butte, I had my own impressions of this town and its people. I'm sure Butte folks had their impressions, many of which may have been less than positive in nature, regarding Missoulians. So be it. People are entitled to have opinions, all of which are neither right nor wrong.

Accompanying my parents during one of my dad's salesman trips, we spent a day and night in Butte. My mother and I went to a movie while dad made his calls on grocery stores in the area, and that night we went to dinner in Meaderville (a section of Butte originally settled by the Italian faction of miners) at a restaurant called The Rocky Mountain. I guess the food outstanding, but for a youth of only six years, my opinion would not have mattered to anyone, so I did not express one.

Years later, as a member of our college tennis team returning to Missoula from a road trip, we were passing through Butte around 7:00 and in need of something to quiet our grumbling stomachs. Our player-coach told us he knew just the place, and we soon parked at The Rocky Mountain. I recalled having eaten there as a small child, but nothing more, although our guide, a Butte native, advised us of its top-notch reputation for anyone visiting the area. I was ravenously hungry and ordered a steak.

Long before the main course arrived, I had been served bread sticks, pasta and salad in sufficient quantities to take care of the majority of my hunger pangs. Next they brought an oversized plate containing my steak, potato and vegetable. Although I declined dessert, I experienced quite a stomach ache from the excessive quantities of food, too delicious to pass up. I still recall that place as having provided me with one of my fonder memories of dining pleasure.

****

As a sophomore in high school, I had signed up for a bus trip to Butte to support our local eleven in this annual rivalry on the gridiron. In subsequent (actually many years later) conversations with various Montanans who had actually played high school ball against Butte, I learned that no one wanted to play them on their home turf.

It was a grass field, technically, but it was also covered with cinders. From time to time, one or more Butte linemen would grasp a handful of said cinders and drop them down the neck of the opposition in a pileup during a running play, or perhaps toss a handful of them toward the face of an opponent while awaiting the snap of the ball. While getting cinders in one's eye or mouth was not to be desired, it could be even worse to have them work their way under shoulder pads, as they served as something akin to portable sandpaper, resulting in bleeding and abrasions.

Certainly not all of Butte's players resorted to this tactic, and I have several friends from Butte for whom I have nothing but the greatest respect. Still, such things happened, and it served to add to Butte's rough and rugged reputation.

But getting back to the bus trip in question, it was basically free of any unpleasantness; that is until after the game was completed, and we had all piled back into our bus for the ride back to Missoula.

Suddenly a group of girls near the window, just a couple rows behind the door, began to shriek and hide their eyes; only to begin giggling and looking outside again, alternately, with more screaming and turning away. When those of us on the other side of the bus questioned their antics, one girl replied that a whole bunch of Butte boys were peeing on the side of the bus, with some even aiming toward the windows.

Fortunately, about that time, some teachers broke up the festivities, and we departed without further incident.

****

Yet another recollection about Butte and its residents relates to a basketball game between our two high schools. The starting lineup for the Butte Bulldogs was announced over the public address system as follows: "Starting at forwards: Les Marinkovich and Mark Stanosich; at guards: Louis Markovich and Bob O'Billovich; at center: Ed Smith."

Now I don't mean to be nit-picky, but why in the world did they allow someone named Smith to break up the rhythmic continuity of the other four starters' names? Perhaps an opposing team's center, getting pummeled by Smith's flying elbows while battling for rebounds, may have referred to him as a "son of a bitch," thereby making for a completely "like sounding" lineup. Just saying, you know?

By the way, the aforementioned O'Billovich went on to become a three-sport letterman at the University of Montana, playing both as starting quarterback and defensive back on the football team, followed by a highly successful career in the Canadian Football League as both a player and later a coach.

****

Sub Chapter 15.2:

"Who Invited Her?"

(And Other Female "Oops" Mishaps)

During my assignment with the Navy in the Province of Newfoundland, one of my collateral duties involved serving as the Chair of an Entertainment Committee, consisting of a Chief Petty Officer, an enlisted representative, and another officer (most likely Don, who was in charge of the Officers' Club, as mentioned earlier). We had the responsibility of booking live entertainment to perform for the military residents of the Argentia Naval Station at the various clubs on base.

Argentia's location was not exactly "on the way" to somewhere else, and could hardly be considered a "plum" on any entertainer's resume. Add in the fact that transportation was generally provided by a noisy, uncomfortable piece of military aircraft, and it was highly unlikely we would ever be able to book any group that actually had a shot at eventual fame in the business.

Still, we had what seemed to be a sizeable assortment of presentations sent to us for consideration, including glossy 8 X 10 photos of the featured singer (nearly always of the feminine gender, of course). Among the more polished acts we did manage to book was a trio called "The Rag Dolls" which was backed up instrumentally by "Mitch Ryder and the Detroit Wheels."

Both of these groups went on to spend some time in the musical limelight, unlike most other acts which visited Newfoundland. The "Dolls" were sort of a female version of "The Four Seasons," with lead singer Jean Thomas being the feminine counterpart to Frankie Valli of the popular male quartet.

Stateside Entertainment

THEY'RE HERE! ! ! The biggest, rockingest, swingingest, group of entertainers to hit the Naval Station since Red Nichols lost his five pennies in the gum machine, are now appearing at your clubs.

There is entertainment for everyone in this show. The Rag Dolls, a trio of talented ladies sing a variety of songs and provide a lovely view while performing. Backing up the Rag Dolls instrumentally, as well as performing on their own, are Mytch Ryder and the Detroit Wheels. You can tell by the name that this group could not possibly be square. If you are one whose musical appreciation tends toward long-hair, the show has plenty of that too, although it's more noticeable on their heads than from their instruments.

The show features the new sound, and for those of you who have played their records on the jukebox in the clubs, you'll definitely want to see and hear the group in person.

So go out to your club and sing along with Mytch (Ryder, that is), rock and roll with his Detroit Wheels, and don't lag in the halls, go see the Rag Dolls.

This was a promo article written by me for "The Foghorn," which was the Naval Station's weekly newspaper. Hey, I know it is cornball at best, but I did have other full-time responsibilities to perform too, don't forget.

******

285

It was part of my duty to greet such groups when they deplaned, and to escort them to the Bachelor Officer Quarters, where they would reside during their stay. Once they had checked in, I would then have them transported to the Enlisted Men's Club to practice a couple of numbers, providing them the opportunity to tune their instruments and check the sound system, while also allowing me to evaluate their material.

There was to be no nudity of any kind; and even the "patter" could not get overly risqué. For example, the front man could say something like "Our female singer may not be a candidate for Rhodes Scholar consideration, but up front, she's GANGBUSTERS!" Whereas references to "boobs" or "knockers" might be acceptable, there was to be no use of words such as "tits," "ass" or even "pissed-off."

I guess this was another wonderful example of our government protecting its citizens (in this instance: hardly innocent, mostly young, Naval Personnel) from what it hypocritically judged not to be in their best interests; while turning a blind eye to the negative aspects of readily accessible cigarettes and booze (practically free, due to the lack of taxes thereon), along with slot machines galore which served to hook many on gambling.

At the time of my initial "preview" of one such act, Johnny Johnson, the Navy Exchange Officer (and my boss), advised that he would accompany me, in case I had any doubt about whether or not something would be considered acceptable by the Navy Base Command Team. (By the way, what follows is in no way connected to the "Rag Doll" booking, as their visit occurred much later.)

Lieutenant Johnson was what is known as a Limited Duty Officer, meaning that he had successfully worked his way through the enlisted ranks, and was promoted to the position of commissioned officer, despite lacking a college education.

The number chosen by the band for practice was "Satin Doll," and they played it well enough to have kept its composer, Duke Ellington, from wincing too much. Their girl singer had a pleasant voice, not to mention a pretty decent (from a visual perspective) set of lungs.

Johnny advised me that everything seemed satisfactory from his perspective, with one minor exception: there appeared to be just a tad too much skin being exposed in the upper torso area of the aforementioned singer. (Having served so many years in the enlisted ranks, and being far worldlier than was I, a fresh-faced Navy Ensign for all of some ten months; what he actually said was more along the lines of "Her Goddamn tits are all but falling out of her costume!" Regardless of the specific terminology, I understood what he meant.)

The group leader assured us that what we may have thought we were seeing was simply an illusion, and he asked us to accompany him and the sweet young thing to a more private corner to demonstrate.

When we did so, he proved his point by having us observe up close and personal, so to speak, that we were not seeing actual skin, but rather a very fine triple layer of flesh colored fabric. He then asked her to peel back, one at a time, each such layer, until she reached her actual skin. She complied with the proper appearance of modesty, although in the process, nearly did have her right boob pop out (much like my eyes had already done).

Having satisfied us that she was adequately attired, we allowed the show to go on, and it was a big hit at all the clubs in which they performed.

About two weeks after the band had departed; I was called to the office of the Naval Station Executive Officer. He advised me it had come to his attention that a certain female member of a musical group that had recently been booked to play at various locations on the base had apparently utilized her room in the Bachelor Officer Quarters for the purpose of entertaining numerous such bachelor officers in a one-on-one setting.

While he no doubt admired her entrepreneurial acumen and keen sense of capitalizing on her knowledge of supply and demand; he could not condone the resulting actions of her having made available her supply of what was obviously in popular demand.

He made it vividly clear that I understood such activity was totally unacceptable, and was never to be allowed to be repeated. After confirming that his message had been received loud and clear, I saluted, made a hasty retreat, and drove back to my office.

Wondering how word had leaked out, I couldn't envision anyone involved saying something that would tend to kill the goose that laid the golden egg, or perhaps more accurately, the gal that "laid" each of them.

While never learning the specific source of the Executive Officer's knowledge of the matter, I had heard a rumor that some nerdy, newly commissioned Ensign had lost his virginity to the (relatively) young lady in question; he had subsequently been observed by some senior officers, who commented that he seemed unable to stifle an ear-to-ear grin, while humming the *South Pacific* tune "There Is Nothin' Like a Dame" over and over during a Sunday morning service in the base chapel. You be the judge.

****

Although to my knowledge, no similar off-stage improprieties by visiting entertainers seeking supplemental income occurred during my time in Argentia, an incident on the final night of yet another evening of imported entertainment caused an even greater uproar.

A trio consisting of two guys and a gal had been well received at all the clubs, and was concluding the week with an encore performance at the Officers' Club, due to the arrival of a visiting Admiral and his wife.

Because of the popularity of the trio at its show earlier in the week at the Officer's Club, positive word-of-mouth comments caused the club to be filled to capacity for this added show. The female vocalist had a voice that might be favorably compared to that of a Julie London, or more recently, Diana Krall; and she just might someday have "made it big" were it not for her basically fatal mistake during the last of the group's three sets that night.

The Guest of Honor for the evening, an Admiral Richard something or other (and no, I really do not recall his last name, not that I'd spell it out for you if I did), was recognized by the Officers' Club Manager over the PA system. (It was not Don, the fellow who was the Club Manager when I first arrived on base. His tour in Newfoundland had long since been completed.) The lights came up and our guest received a hearty round of applause by all those present. Unfortunately, said Admiral was ALSO RECOGNIZED by our group's female singer.

Whether she was on some sort of mind-numbing substance, or just totally lacking in brains, I could not say. Upon looking across the crowd at our distinguished guest, she blurted out, "Why Ricky, honey; I never expected to ever see YOU again! You told me in San Diego that you were in the Navy, by My God, an Admiral!"

The group's leader quickly jumped to the microphone, adlibbing something along the lines of "What a kidder! And you folks thought all she could do was sing. Let's hear it for her improvisational comedy bit, and then we'd like to play one of our favorites for you......."

While most of the audience laughed uproariously, as if the bit HAD been staged, the Admiral's wife wasn't laughing; even from my seat across the room from them, I could see her shooting deadly daggers from evil eyes towards her red-faced husband.

****

Sub Chapter 15.3:
"I've Gotta Stop Doing That!"

I'm aware that I've mentioned the name Doug Baldwin frequently throughout this book. It figures, since we did a lot of stuff together in high school and college. There was also the Doug whose driving skills "preserved the bacon" of a carload of us on an icy highway; I've had any number of classmates and business associates who answer to "Doug" as well; why, I even have a close cousin by that name.

'Tis now time to introduce into this memoir yet another particular Doug; one whose path has criss-crossed mine with some degree of frequency over seven decades. His last name is Hacker.

****

Somewhat short of a thousand days prior to an abusive doctor slapping me on the butt to welcome me into the world, Joe and Dorothy Hacker had already expanded the population of Missoula with what would be their only child.

A few years after we had again taken up residence in Pattee Canyon, the Hacker family built a lovely home just over a quarter of a mile down canyon from us and became neighbors of sorts. Even before that move, Joe and my dad had met as a result of some business dealings. While our respective parents were jointly attending some sort of dinner or similar event, I had my initial contact with Doug, spending the better part of an interesting evening with him in their pre-canyon residence.

Mistakenly, our misguided sets of moms and dads had mutually determined that Doug possessed a sufficient level of maturity to be in charge of the evening's activities in their absence. I can't say with full confidence, but our ages at the time approximated eleven and eight, with me obviously being the junior member of the duo. Shortly after the departure of our parents, rather than playing any of the many board and/or card games that had been laid out for our evening's entertainment, Doug asked if I liked to concoct things in the kitchen.

To make a long story a tiny bit shorter, we spent the entire evening combining nearly every available liquid in their refrigerator and pantry into a large mixing bowl, while adding various portions of the contents of assorted jars, boxes and other containers, interrupted only by the frequent operation of the electric beaters. Included in our undocumented list of ingredients were the following items: chocolate syrup, mustard, cinnamon, sugar, jelly, milk, bananas, ice cream, almond flavoring, half a bottle of Coca Cola, a pealed orange, one raw egg with most of the shell removed, the powdery contents of a box of strawberry Jell-O, a tablespoon of either catsup or ketchup, some unsweetened cocoa, two crumbled up graham crackers, vinegar and, well, you get the idea. Although we wisely made the decision to refrain from eating a bowlful of the resulting mixture, we had frequently paused for a taste test following the adding of each new ingredient. In other words, we had already ingested enough of the concoction that it should have caused serious stomach aches. Why it did not, I'll never know.

****

A three year age difference is of little consequence once one has reached his/her twenties, but it can seem quite significant prior to that point in life. When the Hackers became residents of the canyon, Doug was older than other children residing there. I may have been roughly next in line; but what self respecting young male would want to become close friends with a little kid like me? Therefore I would have to say that while we were occasionally paired up during an evening such as that described previously, or as part of a group playing "Hide and Go Seek" after dark near his house, softball in the field near my house or Monopoly in his basement, it would be a stretch to say we were in any way "friends" in those days. I was, however, often the fall guy for various pranks he initiated.

One evening soon after their move to Pattee Canyon, Dorothy invited the three Coopers to join the three Hackers for dinner, following a tour of their new residence. She had "put on the dog" for the meal, so to speak, complete with a well-pressed linen tablecloth and some brand new dishes. Unlike the fancy (boring looking) glassware for the parents at the table, Doug and I had water glasses decorated with a colorful floral pattern.

Despite having been properly trained at dining skills, such that I had long since abandoned the wearing of a bib, I seemed to be having a problem whenever I would take a sip of my water. It was as if I had moved the glass away from my mouth too quickly, resulting in a dribbling of water onto my plate, the tablecloth or my lap (or some combination of all three). My mother ignored the first such episode, but after a repeat performance, commented in a whisper loud enough to be heard by others besides me, "For heaven's sake, Ken, what is wrong with you?"

Doug then broke out with a serious case of the giggles, at which time his mother apologized, saying that her son had found these "gag drinking glasses" while shopping one day, and absolutely begged to put one at my place when we ate dinner; and she had allowed him to do so. It seems there was a hole in the center of the two flowers near the top of my glass, and when I tipped it to my mouth to take a drink, the water would leak out of the tiny holes, making it look as if the drinker was lacking in coordination.

****

When I described earlier attempts to play softball in the field near our home, I failed to mention it was Doug who convinced me that we ought to assemble a softball team from the residents of the canyon and challenge someone in Missoula to a ballgame. The easy part was to come up with a team name, and we quickly chose the "Pattee Canyon Panthers" as our moniker. It was far more difficult to assemble enough kids to fill out a roster. We finally settled for just eight players, including the much older cousin of two boys on our squad. He was not only old enough to drive, but had a ramshackle vehicle large enough to transport our octet to the Bonner Park softball diamond in town. For the record, we lost that game rather lopsidedly, and the Panthers abbreviated season came to a compassionate close

****

Allow me now to insert a little quirky tie-in with Doug's middle name, which happens to be Barclay, and why it is so easy for me to recall.

One cold winter's evening when in high school and (finally) in possession of a driver's license, I had convinced my parents that I'd finished a rather difficult assignment from my Latin class, and to reward myself, wanted to borrow their car to drive to town to see a movie which was playing at a small neighborhood theatre showing older films.

"The Moon Is Blue" was its title, and while history has not been complimentary regarding reviews of the overall quality of the movie, it had built up significant interest when initially released a couple of years earlier, due to the inclusion of the (at the time forbidden in film) words "virgin" and "seduce" in the dialogue. (Inquisitive minds want to know, especially for a teen aged boy.)

Although I was successful in my sales pitch, I lived to regret my short-term success. As I departed the driveway, snow had been coming down for a couple of hours. Unbeknownst to me, Doug's mom had stopped to deliver something to a family named Barclay, who lived the equivalent of a city block down beyond the Hacker residence. She had parked her car at the side of the road, but with a rather steep drop adjacent to the narrow shoulder, it was situated far more "on" than "off" the actual road.

(The Barclays were the parents of Curt Barclay, a promising pitcher about to be called up to the then New York Giants. As no Missoula residents had ever played in the majors, this anticipated promotion made him a local celebrity of sorts. Curt did subsequently spend two or three years with the Giants before a bum shoulder shortened his playing days. He eventually returned to Missoula where he died at age 53.)

About the time I rounded the corner and observed the parked automobile adjacent to the Barclays, another driver was proceeding up the canyon. As one might expect from the novice that I was, I foolishly slammed on the brakes, hoping to stop until the other vehicle had passed. After the other driver rounded the corner behind me, I continued to keep my foot pressed on the brake pedal. Fortunately I had not been going fast even before hitting the brakes, but I still slid into the rear bumper of the parked car, pushing it into the ditch. The damage to either vehicle was minimal, but it took all three dads (Cooper, Hacker and Barclay) to extract the target of my driving inexperience from said ditch. No, Doug had not been home to provide either assistance or commentary related to the incident.

It was to be another fifty years or so before I had occasion to finally view "The Moon Is Blue," and then only on videotape. While the film may not have been memorable, I have never forgotten my first auto mishap near the Barclay home, nor the tie-in with Doug's middle name related thereto.

****

Our difference in age kept us from much association once Doug began high school. As fate would have it, both Doug and I later attended college in Missoula and even joined the same fraternity, but generally had little contact with each other. Nevertheless, following our respective military obligations, Doug and his wife relocated to Denver, just as did my wife and I. During ensuing decades we have occasionally shared dining experiences at each others homes; attended ballgames when our University of Montana teams played in or near the Denver area; and we've hit more than a few tennis balls back and forth from time to time. Ok, so much for background.

Believe it or not, I am finally getting to the focal point of this particular segment, and how it is exemplified by the esteemed Mr. Hacker. To do so, I must again backtrack to the year when Doug had first moved into Pattee Canyon.

Habit patterns are prevalent in numerous species. Take Loggerhead Turtles and their treacherous nesting function; or the upstream struggle by certain species of salmon in order to spawn before dying. (Do you suppose the "Samuel" salmon display a gill-to-gill grin upon reaching the spawning area with their charming "Samantha" salmon?) Or visualize (but please stop the heavy breathing in so doing) the inevitable "wet t-shirt contests" which break out amongst female college students who have migrated to Fort Lauderdale, Florida, for Spring Break. One might also include certain gestures, nervous responses, obsessive/compulsive behaviors and even superstitions as falling within such habit patterns. I would have to describe Doug as having had a habitual "pain displacement" pattern of response for the entire seven decades that I have known him. Here is the proof.

Doug did not attend Paxson like the rest of us, but rather Roosevelt Elementary, where he'd been enrolled prior to his move from town to his home in the canyon; naturally he had not wished to change schools for just the few remaining months of his final year of grade school. As Roosevelt was situated between the dispatch center and Paxson, Doug was already on board when our transportation arrived to take us home. He hopped out to act as a wrangler of sorts, steering the rest of us younger students into the big, black hearse.

One day, I had somehow managed to both sprain my ankle and badly scrape my knee from a fall playing tag after school, just prior to their arrival. I allowed the other kids to enter, before grabbing hold of the door frame to gingerly pull my injured body into the vehicle. I guess Doug was not paying strict attention to the progress of my entrance, as he slammed the back door so he could hop up front with the driver. I was approximately 98 percent "in" as the door closed. Unfortunately for me, the remaining 2 percent was represented by the hand I'd been using to pull myself in without putting pressure on my knee or ankle.

I cried out, and then cried countless tears. Doug quickly apologized, utilizing the comforting voice of one much older and wiser, as follows: "Gosh Ken, I'm really sorry. Of course, you can look at it this way. At least it has taken your mind off the pain from your ankle and knee."

Fast forward a mere 63 years or so to February, 2012.

Doug's dear wife, Bobbie, had fallen on her slippery front porch while retrieving the newspaper and had just recently been treated for the broken leg, badly bruised arm and serious bump on the head resulting from her tumble. To be even more gruesomely specific, the doctor had also had to drill three holes in Bobbie's cranium to relieve pressure which had built up, causing severe headaches. To add emotional discomfort to physical pain, it was now time for Bobbie to transport 2011 tax info to the accountant handling such matters.

Doug gently assisted Bobbie from the house to the car and made every effort to help her comfortably into it as well. As Bobbie grasped the door frame, shifting slightly to untwist her seat belt, Doug slammed the door. (Sound familiar?)

(Unbelievable as it may seem, some folks from "Candid Camera" happened to be nearby with a live microphone, scouting the area for a possible reincarnation of that formerly popular television show, and strictly by chance, they recorded Doug's words immediately following the slamming of the car door. When they determined not to proceed with the television project, they tossed the audio tape into a trash can. When that can was picked up by the trash company, the recording fell out and somehow got caught in the mechanism near the truck's bumper. When that same trash truck later picked up our weekly disposables, the tape was dislodged and landed in the gutter near our driveway. I noticed it shortly thereafter, and being more than slightly curious, I played it. You can imagine my amazement when I recognized Doug's voice and heard his recorded response, although it didn't make much sense until I later learned what had transpired in total.)

No doubt Doug's immediate thought process after slamming the door was along the lines of "Oh, oh, I did it again. That had to hurt! Better shift into damage control." Here is what he actually said (based on what I heard on the tape, somewhat garbled, due to the painful cries coming from his wife): "Gosh Bobbie, I'm really sorry. Of course, you can look at it this way. At least it has taken your mind off the taxes and your other injuries."

Yes, yes, I made up that "Candid Camera" part; but the door slamming on Bobbie's hand is fully factual. Furthermore, knowing Doug as I do, he might well have repeated the very same comments to Bobbie that he had previously used on me; although I have no doubt her response may have been just a bit more belligerently expressive than was mine.

By the way, when I first had the pleasure of meeting Bobbie, I recall asking her if there was anything from Doug's early life of which she'd like to be made aware. Though she didn't mention any concerns at the time, I'm sure, in retrospect, that she'd have appreciated knowing of Doug's dangerous door slamming habits.

****

Sub Chapter 15.4:

"Dragnet" Protected the Innocent by Changing Names.

Sorry, I'm No Joe Friday

Having identified by either first or full names, numerous individuals whose young lives interacted with mine during the relative innocence of elementary school years, I've undoubtedly tarnished some otherwise unblemished reputations in the process. It is only natural that one or more of them might respond by saying, "No no, that wasn't me; he's talking about some other guy with a similar name." To reject such claims, while realizing I most likely have already have been deleted as a "Friend" by any of them on Facebook®, I might as well go the whole nine yards and provide visual proof as well.

As I was digging through boxes of old photos for this book, I came across a picture taken in our front yard at what I think was my twelfth year birthday party. As it happened to include five of those individuals mentioned by name earlier, I now expose them to you the reader.

Stan Strong (second from your right in the front row) was my partner-in-crime for both the tubing incident in Chapter 2 and the failed movie business in Chapter 5.

Tom (top row, far left) and Jim (front row, far right) Shipkey were the brothers described in Chapter 3's football game featuring a broken leg and a brother galloping off for help.

John Wertz (top row, third from left) was my newspaper route associate in Chapter 5.

Doug Hacker (top row, second from left) was the guilty party who slammed car doors on defenseless hands, just a few paragraphs ago in Chapter 15.

And yes, there I am (front row, second from the left) with my brave little dog, Stuffy, who harassed the relentless mountain lion in Chapter 9.

One final disgusting disclosure: You may have noticed one of those "Cancer Candies" dangling from my fingers in a couple of the photos in this memoir. For the first twenty years of my life I swore that I'd NEVER, EVER get HOOKED on CIGARETTES! No way, no how.

Man plans; God laughs. I do not even recall the reason for ever taking my initial puff, but suddenly I, too, was a smoker. I'd pretend that I could quit at any time, and won several bets with other smokers as to which of us could resist lighting up the longest. While I'd win the bet, I lost the battle and continued to smoke.

It only worsened while I was in the Navy, where I increased my daily usage to three packs. Of course, since I smoked filtered ones, no big deal; right? Stationed in Newfoundland with no taxes applied, cigarettes cost a whopping ten cents per pack (or eleven cents for filters), so there was certainly no financial impetus to quit. I even took up a pipe for a while to cut down on cigarette volume, but failed to make a dent in my three packs per day habit.

Back in civilian life, and upon reaching the age of thirty, during a week long case of the flu accompanied by a very sore throat, I vowed to stop smoking. I did not mention this decision to my wife for several weeks, and when she ultimately commented about all the clean ashtrays, I said merely that I had not had a cigarette for a while.

I've never smoked again, with the exception of joining my two sons in a brief congratulatory cigar ceremony celebrating the birth of our only grandson.

I've had dreams (nightmares, actually) in which I had started smoking again; expressing a huge sigh of relief upon awakening. I knew if I ever had just one cigarette, I'd be hooked again; now, over forty years later, I feel the same way.

Mea culpa! I apologize for any inference that smoking is "cool" by having included those pictures; but as I nearly always had a cigarette in hand, I had no other option.

Sub Chapter 15.5:

"Luck of the Draw"

Be it Blackjack in Vegas, slot machines in Newfoundland, or Colorado Lottery tickets where I currently reside; I have never been bitten by the gambling bug.

As a curious youth, actively seeking what life had to offer in the area of "teenage enlightenment," I was introduced one evening to the game of Roulette. Along with several of my contemporaries from elementary school, I was in the home of a young acquaintance who was describing to us this "really fun Roulette thing" that was just like playing in Vegas, absent the skimpily attired cocktail waitresses. He easily garnered our interest, and even (oh, so generously) volunteered to be the "house" for the evening.

Although I tried to play mostly "safe" bets (odd/even or red/black) in small amounts; before departing, I had managed to lose almost my entire life savings (close to $1.50 to be specific). Looking back, this was probably the best thing that could have happened to me. Had I come out ahead that evening, my thought processes related to games of chance may have been totally different.

****

Regardless of whether or not an individual chooses to include a Power Ball Lottery ticket with each visit to the grocery store, we are all faced with choices related to "chance" daily. Spinning a tennis racquet to determine who serves first; coin flips at football games to decide who is to kickoff or receive; an odd or even number of fingers extended behind the back to see who gets to choose the best donut or apple at lunchtime; drawing a winning name or ticket from a hat; (Hey, maybe young folks today even utilize "Rock, paper, scissors" to determine who gets to be on top

during lovemaking. Things have changed a lot since I was young.)--
-----all are dictated by chance.

Now well into my eighth decade and being present for countless "And the lucky winner is" announcements, I have logged in many hours of politely applauding, as names or numbers were read which did not coincide with mine; however there were THREE occasions when fate was obviously smiling in my direction.

One such drawing occurred when I was in the fourth grade. Local radio station KXLL selected one student from each of the eight or nine elementary schools in Missoula, to share the microphone during a two month time frame with Ray Evans, their regular "on air personality" during a half-hour program on Saturday mornings.

To qualify for the opportunity, any interested student had to first write an essay on some topic, the theme of which I have no recollection. One student from each of our two fourth grade classrooms was chosen as the winner of that preliminary screening process. Somehow or another, I was the youngster selected from my room, after which the decision as to who would win the radio slot came down to pulling a name out of a hat. My name was drawn.

On my designated Saturday morning, I dressed up in my Cub Scout uniform, and was driven to the studio by both of my proud parents. The "runner up" was also in attendance, just in case I had a heart attack or a late case of stage fright, I guess.

"D-J Ray" introduced me to his radio audience as "a young lad in Scout attire," after which I proceeded to explain in great detail what was required to obtain the various badges I had won as a Cub Scout.

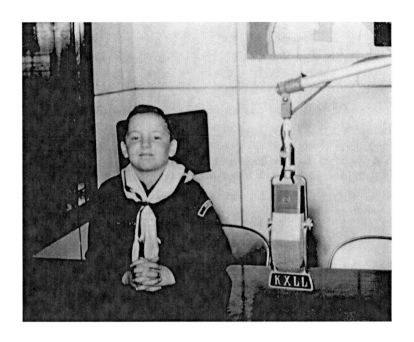

Do you suppose this was how a Howard Stern,
a Tom Brokow or a Johnny Carson got his
start in the radio or television business?

After politely acting impressed, Ray then handed me a brief bit of copy to read over the air, concerning the sponsor of the program, Hefte's Music Shop.

While I was amongst the most prolific shoppers for phonograph records (which is not to say I BOUGHT very many; just that I could probably describe the artists performing, the jacket cover and most of the songs contained therein), I totally blew the commercial, and with it, any future in the broadcasting profession. I sounded as if my mouth was full of mush, and pronounced "music" as either "mugic" or "mushic" on both attempts of reading the sponsor's name. Nevertheless, it was an exciting experience, and I was overjoyed at having had my name picked in that contest.

****

A little over a dozen years later, a door prize came my way on the evening of the Graduation Ball, held at the completion of Naval Officer Candidate School.

Four months earlier, when all the prospective Officer Candidates were initially addressed during our first day of OCS, we were told to look around the table at our fellow classmates. We were advised that at least four of each ten of us would fail to survive the sixteen-week program. My table, and others, contained graduates from the likes of Texas A&M, Stanford, Penn State, Princeton, Michigan and so forth, whereas my credentials listed Montana State University (later changed to the University of Montana), and I figured the deck was heavily stacked against me.

Therefore, when I successfully completed the four month program and earned my commission as an Ensign in the United States Navy, I was already floating in the stratosphere by the night of the Ball.

I had finished marching off all the "red gigs" I had periodically received as a result of my bedding not being tucked quite tightly enough, or for my locker not being arranged exactly right; now all that marching would be replaced by dancing with my lovely and supportive wife. That the Si Zentnor Orchestra was playing for our dancing pleasure, was just icing on the cake.

I was no "90 Day Wonder" (the often derogatory description of those who become commissioned officers in any branch of the military by simply going the OCS route, as opposed to surviving four years attending one of the service academies). I'll have you know we had to endure an entire "16 weeks" of abuse.

Midway through the evening, a drawing was held for an officer's sword, and my name was the one selected. I was nowhere near the top of our class, or even in our division, but the sword was mine, simply due to the sometimes sweet, but never predictable "Lady Luck."

****

My final "luck of the draw" stands out to me, if for no other reason than the ridiculous aspects of the whole thing.

In my role as Assistant Controller, and later Controller, of the Colorado Supermarket Chain, King Soopers, I would occasionally be invited to social and/or sporting events by various companies. Our "buyers" always were invited, as they were they were the individuals who made decisions about whether, or how much of, a product would be purchased, featured in an ad, etc. Now and then, other members of management were included as well. One such event was an annual golf outing sponsored by the local Pepsi Cola folks. It was an all-day affair, beginning with a round of golf (best ball, thank heavens), followed by a meal and drawings for prizes.

In case I failed to mention it earlier, while I was not particularly adept at any sporting activity, I really suck when it comes to golf. Oh, I have learned to drive a motorized cart; know the difference between hooks and slices; can encourage a fellow player with phrases such as "That'll play." or "You really tagged that one!" or "That's a gimme." and can use a ball washer with the best of them. Still, I would just as soon walk a course, without the interruption of having to look for a lost ball, or having to pause to attempt hitting that little, round, pock-marked thing every 100 yards or so.

On this particular golf outing, having lost only half the contents of the sleeves of new golf balls each of us was given at the start of our day, I was just finishing my post round meal, when the prizes were beginning to be handed out. Nearly everyone, it seemed, was destined to win something; the items included caps, towels, windbreakers and golf balls, all with the Pepsi insignia imprinted thereon.

The grand prize was this humongous golf bag and cover, with enough pockets for one to carry jackets, balls, tees, towels, snacks, hats, sunglasses, keys, blankets, beverages and on and on. The "true golfers" in attendance were all drooling over it, so naturally, the greatest imposter of the day, which would be me, was the winner of this grand prize.

When it is said that "Life isn't fair," this would be a perfect case in point.

****

Sub Chapter 15.6:

"Must Be a Terrible Toothache!"

With all the improvements to the education system brought about over the years by the valuable teachers' unions, I suppose today's educators at the elementary school level NEVER have problems with their young charges talking in whispered tones to each other, when they are supposed to be listening to the instructor, or to another student going through a "show and tell" or reading from a report, or focusing on some sort of power point presentation in a given class.

However, such inappropriate behavior did occur on occasion during the 1940s when I was amongst such a collection of youngsters sitting in a classroom. In fact, having basically grown up absent other children being present with which to converse or play, I seemed to have an even greater propensity than my classmates to take advantage of the presence of similarly aged youths to fill this gap (apparently even more than I felt the need to learn every element of what my teachers had in their lesson plans for a given day).

Commencing in poor Miss Lydia Van Hynning's first grade classroom at Paxson Elementary and continuing until a few months into Miss Winship's third grade class, I probably had more "detention periods" at day's end related to unacceptable whispering, than the rest of my class combined. [I also used to play with the pigtails of Marlene Waylett, who sat directly in front of me in Miss Winship's class (we were obviously not seated in any sort of alphabetical order), often attempting to dip them in the inkwell of my desk. However, as that has nothing to do with my whispering antics, I'll not detail it here.]

Included with me in the enrollment of third graders at Paxson were the Forman twins, Frank and Neal. Despite having a twin brother, plus Jimmy, another slightly younger sibling, with whom to share things, Neal and I became all but attached at the hip that year, and referred to each other as "Nelly" and "Kelly" rather than our given names.

We seemed to have an endless array of information to share with each other, and Neal had numerous questions about what it was like living in Pattee Canyon. We would chatter on without ceasing: prior to the ringing of the school bell to commence the day's classes in the morning; following lunchtime; throughout recesses, and, much to Miss Winship's displeasure; during class time as well.

After a few weeks of unsuccessful chastising, she decided she had had it with the two of us, and undertook a form of corporal punishment to resolve the whispering problem.

Years earlier, before the days of readily available quality dental care, a severe toothache might be treated, at least temporarily, by wrapping a rag under the jaw and up over the top of the head of the pained patient, tying it tightly to prevent movement of the jaw. The knot would be placed directly adjacent to the painful tooth to apply pressure, after having applied a drop of whiskey, a ground up aspirin or some other pain reliever on or around the tooth itself.

Miss Winship's solution to our unjustifiable jaw jabbering took a page from that old dental treatment. At the completion of classes on a day during which Neal and I had been reprimanded more than once for disruptive talking; rather than merely having us sit at our desks and read a book, or stand at the blackboard writing "I will not whisper in class" or some other standard method of punishment, she instead produced two white rags and proceeded to tie them beneath our jaws and around our heads, with a large bulky bow at the very top.

While approximately the size of a dish towel, she intentionally used what I think may have been torn pieces of bed sheets, making the wraparound look quite bulky and absurd. At first, she would have each of us sit on opposite sides of her classroom in such ridiculous facial attire; later, she moved us into the hallway directly outside the door to her classroom to allow us to be more readily observable by other teachers and students from all grades who were passing in the halls.

I know that such punishment would today be considered cruel and unusual (and even then it was unusual) and something that could irreparably damage our psyches. But just like the well-timed swat on the butt by my parents when I was caught misbehaving, I am so very glad that Miss Winship had both the courage and inventiveness to make negative examples of our behavior. Neal and I may have continued to communicate before and after class, but our in-class whispering diminished dramatically.

****

Sub Chapter 15.7:

My Doomed Youthful Love Affair with an Automobile

A year after having taken up residence in Pattee Canyon for the second time, my parents acquired what I immediately considered to be the world's most amazing automobile. I would tell you the make, year, model, and other pertinent details related thereto, but for reasons you'll read in a moment, I do not know them; however I will insert a photo so you can see it for yourself.

A boy, a bike and a buggy
Bonding for a lifetime......Or not.

My mother immediately christened it "The Joupe," which was apparently a combination of coupe and Jeep. It drew a lot of attention whenever we drove it down into Missoula, and whenever my mother was dropping me off or picking me up from the home of any of my little friends in town, my young hosts would all but insist that she take them for a spin around the block.

Despite the fact that I was, at the time, less than half the age required to obtain my first driver's license, I confidently advised my parents that as soon as I could drive, I would buy this car from them and would keep it forever. I would learn how to maintain it in top running condition, wash it to avoid rusting problems and never drive recklessly in order to reduce the risk of having it in an accident.

Not too long thereafter, my father decided to part ways with the Folgers Coffee Company and become a salesman for Sweets Candy Company. The change had something to do with the excessive driving required to cover his territory; with the Sweets folks having offered to reduce the monthly mileage substantially by assigning Wyoming to their Colorado representative and the Dakotas to Minnesota's representative, or some such improvements. That still left plenty of acreage to cover in Idaho and the wide open spaces of Montana, but it was certainly a better situation overall.

An unfortunate downside of this change of employers was a significant reduction of income (at least in the near term) for our family. Neither of my parents was adept at budgeting, and had not made any plans to set aside savings for such revenue reductions. (That they never did develop a savings habit and frequently found they were lacking funds to meet any of those little events that arise throughout life, such as family vacations or partial assistance with college tuition for me, may have had an impact on my decision to major in business when I did go to college.)

In any event, they advised me that in order to put food on the table, pay the mortgage and all that sort of thing of absolutely no interest to a child whose age was still in single digits, they unfortunately would have to sell "my car" of the future.

To say I was devastated would be an understatement. I loved that vehicle as much as anyone could love an inanimate object. Had my original game plan of making the car my very own in another 8-10 years come to fruition, I have no doubt I'd have learned every possible detail regarding the vehicle, and what made it tick.

I moped around for several days; then early one morning, a young man appeared at our door with the biggest wad of bills I had ever seen. He had read the newspaper ad about my parents' desire to sell the car, and had brought the exact asking price in cold currency. I think the amount was around $700, but that may not be entirely accurate, nor does it really matter. He spread out on our coffee table a couple $20 bills, several $10s and a great many $5s and $1s to make up the full price. (No, he did not include any silver dollars, so he may have been a recent transplant from out of state.) I don't know how he had scraped together so many bills of different denominations or why he hadn't gone to a bank to swap them for larger ones, unless he wanted to be the first person on the scene with cash in hand, and therefore didn't want to wait for the banks to open. Or perhaps it was a Sunday.

I did not stick around for the completion of the transaction, but instead walked out to the driveway to say a last goodbye to "my car," before going to my bedroom. I then vowed that I would never again allow myself to get as emotionally attached to something as ridiculous as an automobile, which was really nothing more than an impersonal conveyance utilized to transport people from place to place. Maybe with a horse and buggy, as had been utilized for transportation years earlier, one might conceivably develop a relationship with the animal portion of that combination; but an automobile was just so much metal, rubber and glass.

If I knew at the time the name of that vehicle which, had things worked out, was to have been mine, I quickly forgot it. As I grew older and my dad would ask if I might like to learn about the under the hood workings of any cars we had in following years, I politely declined his offer.

You'd be correct to say that I may have gone overboard in trying to avoid any interest in cars; my only description of them over subsequent years has generally been limited to color; not make, nor model. Unlike many of my counterparts who can look through a brochure of new vehicles and drool over various aspects of them, my only concern over the ensuing decades has been whether or not a given vehicle would get me from point A to point B with a relative degree of reliability.

As a result, my wife and family have had to put up with some terribly boring station wagons, bland sedans, embarrassingly dull mini-vans and the like.

The sole diversion during nearly six decades of "bland and boring" was a regrettable detour to "dumb and dumber" which occurred when we purchased one of those goofy Gremlins, a vehicle that appeared to have lost out in attempting to outrun a giant sized lawn mower, with a sizeable chunk of its butt being sheared off in the process. Oh, yes, if you are interested in the more critical and/or technical specs of that particular Gremlin; it was red.

****

Sub Chapter 15.8:

"What Was That Again?"

We've all read those cute quotations of kids in kindergarten up through about third grade, where they misstate verses from the Bible or the National Anthem or some famous quotation, because "it sounded like that" to them.

I had one from my own childhood which, while it may not fall into the "cute" category, pops into my head whenever I read or hear of such innocent misstatements by little tykes today.

It related to some sort of smelly "analgesic" liniment that my mother rubbed on an injury I had incurred in the calf/ankle area. I always thought she was calling it "Ankle Jesus." Naturally when I experienced subsequent bumps and bruises requiring my mother's tender love and care, I would ask her to be sure to get out the "Ankle Jesus" to make it well again.

****

Another example was provided to me quite recently by our younger son, Andy, describing an incident involving his daughter, Chloe, (our youngest granddaughter), age five.

They were in his pickup truck, driving through a wooded area west of Denver when they rounded a curve and came upon a mother deer with two recently born fawns. He pulled over so they could observe the trio cross the road. As he pointed them out to her, he said, "Chloe, look at that! It's a doe taking her new babies out for breakfast. Do you suppose those fawns are boys, girls, or one of each?"

"They're both girls, daddy," Chloe replied.

"Oh, how can you tell?"

"No peanuts."

****

Most of us old codgers can readily recall the novelty song from the 1940s entitled "Mairzy Doats," which initially sounds like so much double-talk, until the song itself basically advises the listener to simply say the words slowly, so that you hear "Mares eat oats" and so forth and so on.

In a remotely similar vein, my mother taught me a word grouping, which once again, if said very slowly, made perfect sense; but if spoken at typical talking speed, resembled complete gibberish. It went like this, using the actual correct spelling, but without any spaces or punctuation included, to more closely relate to the spoken word:

"inmudeelsareinclaynoneareinpinetarisinoaknoneis"

I would then teach it to various other friends to, in turn, confuse their parents, siblings or buddies. Once one breaks down those 47 letters into 16 short words, inserts the required 15 spaces, and tosses in 4 each of initial caps and periods, the mystery is solved. While not exactly worthy of inclusion in a listing of critical information essential to all thinking members of the human race; the resulting statements are factual.

****

In the life of a CPA, there are an incredible number of acronyms utilized in the profession, which, to the lay person, may sound like gibberish as well.

To list but a few of them: FASB, GAAP, EBITD (not to mention EBITDA), IFRS, DEBITS or CREDITS, GAAS (even worse than just moderate GAS), SARBANES-OXLEY, and (You say) FIFO (but I say) LIFO; and that's just for openers.

After a few dozen business school classes focused on accounting, a CPA Review course, and perhaps an internship with a practicing CPA; these acronyms will be as clear to the aspiring Accountant / Auditor / Tax Expert / Management Consultant as are the words in those "Mares munching on buckets of oats" or "Eels existing in mud" phrases listed earlier.

****

Therefore, should you choose, as did I, the career of a CPA, more power to you.

While it is doubtful that Hollywood will ever see fit to cast George Clooney in the role of an accountant, or portray the CPA as the hero in one of their films; the next time the Academy Awards are televised, you just might be the distinguished lady or gentleman from Price Waterhouse Coopers (the CPA firm which tallies up all those ballots; and no, I am not in any way related, despite the name similarity), who hands the envelope to a celebrity presenter for "Best Performance by an Actor in a Cross-Dressing Role While Still in Rehab Who Is Between Marriages And Currently Out on Parole for Possession of the Illegal Substances Which Brought About the Need for Rehab in the First Place" or similar Oscar nominations.

CPSIA information can be obtained at www.ICGtesting.com
Printed in the USA
LVOW081636061112

306118LV00011B/134/P